The Manipulation of Literature

First published in 1985, the essays in this edited collection offer a representative sample of the descriptive and systematic approach to the study of literary translation. The book is a reflection of the theoretical thinking and practical research carried out by an international group of scholars who share a common standpoint. They argue the need for a rigorous scientific approach to the phenomena of translation – one of the most significant branches of Comparative Literature – and regard it as essential to link the study of particular translated texts with a broader methodological position. Considering both broadly theoretical topics and particular cases and traditions, this volume will appeal to a wide range of students and scholars across disciplines.

CW01497091

The Manipulation of Literature

Studies in Literary Translation

Edited by
Theo Hermans

Routledge
Taylor & Franc s Group

First published in 1985
by Croom Helm, Ltd

This edition first published in 2014 by Routledge
2 Park Square, Milton Park, Abingdon, Oxon, OX14 4RN
and by Routledge
711 Third Avenue, New York, NY 10017

Routledge is an imprint of the Taylor & Francis Group, an informa business

© 1985 Theo Hermans and Contributors

The right of Theo Hermans to be identified as editor of this work has been
asserted by him in accordance with sections 77 and 78 of the Copyright,
Designs and Patents Act 1988.

All rights reserved. No part of this book may be reprinted or reproduced or
utilised in any form or by any electronic, mechanical, or other means, now
known or hereafter invented, including photocopying and recording, or in any
information storage or retrieval system, without permission in writing from the
publishers.

Publisher's Note
The publisher has gone to great lengths to ensure the quality of this reprint but
points out that some imperfections in the original copies may be apparent.

Disclaimer
The publisher has made every effort to trace copyright holders and welcomes
correspondence from those they have been unable to contact.

A Library of Congress record exists under LC control number: 72193299

ISBN 13: 978-1-138-79475-7 (hbk)
ISBN 13: 978-1-315-75902-9 (ebk)
ISBN 13: 978-1-138-79477-1 (pbk)

The Manipulation of Literature

Studies in Literary Translation

Edited by THEO HERMANS

CROOM HELM
London & Sydney

© 1985 Theo Hermans and Contributors
Croom Helm Ltd, Provident House, Burrell Row,
Beckenham, Kent BR3 1AT
Croom Helm Australia Pty Ltd, Suite 4, 6th Floor,
64-76 Kippax Street, Surry Hills, NSW 2010, Australia

British Library Cataloguing in Publication Data

The Manipulation of literature : studies in
  literary translation.
  1. Translation.
  1. Translating and interpreting
  I. Hermans, Theo
  418'.02   P306

  ISBN 0-7099-1276-5

Printed and bound in Great Britain
by Billing & Sons Limited, Worcester.

CONTENTS

PREFACE

Thanks are due to Susan Bassnett, Leon Burnett,
Jane Fenoulhet, Lesley Gilbert, Mara Hasenstrauch,
Maarten Kruizenga, André Lefevere and Frances Mills,
for various kinds of editorial assistance; and,
of course, to Marion, for typing.

INTRODUCTION

Translation Studies and a New Paradigm

Theo Hermans

It is nothing new to say that the position occupied
by Translation Studies in the study of literature
generally today is, at best, marginal. Handbooks on
literary theory and works of literary criticism almost universally ignore the phenomenon of literary
translation; literary histories even those that
cover more than one national literature, rarely make
more than a passing reference to the existence of
translated texts. Educational institutions, which
tend to link the study of language and literature
along monolingual lines - one language and one literature at a time - treat translations with barely
veiled condescension.

There are, of course, many reasons for this
neglect, some merely practical, others more deeply
rooted. In the end, they can probably be traced back
to certain influential views on the nature of literature and of the relation between language and literature. The ultimate provenance of these views, it
seems, lies in a number of naively romantic concepts
of 'artistic genius', 'originality', 'creativity',
and a severely restricted notion of what constitutes
a 'national literature'. If the literary artist is
viewed as a uniquely gifted creative genius endowed
with profound insight and a mastery of his native
language, the work he produces will naturally come
to be regarded as exalted, untouchable, inimitable,
hallowed. If, in addition, language is conceived as
closely correlated with nationhood and the national
spirit, the canonized set of texts that together
make up a given national literature will also assume
an aura of sacred untouchability. In such circumstances, any attempt to tamper with a literary text
by rendering it into another language must be condemned as a foolhardy and barely permissible under-
taking, doomed from the start and to be judged, at

best, in terms of relative fidelity, and at worst as outright sacrilege.

The strongly evaluative orientation of literary criticism, moreover, has meant that the hierarchy of canonized texts in a given national literature may occasionally be reshuffled in accordance with changes in the dominant poetics, but this does not affect the basic parameters, for the ultimate criterion remains the question of quality, of creativity, originality and aesthetic excellence. As a result, translation has found itself consistently relegated to the periphery, together with, for example, parody, pastiche, stage and screen adaptations, children's literature, popular literature and other such products of 'minor significance'.

Of course, faced with the rather obvious presence of translated texts in the total literary production of most countries, and with the equally obvious historical importance of translations in the development of most national literatures, literary criticism has shown signs, periodically, of a bad conscience. The saving grace, however, always lay in the evaluative yardstick, i.e. in comparing the rich and subtle texture of the original with the translation, only to find the latter wanting, because its texture was never quite the same as that of the original. In those rare cases where translations seemed to be aesthetically on a par with their originals, a subterfuge could always be used by simply coopting the translator into the pantheon of creative artists and incorporating his work into the canon on that basis.

The conventional approach to literary translation, then, starts from the assumption that translations are not only second-hand, but also generally second-rate, and hence not worth too much serious attention. A translation may have its limited use as a stepping-stone to an original work, but it cannot presume to form part of the recognized corpus of literary texts. The fact, incidentally, that many of us have a vague notion of what we take to be world literature through reading, say, Euripides, Dante, Dostoyevsky, Ibsen, Li Po, the *Thousand and One Nights* and the *Tale of Genji* in translation, is not allowed to impinge on the oft-repeated exhortation that literature should be read in the original and not through some substitute. Taking the supremacy of the original for granted from the start, the study of translation then serves merely to demonstrate that original's outstanding qualities by highlighting the errors and inadequacies of any number of translations of it.

The outcome, needless to say, is an invariably source-oriented exercise, which, by constantly hold ing the original up as an absolute standard and touchstone, becomes repetitive, predictable and prescriptive - the implicit norm being a transcendental and utopian conception of translation as reproducing the original, the whole original and nothing but the original. A watered-down version of this procedure may consist in the application of an *ad hoc* norm devised for the critic's own convenience, but mostly the results are equally unproductive, even if they are accompanied by the umpteenth call for better translations.

In so far as translations have received sustained attention in modern literary studies, it has been, not surprisingly, in the area of comparative literature. But here, too, the study of translation has usually been carried out in the context of influence studies, i.e. of genetic relations between literatures and writers, whereby the emphasis remained firmly on the original works to follow. Even in the study of the migration of themes and motifs, translators are rarely regarded as more than industrious intermediaries, running messages between two national literatures. Although comparatists have undoubtedly kept the phenomenon of translation in their sights, they have still, on the whole, left the field fragmented and compartmentalized. They have rarely, if ever, come to terms with the totality of translated texts as a separate class of texts, or with the place and function of translated texts within the whole of a given literature and its development.

It must be admitted, on the other hand, that translation scholars have often been their own worst enemies, not just for failing to question the normative and source-oriented approaches typical of most traditional thinking about translation, but also for continuing to ask similarly unproductive essentialist questions (how is translation to be defined?, is translation actually possible?, what is a 'good' translation?) - with or without the dubious excuse that pedagogical considerations (we need to train translators, good translators) justified such questions.

True, some scholars have sought to make progress in other directions, most notably, in recent decades, via psychology and linguistics. The results have not been encouraging. The attempt via psychology, even if backed up by some impressive semiotic terminology, produced complex schemes and diagrams illustrating the mental processes of decoding messages in one

medium and encoding them again in another, but since
the conversion inevitably took place within the human
mind, that blackest of black boxes always turned out
to be the centrepiece. For a time, the modern advances in linguistics, too, held a particular fasci-
nation for students of literature and of translation.
Linguistics has undoubtedly benefited our understanding of translation as far as the treatment of un-
marked, non-literary texts is concerned. But as it
proved too restricted in scope to be of much use to
literary studies generally - witness the frantic attempts in recent years to construct a text linguistics - and unable to deal with the manifold complexities of literary works, it became obvious that it
could not serve as a proper basis for the study of
literary translation either. Thus, whereas linguistics disqualified itself on account of its self-
imposed limitations, the psychological study of the
translation process condemned itself to speculating
about essentially unobservable phenomena. Furthermore,
with literary translation excluded as a suitable
subject for serious study by a constricting view of
literature and by institutionalized pedagogical concerns, it is hardly surprising that there grew a
feeling that the discipline had reached an impasse.

*

Since about the mid-1970s, a loosely-knit international group of scholars has been attempting to break
the deadlock in which the study of literary translation found itself. Their approach differs in some
fundamental respects from most traditional work in
the field. Their aim is, quite simply, to establish
a new paradigm for the study of literary translation,
on the basis of a comprehensive theory and ongoing
practical research. It is their work which is represented in the present book.
    The group is not a school, but a geographically
scattered collection of individuals with widely vary-
ing interests, who are, however, broadly in agreement
on some basic assumptions - even if that agreement,
too, is no more than relative, a common ground for
discussion rather than a matter of doctrine. What
they have in common is, briefly, a view of literature
as a complex and dynamic system; a conviction that
there should be a continual interplay between theoretical models and practical case studies; an approach
to literary translation which is descriptive, target-
oriented, functional and systemic; and an interest
in the norms and constraints that govern the produc-

tion and reception of translations, in the relation
between translation and other types of text proces-
sing, and in the place and role of translations both
within a given literature and in the interaction between literatures.

The conception of literature as a system, i.e.
as a hierarchically structured set of elements, goes
back to the Russian Formalists (Tynianov, Jakobson)
and the Czech Structuralists (Mukařovský, Vodička).
Today it is to be found in the writings of scholars
like Yury Lotman, Claudio Guillén, Siegfried Schmidt,
Itamar Even-Zohar and others. The work of Itamar Even-
Zohar (University of Tel Aviv) in particular is
directly associated with the new approach to translation studies. In a series of essays (see General
Bibliography, Even-Zohar 1978 and 1979) he reformu-
lated some basic insights stemming from Tynianov especially, and developed the notion of literature as
a 'polysystem', i.e. as a differentiated and dynamic
'conglomerate of systems' characterized by internal
oppositions and continual shifts. Among the oppositions are those between 'primary' (or innovatory)
and 'secondary' (or conservative) models and types,
between the centre of the system and its periphery,
between canonized and non-canonized strata, between
more or less strongly codified forms, between the
various genres, etc. The dynamic aspect results from
the tensions and conflicts generated by these multiple oppositions, so that the polysystem as a whole,
and its constituent systems and subsystems, are in
a state of perpetual flux, forever unstable. Since
the literary polysystem is correlated with other
cultural systems and embedded in the ideological and
socio-economic structures of society, its dynamism
is far from mechanistic.

The theory of the polysystem sees literary
translation as one element among many in the constant
struggle for domination between the system's various
layers and subdivisions. In a given literature,
translations may at certain times constitute a separate subsystem, with its own characteristics and
models, or be more or less fully integrated into the
indigenous system; they may form part of the system's
prestigious centre or remain a peripheral phenomenon; they may be used as 'primary' polemical weapons
to challenge the dominant poetics, or they may shore
up and reinforce the prevailing conventions. From the
point of view of the target literature, all translation implies a degree of manipulation of the source
text for a certain purpose. In addition, translation
represents a crucial instance of what happens at the

interface between different linguistic, literary and cultural codes, and since notions of interference, functional transformation and code-switching are essential aspects of the polysystem theory, translation may provide clues for the study of other types of intra- and intersystemic transfer as well (as indeed Even-Zohar has suggested; see Even-Zohar 1981).

As a theoretical model the polysystem theory appears to provide an adequate framework for the systematic study of translated literature. It is simple and bold enough to be attractive as a cognitive tool, and yet flexible and inclusive enough to adapt itself to different cases and situations. But it is important to be clear about the notion of 'theory'. The term is here taken to mean a systematic framework for collecting, ordering and explaining data. Although a theory is first and foremost a conceptual pattern, it also functions as an instrument of exploration, and thus has both heuristic and cognitive value. Indeed, a theory increases its attractiveness as it generates new ways of looking and interpreting. While the testability of a theory of literature is naturally low, its acceptability "depends mainly on the fruitfulness of the application of the theory and on the degree of enlightenment derived from it" (Mooij 1979:133).

Practical fieldwork and case studies are therefore a necessity, since ultimately the theory remains a tentative construct which stands or falls with the success of its applications. Ideally, the process works both ways: case studies are guided by the theoretical framework, and the feedback from practical research then results in corroboration or modification of the theoretical apparatus. In practice, the relation between the two is less straightforward. Case studies vary greatly in scope and emphasis, and may develop their own momentum. On the other hand, the theory consists of an aggregate of hypotheses which tend to be used highly selectively by individual researchers, and even in its entirety it offers no more than a simplified and abstract model at one remove from the real world.

On the whole, however, the polysystem theory seems sufficiently inclusive and adaptable to stimulate research in a variety of fields, not least that of literary translation. In contrast with most conventional work on translation, the approach based on the systems concept of literature is not prescriptive. Instead of providing guidelines for the next translation to be made and passing judgement on any number of existing ones, the descriptive method takes the

12

translated text as it is and tries to determine the various factors that may account for its particular nature. This position implies that the researcher has to work without preconceived notions of what actually constitutes 'translation' or where exactly the dividing line between translation and non-translation is to be drawn, for such notions would inevitably reveal themselves to be normative and restrictive. As in the case of concepts like 'literature', 'poetry' or 'art', a tautological or - to put it more kindly - a sociological and pragmatic circumscription seems the best that can be hoped for: a (literary) translation is that which is regarded as a (literary) translation by a certain cultural community at a certain time. A working definition of this kind also points up the necessity of a target-oriented approach, as a corollary to the descriptive orientation. As Gideon Toury's essay in the present book argues, the investigation of translational phenomena should start from the empirical fact, i.e. from the translated text itself.

In consequence, much of the practical work done in this descriptive and target-oriented context is also of an historical nature, because it deals with existing texts which, to all intents and purposes, are (or were, at the time) regarded as translations by the cultural community concerned. That being the case, the old essentialist questions about the prototypical essence of translation are simply dissolved, and the way is open for a functional view. The new approach tries to account in functional terms for the textual strategies that determine the way a given translation looks, and, more broadly, for the way translations function in the receptor (or target) literature. In the first case the focus is primarily on translational norms and on the various constraints and assumptions, of whatever hue, that may have influenced the method of translating and the ensuing product. In the second case explanations are sought for the impact the translation has on its new environment, i.e. for the acceptance or rejection of a given translation (or, of course, a number of translations) by the target system.

The explanations are of the functional and pragmatic type, which means - given the theoretical context - that they are in most cases also systemic. They aim to go beyond isolated occurrences or texts and to take into consideration larger wholes (collective norms, audience expectations, period codes, synchronic and diachronic cross-sections of the literary system or parts of it, interrelations with surrounding literary or non-literary systems, etc.) in order to provide a broad contextual framework for individual phenomena. At the same time they want to extend findings bearing on particular instances to more substantial corpora, so as to be able to discover large-scale and long-term patterns and trends.

The net result of the new approach to translation is, on the one hand, a considerable widening of the horizon, since any and all phenomena relating to translation, in the broadest sense, become objects of study; and, on the other hand, it provides a more coherent and goal-directed type of investigation, because it operates within a definite conception of literature and remains aware of the interplay between theory and practice. The diversity of personal styles and interests within the group, which is evident also in the present collection, does not detract from that fundamental coherence.

As the group has been meeting and publishing for close on a decade, a number of developments have taken place on the theoretical level as well. Although, generally speaking, the polysystem concept of litera-ture appears to have successfully inspired a number of case studies on translation, some aspects of it have been elaborated further. Thus José Lambert and Hendrik van Gorp have stressed the importance of working with comprehensive communication schemes in the description of translations, whereby the various relations and parameters thrown up by the scheme present so many potential objects of study (see Lambert 1983 and Lambert & Van Gorp in the present book). Whereas in the 1970s André Lefevere's main contribution lay on the metatheoretical level (see, for example, Lefevere 1978), in recent years he has been strongly advocating the integration of translation studies into the study of the many types of 'rewriting' and 'refraction' that shape a given culture. At the same time he has argued in favour of a more determined effort to in-corporate into the polysystem concept the notion of a 'control mechanism', which he proposes to call 'patronage' and which regulates – and often manipu-lates – the literary system from inside the socio-economic and ideological structures of society (for a full exposition, see Lefevere 1984 and his essay in the present volume).

The group of people who may be identified with the new approach as illustrated in the following pages, were brought together at a series of symposia on literary translation, the first at the University of Louvain in 1976 (the proceedings were published in 1978 as *Literature and Translation: New Perspectives in Literary Studies*, eds. J.S.Holmes, J.Lambert & R. van

14

den Broeck), the second at the University of Tel Aviv in 1978 (with the proceedings in a special issue of *Poetics Today*, Summer-Autumn 1981, eds. I.Even-Zohar and G.Toury), and the third at the University of Antwerp in 1980 (proceedings in the translation issue of *Dispositio,* 1982, eds. A.Lefevere and K.D.Jackson). Among the group's major theoretical texts are Even-Zohar's essay on 'Polysystem Theory' in *Poetics Today* (1979), Lefevere's *Literary Knowledge* (1977) and Toury's *In Search of a Theory of Translation* (1980). Many of the case studies carried out by members of the group have appeared in widely scattered journals or in preprints, or are available only in the form of unpublished doctoral disserations. Much of this work appeared in Belgium, the Netherlands and Israel, and is written in Dutch, French or Hebrew.

The essays in the present book, then, amount to a collective profile of the group in a form accessible to a wide audience in the English-speaking world. Together they offer a representative sample of the new descriptive and systemic approach to the study of literary translation.

The General Bibliography at the end lists further names and titles. Although most of the essays in the present book were written on recuest, some are based on previous publications. Hendrik van Gorp's contribution is slightly amended from Van Gorp 1981. Ria Vanderauwera's piece builds on material discussed in her (unpublished) doctoral thesis (Vanderauwera 1982). Maria Tymoczko's essay is the expanded and amended text of a paper presented to the Tenth Congress of the International Comparative Literature Association (New York, August 1982), and Gideon Toury's article is a revised version of Toury 1982.

A RATIONALE FOR DESCRIPTIVE TRANSLATION

STUDIES

Gideon Toury

1. A Case for Descriptive Translation Studies

No empirical science can make a claim for complete-
ness and (relative) autonomy unless it has developed
a descriptive branch. The reason for this is that an
empirical discipline, in contradistinction to non-
empirical sciences, is initially devised to study,
describe and explain (to which certain philosophers
of science would add: predict), in a systematic and
controlled way, that segment of 'the real world'
which it takes as its object.*
        An empirical science refers to its subject-
matter on the basis of a theory, which is formulated
for that very purpose; in addition to the description
(etc.) of the object-level being the main goal of -
and only justification for - the entire discipline,
descriptive studies are actually the best means of
testing, refuting, and especially modifying and
amending the underlying theory, on the basis of which
they are executed. This reciprocal relation between
the theoretical and descriptive branches of the same
discipline makes it possible to produce ever better,
more refined and more significant descriptive studies
and thus advances the understanding of that section
of 'reality' to which the science in question refers.
        Since the object-level of translation studies
consists of actual facts of 'real life' - whether
they be actual texts, intertextual relationships, or
models and norms of behaviour - rather than the merely speculative outcome of preconceived theoretical
hypotheses and models, it is undoubtedly, in essence,
an empirical science. However, despite attempts in
recent decades to raise translation studies to the
status of a scientific discipline, it is still a
discipline-in-the-making. This situation is reflected
in that, among other things, it has not yet developed

a descriptive branch, and therefore is hardly in a position to test its own hypotheses, insofar as the hypotheses which serve it should indeed be formed within the discipline itself and in accordance with its own basic assumptions, and not simply imported wholesale from other theoretical frameworks which for one reason or another are regarded as the "Voraussetzungswissenschaften für die Übersetzungswissenschaft" (as the 'ideological' platform for a recent International Colloquium on Contrastive Linguistics and Translation Studies had it; Kühlwein *et al.* 1981: 15).

One of the main reasons for the prevailing lack of descriptive translation studies has no doubt been the overall orientation of the discipline towards its practical applications. Thus, whereas for a fully-fledged empirical science such applications - important as they may be - are only extensions of the discipline into 'the real world', the applications of translation studies in the form we usually know them (such as translation didactics, translation criticism, 'translation quality assessment' (House 1977), and even foreign language teaching) represent the main constraint on the very formulation of the theory which underlies them, if not the very reason why its formulation is imperative. Small wonder that a theoretical approach oriented towards practical applications should show preference for *prescriptive* pronouncements which, as a rule, derive either from sheer speculation or from theoretical and descriptive work done within the framework of *cther*, more 'basic' disciplines such as contrastive linguistics, contrastive textology (Hartmann 1980), or *stylistique comparée*. What it does not wish to do is to rely on research carried out within its *own* framework - which is why the lack of descriptive translation studies has never really bothered translation scholars.

All this is not to say that no attempts have been made to study, describe and explain actual translations or translating practices and procedures. What we need, however, is not isolated attempts reflecting excellent intuitions and supplying fine insights (which many of the existing studies certainly provide) but a *systematic* scientific branch, seen as an inherent component of an overall discipline of *translation studies*, based on clear assumptions and armed with a methodology and research techniques made as explicit as possible. Only a branch of this sort can ensure that the findings of individual case studies carried out within its framework will be both relevant and intersubjectively testable, and the studies themselves repeatable.

In what follows I intend to sketch a tentative rationale for such a branch of Descriptive Translation Studies (DTS),[1] by putting forward a set of ordered principles and guidelines for its gradual establishment, on the one hand, and for its operation, on the other. The step-by-step exposé of the principles themselves will be accompanied not only by small-scale illustrations for this or that point in the presentation, but also by a corresponding step-by-step unfolding (in small type) of an exemplary 'study in descriptive studies', focusing on one common type of textual-linguistic phenomenon (namely, the use of binomials of synonyms and near-synonyms) as it has presented itself in literary translation into Hebrew during the last hundred years or so.

2. The Kind of Facts Translations Are

Translated texts and their constitutive elements are *observational* facts, directly accessible to the eye. In contrast, translating processes, i.e. those series of operations whereby actual translations are derived from actual source texts, though no doubt also empirical facts and as such a legitimate part of the object-level of translation studies, are only *indirectly* available for study, as they are a kind of 'black box' whose internal structure can only be guessed, or tentatively reconstructed. To be sure, from time to time suggestions have been made for more direct approaches to the mental processes involved in translating (see, for example, Sandrock 1982 and the literature described and criticized there), but the main way to get to know those processes is still through a retrospective reconstruction on the basis of the (translational) relationships between the observable output and input of single processes, with the aid of further theoretical assumptions and hypotheses established in translation studies proper as well as in the framework of adjacent disciplines such as psychology and psycholinguistics. So far, only this type of reconstruction seems to ensure a degree of intersubjective testability.

It is only reasonable to assume that any research into translation should start with observational facts, i.e. the translated utterances themselves (and their constitutive elements, on various levels), proceeding from there towards the reconstruction of non-observational facts, and not the other way around. Nor is this order at odds with translation practice itself. Semiotically speaking, it will be clear that it is the *target* or *recipient culture*, or a certain section of it, which serves as the *initiator* of the decision to translate and of the translating process (see Toury 1980:16;1984; Yahalom 1978:1). Translating as a teleological activity *par excellence* is to a large extent conditioned by the goals it is designed to serve, and these goals are set in, and by, the prospective receptor system(s). Consequently, translators operate first and foremost in the interest of the culture *into* which they are translating, and not in the interest of the source text, let alone the source culture.

The basic assumption of DTS is therefore diametrically opposed to that which is usually maintained by the practitioners of any process-based, application-oriented paradigm of translation theory. DTS starts from the notion that any research into translation, whether it is confined to the product itself or intends to proceed to the reconstruction of the process which yielded it (and on from there), should start from the hypothesis that *translations are facts of one system only*: the target system. It is clear that, from the standpoint of the source text and source system, translations have hardly any significance at all, even if everybody in the source culture 'knows' of their factual existence (which is rarely the case anyway). Not only have they left the source system behind, but they are in no position to affect its linguistic and textual rules and norms, its textual history, or the source text as such. On the other hand, they may well influence the recipient culture and language, if only because every translation is initially perceived as a target-language utterance. Of course, there is a real possibility that translated utterances in a certain language or culture will come to form a special system, or special systems, of their own (see, for example, Dressler 1972), if only because of the universality of interference occurring in translated texts (Toury 1980:71-78;1982). However, these systems will probably always turn out to be more of the nature of *sub* systems of the encompassing target system rather than autonomous systemic entities.

3. Establishment of the Corpus and Discovery Procedures

To say that translations are facts of the target system is by no means to claim that every fact of the target system is (a candidate for) a translation. How then are translations to be distinguished from non-translations within the target culture, if such a distinction is to serve as a basis for the establishment of corpora, appropriate for study within DTS?

The answer is that, if one does not wish to make too many assumptions which may prove difficult or impossible to maintain in the face of the empirical data, one really has no foolproof criterion for making such a distinction *a priori*. The only feasible path to take seems to be to proceed from the assumption that, for the purpose of a descriptive study, a 'translation' will be taken to be any target-language utterance which is presented or regarded as such within the target culture, on whatever grounds (see Toury 1980:37,43-45).

By definition, the presentation of a target-language utterance as a translation, or its being regarded as such, entails the assumption that there is another utterance, a textual-linguistic fact of another system, which has chronological as well as logical priority over the translation in question: the source text precedes the translation in time and serves as the basis for the latter's creation.

To be sure, the source utterance as such is *not* part of the basic conditions for a descriptive study within DTS. It is the *assumption* of its existence, based on the observation that a target-language utterance is being presented or regarded as a translation, and not its existence in fact, which serves as a defining factor for a translation from the point of view of the target system, which has been adopted as a starting-point for DTS. In the more advanced stages of the study, when the source utterance is finally brought into the picture, some of the phenomena which have been tentatively marked as translations may well turn out to be *pseudotranslations*. This prospect is of no consequence, however, for the initial phase. In other words, pseudotranslations are just as legitimate objects for study within DTS as genuine translations. They may even prove to be highly instructive for the establishment of the general notion of translation, as shared by the members of a certain target-language community (Toury 1983;1984, Section V). This fact may serve to reinforce the requirement that the *theoretical* branch of translation studies should be equipped to account for phenomena of this kind too; which so far it is not.

For the purposes of descriptive research, translations should therefore be regarded as functions which map target-language utterances, along with their position in the relevant target systems, on source-language utterances and their analogous position. The source utterances, at least up to a certain point in the study, may comprise not only actual linguistic utterances, but also hypothetical ones, reconstructed, as it were, on the basis of the target utterance (in the case of pseudotranslations the corresponding source utterances will remain hypothetical; see Toury 1980:45-46). Thus, the actual subject-matter for descriptive studies within DTS consists first and foremost of *functional-relational concepts* (rather than their surface textual-linguistic representations), such as textual elements or linguistic units in relation to their positions in the translated utterances as systemic wholes; the translated utterances in relation to the target system(s) in which they are situated; or, finally, the translated utterances in relation to the utterances established as their (actual or hypothetical) sources.

Of course, it is the very fact that these functional-relational concepts *have* linguistic representations which serves to distinguish them from their counterparts in the theory, and therefore the surface realizations should not be ignored during the research. However, they should be assigned their proper position, namely as 'functors' fulfilling certain functions which do not owe their own existence to them: one and the same function could have an indefinite number of (superficially different) realizations which are, for that very reason, functionally equivalent and hence equally significant from the point of view of the theory. Moreover, only with regard to the underlying, common function can the question be asked why the functor actually present in a translation has been selected from the range of equivalent 'functors'. Thus, even if surface representations take priority in terms of mere *description*, their *explanation* can be attempted only on the basis of their underlying functions, which have therefore to be extracted from the utterance.

It is advisable, then, first to take up target texts which are regarded as TRANSLATIONS from the intrinsic point of view of the target culture, without reference to their corresponding source texts, or rather, irrespective of the very question of the *existence* of those texts, and to study them from the viewpoint of their ACCEPTABILITY in their respective 'home' systems, as target-language texts and/or as translations into that language. The second step will be to map these texts, via their constitutive elements as TRANSLATIONAL PHENOMENA, on their counterparts in the appropriate source system and text, identified as such in the course of a comparative analysis, as SOLUTIONS to TRANSLATIONAL PROBLEMS; next, to identify and describe the (one-directional, irreversible) RELATIONSHIPS obtaining between the members of each pair; and finally to go on to refer these relationships - by means of the mediating functional-relational notion of TRANSLATION EQUIVALENCE, established as pertinent to the corpus under study - to the overall CONCEPT OF TRANSLATION underlying the corpus. It is these last two concepts which form the ultimate goal of systematic studies within DTS which are after explanation too: nothing on the way to the establishment of the dominant norm of translation equivalence and of the underlying concept of translation can be fully accounted for without reference to these concepts, but they themselves cannot be established in any controlled way prior to the execution of the entire set of *discovery procedures*, and in the proposed order, even though good intuitions as to their nature may be present much earlier.

Only at this stage, when the nature of the prevailing concept of translation has been established, will it become possible to reconstruct the possible process of CONSIDERATION and DECISION-MAKING which was involved in the act of translating in question, as well as the set of CONSTRAINTS which were actually accepted by the translator. This reconstruction will be formulated in terms of the confrontation of the contending models and norms of the target and source texts and systems which were responsible for the establishment of the 'problems' and their 'solutions', including the relationships obtaining between them (that is, the above-mentioned 'translational relationships'), and, ultimately, for the surface realizations of these 'solutions' (standing in these relationships to their respective 'problems') in textual-linguistic substance - the very substance originally identified in the 'translations' as 'translational phenomena'. The order of the *justification procedure* in DTS is thus a complete mirror image of that of the discovery procedures.

Let us now examine a little more closely the main phases of the discovery procedure and the basic notions mentioned (in capital letters) in the course of their brief presentation.

4. Translational Phenomena and their Acceptability

When proceeding from the target system, what lends itself to observation first is, of course, the texts themselves, which are approached on the assumption that they are translations.

There may be various reasons for marking a target-language text as a possible translation, ranging from its explicit presentation as one, through the identification in it of textual-linguistic features which, in the culture in question, are habitu-

ally associated with translations, to the prior knowledge of the existence of a certain text in another
language/culture, which is tentatively taken as a
translational source for a certain target-language
text. This last is valid especially in the study of
cultures or historical periods where the presentation
of a translated text as such is not obligatory, or
cultures which do not at all distinguish - on the
product level, that is (since the translation procedure should be regarded as universally acknowledged
in situations where translating is indeed performed)
- between original compositions in the target language and translations into it. On the face of it,
this method seems to entail the reversal of the recommended order of the discovery procedures, but this
is not so: only when a target-language text has been
established as a possible translation does research
work within DTS proper commence, and from that point
on it proceeds in the recommended order, putting the
source text aside during the initial stages.

Thus, whatever the reasons for the tentative
marking of a text as a translation, at the first
stage ASSUMED TRANSLATIONS are studied from the point
of view of their (type and extent of) ACCEPTABILITY
in the target system(s), i.e. in terms of their sub-
scription to the norms which dominate these systems.

However, even under such a superficial observation, *translation description* may be said to take place,
both in cases where, in terms of substance (that is,
from the point of view of the textual-linguistic
phenomena proper), texts regarded as translations
appear as *identical* to texts regarded as original compositions in the target language, and in cases where
the surface representations of these two types look
different. This is true especially if, and when, the
differences show regularities which may - tentatively, at least - be attributed to the texts as members
of distinct subsystems, governed by different sets
of norms. Some of these differences will no doubt
find their explanation, at a later stage of the study,
as realizations of *formal* relationships to the corresponding source texts (see Section 8 below). Relations
of this type may also be found to obtain between
pseudotranslations and the reconstructed pseudo-source
texts.

This also means that the study of translation,
and DTS as a branch of translation studies, is not
to be reduced to comparative or contrastive analyses
of target and source texts (or items). Moreover, it
is clear that this type of comparative study is not
really justifiable within DTS (in contradistinction

to disciplines such as contrastive linguistics), unless on the basis of the identification of the target text and its constitutive elements as TRANSLATIONAL PHENOMENA from the intrinsic point of view of the *target* system; for it is this identification which presupposes the existence of translational relationships and translation equivalence, and which necessitates their extraction by means of confrontation.

However, there is room for a kind of comparative study even at this initial stage, when source texts have not yet been brought into the picture. This may, moreover, add another dimension to the functional description of (the acceptability of) translational phenomena in the target system, namely, the comparison of different translations of one and the same text (see for example Reiss 1981). Thus, one may compare several translations into one language done by different translators, either in the same period or in different periods of time (in which case the notion of *one* 'target language' may well have to undergo some modification); or one may compare different phases in the establishment of one translation, in order to reconstruct the interplay of 'acceptability' and 'adequacy' during its genesis (e.g. Hartmann 1980: 69-71;1981:204-207); or, finally, several translations of what is assumed to be the same text into different languages, as an initial means of establishing the effects of different cultural, literary and linguistic factors on the modelling of a translation.

Any examination of literary translations into Hebrew during the last hundred years or so immediately reveals a host of *binomials of synonyms and near-synonyms*: combinations of two (or sometimes more than two) (near-)synonymous lexemes of the same part of speech (see especially Malkiel 1968).

Obviously, *any* language may have binomials of this type, and probably does have them to a certain extent, so that they may be taken as a *universal of language* inasmuch as (near-)synonymity and conjunction are semantic and grammatical universals, respectively. However, the extent to which this universal potential is actually realized in a language, and the exact ways of its realization, are norm-governed, and therefore vary considerably from language to language, and even – within one language – between different dialects, registers, stylistic variants, periods in the history of the language, etc. (For Modern English, see Gustafsson 1975; for Old and Early Middle English, Koskenniemi 1968.)

The Hebrew language as a whole abounds in binomials of (near-)synonyms, most of which appear as fixed collocations. However, in translation into Hebrew they occur: (a) in a *much greater frequency* than in texts originally written in Hebrew;

(b) very often *as free combinations*, that is, as a result of the productive use of the technique. They keep occurring when, in original literary writing in Hebrew, the device has already been pushed to the periphery (mainly children's literature).

These facts taken together account for a slightly reduced rate of acceptability of this phenomenon, and a feeling of un-usualness is sometimes aroused in the reader, which tends to be interpreted as a sign of 'translationese'. In other words, every attentive reader of Hebrew literature is likely to mark certain texts as candidates for classification as translations on the mere evidence of a high frequency of the occurrence of this linguistic device, the more so since these binomials usually co-occur with other textual-linguistic features which lead to the same tentative hypothesis.

5. Translational Solutions and Translational Problems

The functional relationships which obtain between translated texts and other members of their 'home' systems, and these systems as wholes, are, by defini-tion, supplemented by a second set of relationships, those between target and source. These relationships, which have traditionally been presented as 'transla-tional' relationships proper, make target facts which have been regarded, at the first stage of the study, as *translational phenomena*, into TRANSLATIONAL SOLUTIONS by referring them to corresponding PROBLEMS in the source text(s) – existing ones, in the case of genuine translations, assumed (or reconstructed) ones, at least in part, in cases where the source text has not been or cannot be located, such as in cases of pseudo-translation. The TRANSLATIONAL RELATIONSHIPS themsel-ves will then be established on the basis of the pairs of problem + solution (see Section 8 below).

Thus, within the descriptive framework, a target 'solution' does not merely *imply* a corresponding source 'problem'. Rather, the two are *mutually* established in the course of the comparative analysis; they inevita-bly present themselves as *a coupled pair*.

The last assertion rests on the assumption that, since the subject-matter of DTS consists, by defini-tion, of actual instances of performance which belong in defined sets of socio-cultural circumstances, it is valid to examine only those facts of the source text which can be shown actually to have posed trans-lational problems in those particular circumstances. This status can be established only through the iden-tification of the respective solutions at the same time (including, of course, 'zero' solutions, i.e. omissions). It is often quite misleading to regard as translational problems all, and only those, phe-

nomena in the source text which may be established
as *potential* difficulties from the contrastive angle
of the *systems* underlying the two texts involved (see
for example Wilss 1982, Chapter VIII). To be sure,
even if all of them prove to be actual, realized problems for the case in question, additional facts
which present no difficulties from the *a priori* standpoint of one of the 'base' disciplines may well turn
out not merely to be problems, but even to be major
ones, from the *a posteriori* point of view of DTS, as
revealed by the solutions which have been given to
these problems. Facts of this kind may go unnoticed
unless *all* the translational problems are established
from the direction of the target pole. For the purposes of a descriptive-explanatory study in translational terms, there is even less point in regarding
as problems all those source phenomena which appear
'problematic' (however we understand that notion)
from the intrinsic point of view of the *source text*.
Such an approach - the protection of the 'legitimate
rights' of the original, as it were (Toury 1984,
Section III) - is likely to induce one to rest content with a simple enumeration of the 'sins' commit-
ted against the original text. Such a practice may
be part of translation criticism as one of the applied
extensions of translation studies, but it has no room
in a scholarly branch such as DTS.

A striking example of the inadequacies of the
more or less automatic transference of models and
methods from the 'base' disciplines to the treatment
of translational phenomena, and one which fails to
realize and apply the differences between the *a priori*
and the *a posteriori* points of view, is that of 'metaphor
as a translation problem'. The nature of the linguis-
tic-textual phenomenon of metaphor as a problem (or
a set of related problems) has always been established
in the *source* pole, on the basis of the source-language
metaphor, according to linguistic (Dagut 1976;1978:
91-120), or, better, according to textual *and* linguistic (Van den Broeck 1981) criteria. Each problem was
then given tentative solutions, which were presented
as the 'required', the 'best', or even the 'only possible' ones. On no occasion has the focus been on the
solutions *as they really are*, and on the problems as they
appear from the vantage point of these solutions.

Thus, it is symptomatic that the pairs of 'problem + solution' established by those scholars who
worked on 'metaphor as a translation problem' usually
fall into one of only three categories, namely:
  (1) metaphor *into* same metaphor
  (2) metaphor *into* different metaphor

(3) metaphor *into* non-metaphor[2]

Even among the alternatives which proceed from the source text metaphor, one rather common possibility is usually neglected:

(4) metaphor *into* Ø (i.e. complete omission) which is no doubt due to the *a priori*, prescriptive orientation of translation scholars, who are reluctant to accept omissions as 'legitimate' solutions. However, from the point of view of DTS, these four pairs of 'problem + solution' should be supplemented by the two following inverted alternatives, which are characterized by the appearance of the notion of 'metaphor' in the *target* rather than the source pole:

(5) non-metaphor *into* metaphor

(6) Ø *into* metaphor

This addition may facilitate, for instance, the description of a 'compensation mechanism', if such a mechanism is active in the corpus under study, a phenomenon which it is impossible to detect if only the source metaphors and their replacements in the target text are taken into account.

The addition of alternatives (5) and (6) may also lead to the formulation of other hypotheses of a descriptive and explanatory nature – for example the hypothesis that, on occasion, the use of metaphors in the target text is hindered by certain norms originating in the target system, and not by anything in the nature of the source metaphors themselves. Such a hypothesis would be reinforced by the absence of instances of alternatives (5) and (6), and weakened in direct proportion to their occurrence.

6. The Coupled Pair 'Problem + Solution' as the Unit of Comparative Analysis

A further question which deserves our attention in connection with the coupled pair 'problem + solution', the answer to which will ultimately make this pair a justifiable unit of comparative analysis, concerns its *boundaries*: how will one know that something has been established which deserves to be regarded as a coupled pair of this type?

The difficultly in giving a satisfactory answer to this question derives from two basic facts:

(a) any entity, at any textual-linguistic level and of any scope, may in principle turn out to represent a translational problem in relation to a certain target-text solution, or vice versa; and

(b) there is no need for the replaced entity in a translation (or that which is established, in the course of this initial phase of the comparative analysis, as the 'problem') to be identical, in rank or in scope, to the replacing one (i.e., that which is simultaneously defined as the corresponding 'solution').

The solution to this question, which is methodological in nature but may also have important theoretical implications, seems likely to run along the following lines:

The analyst, proceeding from the target pole, will have to establish a certain segment in the target-language text, for which it will be possible to claim that - beyond its boundaries - there are no 'leftovers' of the solution to a certain translational problem which is posed by one of the source text's segments, whether similar or different in rank and scope. It is this procedure which I had in mind when I mentioned the *mutuality* of the determination of the two members of the coupled pair.

Within DTS, then, translational problems are always *reconstructed* rather than given. They are reconstructed through *target–source comparison* rather than on the basis of the source text alone, or even of the source text in its relation to the overall possibilities of the target language to recode its (relevant) features, (that is, on the basis of the initial 'translatability' of the source text into the target language). Consequently, it is clear that what is established as a 'problem' during one study, i.e. for one pair of translation and source text segments, will not necessarily prove to be a problem at all, let alone a problem of the same type, in the framework of another study, even if that second study only compares another translation (into another, or even into the same target language) with the same source text.

Let us consider a concrete example.

The German author Wilhelm Busch (1832-1908) writes in his famous 'Juvenile History in Seven Tricks', *Max und Moritz*, first published in 1865:

> Durch den Schornstein mit Vergnügen
> Sehen sie die Hühner liegen
> Die schon ohne Kopf und Gurgeln
> Lieblich in der Pfanne schmurgeln.   (Busch 1949:7)

These verses are, in themselves, a mere textual fact of the original text, not even, one must admit, a very central one. Their status as a translational problem, and as *one* 'unit' of a problem which is not to be further broken down, is established in relation to the following lines from the first Hebrew translation (here in a literal English rendering):

28

Through the chimney they see
on the stove pots full
of cooking chicken
which are thoroughly roasting;
in fat soup the legs,
the wings, the upper legs
float tenderly, and from sheer delight
they almost melt there like wax. (Luboshitsky 1898:9)

These verses, in turn, are simultaneously established
as the solution for that problem, and the coupled
pair of these two textual segments can now be further
analyzed and its members compared with each other.

As it turns out, it is the confrontation of two
contending sets of norms which can be held responsible for the establishment of the coupled pair as one
unit, namely two incompatible modes (or 'models') of
cooking chicken. Of course, the mere existence of
such an incompatibility, on the cultural or on any
other level, does not necessarily lead to the triumph
of the *target* model, as it did here. The norms expressed in and by the source text may well be preferred,
at the expense of the acceptability of the target
text, or a third model may be adopted, or, finally,
some compromise between the two contending sets of
norms may be accepted. The point, however, is that
in each one of these cases the pair of 'problem +
solution' established during the first phase of the
comparative study (and not, of course, the solution
alone!) will be different.

The fact that the 'problem', and the coupled
pair, that we have established in our example is
neither an inherent feature of the source text nor a
contrastive property of the two languages or literatures underlying the two texts (even though the latter may be involved in its establishment), but an *ad
hoc relational notion*, clearly manifests itself when we
try to couple the original German verses with another
Hebrew translation of *Max und Moritz* (again in literal
English rendering):

They smell the meal,
they peep through the chimney,
without heads, without throats
the cock and each one of the hens
are already in the pan. (Busch 1939:12)

It is even doubtful whether these five lines should
be regarded as *one* unit, and not further broken down,
along with the corresponding German segment, until
some smaller-scale coupled pairs of 'problem + solution' are established, in keeping with the condition

that no 'leftovers' be found outside the boundaries of their respective members.

Finally, the only thing found in a third Hebrew translation of the book (Amir 1939:14) is the Hebrew word for 'roast meat', *tsli*. This word, taken as a solution, obviously suggests an altogether different translational problem posed by the source text segment.

When single pairs of 'problem + solution' have been established, an attempt can be made to trace *regular patterns* which may govern them (or sub-groups of them). The following two parallel texts consist of an English poem by James Joyce (*Chamber Music* XXXV) and its transliterated Hebrew version:

All day I hear the noise of waters	ani shome'a qol ha-mayim
Making moan,	ha-homim,
Sad as the sea-bird is, when going	ke-etsev of boded, shome'a
Forth alone,	al yamim
He hears the winds cry to the	tsivkhat rukhot, qolot
waters'	ha-mayim
Monotone.	amumim.
The grey winds, the cold winds	ru'akh afor, drakhay
are blowing	yishmor hu
Where I go.	ve-yehom,
I hear the noise of many waters	eshma et qol hamon ha-mayim
Far below.	ba-tehom.
All day, all night, I hear them	yomam va-lel, eshma
flowing	yakhzoru
To and fro.	ad halom.

(Joyce 1972:XXXV)

A simplified 'flow chart' of the kind reproduced below may be used to give an overview of the coupled pairs of 'problem + solution' pertinent to these two texts, under a semanto-syntactic observation. (The segments accounted for in the chart are also subject to initial constraints of metre and rhyme, which are only implicitly represented in it.)

Incidentally, since a flow chart is nothing but a graphic representation of an *algorithm*, what we may have here is not only a presentation of the pairs themselves, but also of the *regularities* which govern their establishment, expressed as a *set of ordered rules*. The chart can therefore also be read as an indication of the actual (reconstructed) process of consideration and decision-making on the semanto-syntactic level, that is, not only in the context of discovery, but in the context of justification and explanation as well. Indeed, when the coupled pairs are taken as

30

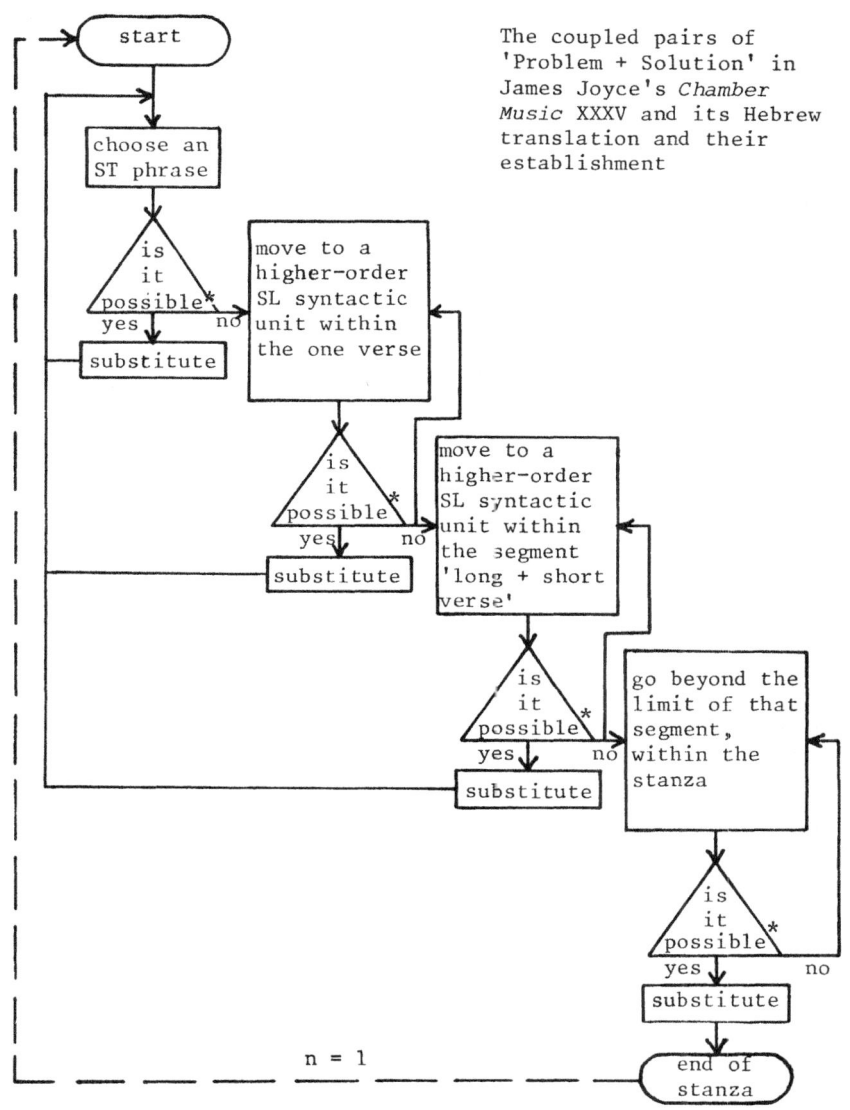

The coupled pairs of
'Problem + Solution' in
James Joyce's *Chamber
Music* XXXV and its Hebrew
translation and their
establishment

start

choose an
ST phrase

is
it
possible*
yes   no

move to a
higher-order
SL syntactic
unit within
the one verse

substitute

is
it
possible*
yes   no

move to a
higher-order
SL syntactic
unit within
the segment
'long + short
verse'

substitute

is
it
possible*
yes   no

go beyond the
limit of that
segment,
within the
stanza

substitute

is
it
possible*
yes   no

substitute

n = 1

end of
stanza

*to substitute a semanto-
syntactic TL unit for it

31

units for further comparative analysis, many correlations are found to exist between the translator's (reconstructed) decisions on the semanto-syntactic and on other, mainly lower, levels. This in turn gives rise to a first tentative hypothesis concerning not only the 'translation unit' pertinent to these two texts, but also the overall concept of translation which directed this translator, at least in the translation of this text.

7. Comparative Analysis and the Establishment of Shifts

As we have seen in our last example, the solutions and problems, and with them the textual segments which together form the coupled pairs, are established in relation to the type of comparison which will be executed on the pair. This is so first and foremost because of the limitations on human perception. As is well known, every comparison, especially of complex objects, is inevitably *partial*: it is performed only on a certain aspect, or certain aspects, of the two objects. It is precisely these aspects which govern the determination of the source and target segments with respect to the 'solution' of a certain translational 'problem'. Moreover, a comparison is also *indirect* in nature: it can proceed only by means of intermediary concepts, which are related both to the aspects to be compared and to the theory which underlies the comparison.

Thus, it is the underlying theory, the aspects to be compared and the intermediary concepts (which may also be regarded as the 'invariant of the comparison', i.e. the famous *tertium comparationis*), which ultimately determine the establishment of the coupled pair as the basic unit of the comparative analysis that will ensue. (For a systematic presentation of these principles and their implications, see Toury 1977:85-94.) The members of each single pair can then be compared with each other.

First, an attempt will be made to identify the SHIFTS exhibited by the target text items in relation to their counterparts in the source text, or rather in relation to the hypothetical construct of the 'adequate translation' of that text into the target language/literature in question, which may serve as a convenient *tertium comparationis* (Toury 1980:112-121). It should be emphasized, however, that the establishment of translational shifts is never an end in itself, but merely a step on the way to the formulation of explanatory hypotheses. Incidentally, the same holds true for comparative studies in general, which

should be seen in perspective and assigned their
appropriate position and role in the descriptive
study as a whole. Consequently, within DTS, a study
is never to be reduced to mere comparison, as other
kinds of study in translational phenomena would
often like it to be.

When Hebrew binomials of (near-)synonyms, encountered in literary translations into the language, are mapped on their counterparts in the respective source texts, it turns out that they
very often replace *non*-binomials, especially single lexemes. In
extreme cases they even replace 'zero' lexical substance in the
source texts, that is, they are 'additions' (Levenston 1976:67;
Toury 1977:162-171,265-266). On the other hand, cases where an
original binomial is *not* replaced by a corresponding Hebrew one
seem very rare indeed, and most of them should probably be attributed to an accidental lack of appropriate pairs of (near-)
synonyms in the Hebrew lexicon or to the original binomial
being an idiom, whose overall meaning (which is not an additive
function of the meanings of its constituents) has been preferred
both to the latter and to the formal identity of the combination
as a binomial.

As a result of the *length* of the binomial, at least in
relation to its constituents, its *semantic repetitiveness* and
its *combinatorial structure* ($x_1 + x_2$), the main shift caused by
its utilization as a substitute for a single lexeme seems to be
the *redistribution of the information*, that is, a change in the
relationships between the linguistic means (in this case, usually at the word level) and the semantic load carried by them,
which may manifest itself as either informational *redundancy* or
intensification, depending on the surrounding context. This
kind of shift gains prominence in direct proportion to the abun-
dance of the use of the device, up to an overall change in the
semantic structure of the text. (For more details see Toury
1977:168-171.)

Another kind of common shift, which originates in the
stylistic markedness of many of the fixed collocations in the
binomial structure as well as of the technique of binomializa-
tion itself, may be *stylistic elevation* (*ibid*.:150-151,170;
1980:128).

The following Hebrew translation of Goethe's famous
'Wanderers Nachtlied'[3] is a particularly striking case in point.
It illustrates in extreme form, yet without sliding into parody
(which, to be sure, does exist in the corpus; *ibid*.:167-168),
the use of binomials of (near-)synonyms at the end of the nineteenth century (the binomials are italicized):

    mi-kol *kípot u-shfáyim*
    m(e)al kol gív(ꞏ)a rama
    takshévna ha-oznáyim -
    akh *háshqet u-dmáma;*

ba('a)le *kánaf va-éver*
ba-yá('a)r yishnu áta,
khaké na m(e)at ha-géver,
od tanú'akh gam áta!   (Mandelkern 1889:102)
(From all peaks and bare heights / from every high hill / the
ears hear - / but quietness and stillness; / winged and pinion-
ed creatures / are asleep now in the forest, / just wait a
little, o man, / you too will yet come to rest.)[4]

Any attempt at translating a German (or English) metrical
text into Hebrew while trying to retain the prosodic traits of
the original, even in part, produces an inescapable need to
omit some of the semantic-lexical substance, because of the
greater average length in syllables of the Hebrew word.[5] In our
example the translator obviously subscribed to this need, but
at the same time did not hesitate to spend a substantial part
of the limited textual space that he had at his disposal on binomials of near-synonyms, where - on account of both the original formulation and the rules of the target language - he could
make do with one of their constituents only: 14 (and if we take
the first two lines of the translation as an additional bino-
mial:20) out of 53 metrical syllables, that is, 26.4% (or 37.7%),
are devoted to them - 8 (or even 14) superfluous syllables from
the point of view of both the translator's prosodic constraints
and an initial norm of adequate translation.

8. Translational Relationships and the Concept of Translation

One of the main objectives of the coupling of the
pairs 'problem + solution' and of the establishment
of the translational shifts (or of the comparative
analysis in general) is to render possible the description and explanation of the TRANSLATIONAL RELA-
TIONSHIP obtaining between the members of the pairs,
as a means towards the establishment of the overall
CONCEPT OF TRANSLATION underlying the corpus under
study.
    The apparatus for the description of these re-
lationships, and for the description of *all* the relationships that may obtain between target and source
items, segments and texts, is one of the tools that
DTS should be supplied with by the *theoretical* branch
of translation studies. Fortunately, in this respect
translation theory is of much greater help than in
any other, primarily because of the long tradition
of its preoccupation with problems of 'equivalence'
versus 'formal correspondence' (from Nida 1964 and
Catford 1965 to Ivir 1981). It must still rid itself,
however, of the prescriptive bias inherent in most
treatments of these questions. The prescriptive element may eventually find its place in the *applied* ex-

tensions of the discipline.

It appears, then, that theoretical, descriptive and applied translation studies - the three branches of a prospective fully-fledged and relatively autonomous discipline (see Holmes 1972) - may and should be distinguished in terms of three levels of translational relationships, along with the criteria (or types of conditions) for their establishment, which find their superficial expression in the use of verbs of three different categories:

Type of Relationship	Criterion (or Type of Condition,	Appropriate Verbs, e.g.	Branch of Translation Studies
possible	theoretical	can (under certain circumstances,	translation theory
existing	empirical	is	descriptive translation studies (DTS)
required	a priori	should be	applied translation studies

Of course, both the existing and the required relationships should turn out to be sub-classes of the overall range of possible relationships (with possible overlappings between the two), otherwise there would be something very wrong with the underlying theory, which, as a result, cannot be trusted to account for every possible translational relationship.

As for the establishment of translational relationships, the key concept is that of the 'invariant under transformation'. This invariant, the nucleus which the members of each coupled pair have in common, may be established in terms of either substance or function, on the purely linguistic (i.e. habitual) as well as on the ad hoc textual level. Consequently, translational relationships may be defined as either *formal* or *functional* on either level. The important *methodological* implication of this assertion is that terms of the same type and rank be applied to both members of the coupled pair, namely on the basis of the invariant which they are actually found to have in common. (For further methodological implications see Toury 1980:89-111.)

Of course, every textual-linguistic segment,

whether the representation of the 'problem' or of
the 'solution', is at once a set of elements of a
lower order and an element in another entity of a
higher order (see, for example, Roman Jakobson's
classic presentation of the issue of 'parts and
wholes in language', Jakobson 1963). Translational
relationships for every pair may therefore turn out
to be functional on certain levels and formal on
others. However, it will never do to settle for a
mere enumeration of all the types of relationship
pertinent to each one of the pairs, even if an explicit reference to the level(s) to which they apply
is added. Rather, a *hierarchy* of relationships should
always be established, in terms of diminishing centrality and growing peripherality. This ordered set
will, in turn, be taken as an indication of the *overall* translational relationship exhibited by the pair
in question.

Similar sets, established for a significant
number of coupled pairs 'problem + solution' and
weighted against each other, will finally yield the
hierarchy of translational relationships pertinent
to the entire corpus under study, be it one text, a
body of texts, or even a set of defined translational
phenomena extracted from the textual-linguistic corpus (like our discussion of the binomial of (near-)
synonyms as a 'translational solution'). At which
point the notion of TRANSLATION EQUIVALENCE has to
be introduced.

The notion of equivalence as it is used here
(following Toury 1980, especially 66-69) differs from
current concepts of translation equivalence in that
it is not one single target—source relationship established on the basis of this or that type of invariant, but another *functional-relational concept*, namely,
that relationship (or set of ordered relationships)
which, by definition, distinguishes between translation and non-translation in certain specific socio-
cultural circumstances of the target language, i.e.
between adequate and inadequate instances of performance with respect to the governing model(s) and to
the norms deriving from these models.

It is therefore the entire set of possible relationships which, for the purposes of descriptive
translation studies, functions as POTENTIAL EQUIVA-
LENCE; the place of this notion is in the theoretical
branch of the discipline. Any part of this initial
potential may on occasion function - within some observational phenomena - as a distinguishing factor,
and in that case we have ACTUAL (or realized) EQUIV-
ALENCE, whose proper place is, of course, DTS.

Finally, any relationship that is POSTULATED as EQUIVALENCE, on whatever ground and for whatever purpose, belongs in the domain of the applied extensions of translation studies.

The notion of equivalence, again, has little importance in itself and, at any rate, should not be regarded as all-inclusive, in DTS or the theory that underlies it. There is a point in establishing it in the course of a descriptive study only as a means, that is, insofar as it can be put to further use. It is most likely to be used as a basis for the establishment of the overall CONCEPT OF TRANSLATION underlying the corpus under study, if only at a semi-conscious or even entirely unconscious level. It may also be used for the tentative reconstruction of the TRANSLATIONAL PROCEDURE in which this concept was gradually realized, namely in terms of CONSTRAINTS of various types and of DECISION-MAKING under these constraints (for a detailed presentation of a process of decision-making, see Even-Zohar 1975). Finally, it may serve the explanation – in an order which is the reverse of the order of the discovery procedures described so far – of the entire network of translational relationships, the individual pairs 'problem + solution' (for example, as representing actual translation units under the dominant norm of translation equivalence) and the textual-linguistic representation of the translational solutions, which has made them into (surface) translational phenomena.

Obviously, the mapping of each Hebrew binomial on its counterpart in the source text yields, in addition to the mere shifts, the target—source relationships obtaining between the members of the pairs.

In a small percentage of the examples, the binomials of (near-)synonyms may be locally explained as an attempt to establish translational equivalence on the *referential* level, as a kind of 'hendiadys' ("the use of words with different but overlapping semantic spectra to denote the area of overlap", Beeston 1970:112), at the cost of both non-equivalence at the level of meaning—carriers, that is, of the ratio of linguistic means and the information carried by them (see Section 7 above), and a lower rate of acceptability as the constituents of an (original) Hebrew text (see Section 4 above). The hendiadys explanation has been given, for example, to parallel phenomena in translations into Arabic (Somekh 1975:6-7;1981) and from Sanskrit into Tokharian (Aalto 1964:69). However, in the case of modern translation into Hebrew, the rarity of the cases where this seems to be the best (let alone the only) explanation, the enormous diversity of the relationships exhibited by the binomials to their counterparts in the source texts, and especially the irregularity of these relationships, lead one to the tentative hypothesis that it is not at all a wish to retain a certain semantic invariant which underlies the frequent use of this device, that is, not a source-governed consideration, but a target-language or target-literature norm. Compare the "Schönheit" interpretation given in Leisi 1947:111-113 to the use of this device in Caxton's *Eneydos*.

The norm which governs the abundant use of binomials of (near-)synonyms can be described as the norm of 'authentic Hebrew' pushed almost to absurd limits. The centralization of a rather peripheral trait (and one which is becoming more and more peripheral), or the petrification of norms which are already outdated and practically obliterated in the centre of the target system is characteristic of a secondary or epigonic activity - the position which translation usually assumes within the target system (see Even-Zohar 1978 and 1979). Further descriptive studies into this phenomenon, in translation into other languages in various periods and under different circumstances, might even lead to a more general hypothesis, namely that the device may be a *universal of translation into young or otherwise 'weak' systems* (Even-Zohar 1978:24-25), perhaps as part of the attempt to develop indigenous linguistic possibilities. A few existing studies such as Leisi's dissertation (Leisi 1947), or the survey of the use of the device in German translations during the fourteenth and fifteenth centuries (Wenzlau 1906), or the tentative discussion of literary translation into Arabic in the nineteenth century (Somekh 1981) already hint at the feasibility of such a hypothesis. Unfortunately, these studies have been carried out under diverse methodologies and for many different purposes (see Section 1 above), which render their findings difficult to compare.

NOTES

* This is a revised and expanded version of an article, under the same title, published in *Dispositio*, 19-21,1982:23-40. I would like to thank all those who have cared to comment on its earlier versions, especially Theo Hermans, André Lefevere and my students at Tel Aviv University.

1. I will, from now on, use the abbreviation DTS, launched by Holmes (1972:Section 3.1), whenever I refer to the scientific branch. The longer denomination will be used to refer to research activities within this branch.

2. These are Dagut's terms. Van den Broeck employs a different terminology, which, however, refers to more or less the same categories: he calls (1) - translation 'sensu stricto', (2) - substitution, and (3) - paraphrase.

3. "Über allen Gipfeln / Ist Ruh. / In allen Wipfeln / Spürest du / Kaum einen Hauch; / Die Vögelein schweigen im Walde. / Warte nur, balde / Ruhest du auch."

4. Since Mandelkern's translation leans heavily on biblical structures and lexical items, it was only reasonable to
base the English literal rendering of his version on an older
English translation of the Bible; I have chosen the Revised
Standard Version for that purpose.
   5. Goethe's poem consists of 24 words and 38 syllables,
an average of 1.58 syllables per word. Mandelkern's Hebrew
translation comprises 26 words and 53 metrical syllables (some
of the grammatical syllables are compressed in the metrical
reading, as indicated by the parenthesized elements in the
transliteration), an average of 2.038 metrical syllables per
word, or almost 1.3 times the average length of an original
word. It may be interesting to note that more modern Hebrew
translations of the poem not only shun the binomials and try
to retain a greater part of the original semantic substance,
but also try their best to use *short* words. Some of them even
coin new ones for that purpose, a practice which is in keeping
with another target-literature norm of that period. Along with
this, the number of metrical syllables in the translations
approaches that of the source text and the average length of a
target-language word drops to about 1.85.

REFERENCES

AALTO, Pentti
1964   'Word-Pairs in Tokharian and Other Languages',
           Linguistics, 5:69-78
AMIR (PINKERFELD), Anda
1939   *Fad ve-Dan*. Tel Aviv, Yavne
BEESTON, A.F.L.
1970   *The Arabic Language Today*. London, Hutchinson
BROECK, Raymond van den
1981   'The Limits of Translatability Exemplified by Meta-
           phor Translations', *Poetics Today*, ii,4:73-87
BUSCH, Wilhelm
1939   *Max u-Moritz zomeme ha-mezimot*. Transl. Chava Carmi.
           Tel Aviv, Joachim Goldstein
1949   *Wilhelm Busch-Album für die Jugend*. Zurich, Raschner
CATFORD, J.C.
1965   *A Linguistic Theory of Translation*. London, Oxford UP
DAGUT, Menachem
1976   'Can "Metaphor" be Translated?', *Babel*, xii:21-33
1978   *Hebrew-English Translation: A Linguistic Analysis of
           some Semantic Problems*. Haifa, University of Haifa
DRESSLER, Wolfgang
1972   'Textgrammatische Invarianz in Uebersetzungen?', in
           E.Gülich & W.Raible (eds.), *Textsorten: Differenzie-
           rungskriterien aus linguistischer Sicht* (Frankfurt
           a.M., Athenäum):98-106
EVEN-ZOHAR, Itamar
1971   *Mavo le-te'orya shel ha-tirgum ha-sifruti*. Tel Aviv
           (Unpublished PhD thesis)

EVEN-ZOHAR, Itamar
1975   '"Spleen" le-Baudelaire be-tirgum Lea Goldberg: Le-
            ofi ha-hakhra'ot be-tirgum shira', *Ha-sifrut/Litera-
            ture*, 21:32-45
1978   'The Position of Translated Literature within the
            Literary Polysystem', in his *Papers in Historical
            Poetics* (Tel Aviv, Porter Institute for Poetics and
            Semiotics):21-27
1979   'Polysystem Theory', *Poetics Today*, i,1-2:287-310
GUSTAFSSON, Marita
1975   *Binomial Expressions in Present-Day English*. Turku,
            Turun Yiliopisto
HARTMANN, R.R.K.
1980   *Contrastive Textology*. Heidelberg, Julius Groos
1981   'Contrastive Textology and Translation', in W.Kühlwein
            et al. 1981:200-208
HOLMES, James S.
1972   *The Name and Nature of Translation Studies*. Amsterdam
            (Mimeograph)
HOUSE, Juliana
1977   *A Model for Translation Quality Assessment*. Tübingen,
            Gunter Narr
IVIR, Vladimir
1981   'Formal Correspondence vs. Translation Equivalence
            Revisited', *Poetics Today*, ii,4:51-59
JAKOBSON, Roman
1963   'Parts and Wholes in Language', in D.Lerner (ed.),
            Parts and Wholes (New York, Free Press of Glencoe):
            157-162
JOYCE, James
1972   *Musiqa qamerit*. Transl. Moshe Hana'ami. Tel Aviv,
            Mahborot le-sifrut
KOSKENNIEMI, Inna
1968   *Repetitive Word Pairs in Old and Early Middle English
            Prose*. Turku, Turun Yiliopisto
KUEHLWEIN, Wolfgang; THOME, Gisela & WILSS, Wolfram
1981   (Eds.) *Kontrastive Linguistik und Uebersetzungswis-
            senschaft*. Munich, W.Fink
LEISI, Ernst
1947   *Die tautologischen Wortpaare in Caxton's 'Eneydos'.
            Zur synchronischen Bedeutungs- und Ursachenforschung*.
            Zurich/New York, G.E.Stechert
LEVENSTON, E.A.
1976   'Liqrat stilistiqa hashva'atit shel ha-anglit ve-ha-
            ivrit', in B.-Z.Fischler & R.Nir (eds.), *Chaim Rabin
            Jubilee Volume* (Jerusalem, Council on the Teaching
            of Hebrew):59-67
LUBOSHITSKY, Aaron
1898   *Shim'on ve-Levi*. Warsaw/St. Petersburg, Tushiya
MALKIEL, Yakov
1968   'Studies in Irreversible Binomials', in his *Essays on

Linguistic Themes (Oxford, Blackwell):311-355
MANDELKERN, Shlomo
1889   *Shire sfat ever*, II. Leipzig, E.W.Vollrath
NIDA, Eugene
1964   *Toward a Science of Translating*, Leiden, E.J.Brill
REISS, Katharina
1981   'Der Uebersetzungsvergleich: Formen - Funktionen -
            Anwendbarkeit', in W.Kühlwein *et al.* 1981:311-319
SANDROCK, Ursula
1982   *'Thinking-Aloud-Protocols' (TAPs) - Ein Instrument
            zur Dekomposition des komplexen Prozesses 'Ueberset-
            zen'.* Kassel (Mimeograph)
SOMEKH, Sasson
1975   *Two Versions of Dialogue in Mahmūd Tamyūr's Drama.*
            Princeton, Princeton UP
1981   'The Emergence of Two Sets of Stylistic Norms in the
            Early Literary Translation into Modern Arabic Prose',
            Poetics Today, ii,4:193-200
TOURY, Gideon
1977   *Normot shel tirgum ve-ha-tirgum ha-sifruti le-ivrit
            ba-shanim 1930-1945.* Tel Aviv, Porter Institute for
            Poetics and Semiotics
1980   *In Search of a Theory of Translation.* Tel Aviv,
            Porter Institute for Poetics and Semiotics
1982   'Transfer as a Universal of Verbal Performance of L2
            Learners in Situations of Communication in Translated
            Utterances', *FINLANCE*, ii:63-78
1983   'Ha-psevdo-tirgum ke-uvda Sifrutit: Ha-miqre shel
            Papa Hamlet', Ha-sifrut/Literature 32:63-68
1984   'Translation, Literary Translation and Pseudo-trans-
            lation', *Comparative Criticism*, 6:73-85
WENZLAU, Friedrich
1906   *Zwei- un Dreigliedrigkeit in der deutschen Prosa des
            14. und 15. Jahrhunderts.* Halle (Inaugural-Disserta-
            tion)
WILSS, Wolfram
1982   *The Science of Translation.* Tübingen, Gunter Narr
YAHALOM, Shelly
1978   *Ha-yekhasim ben ha-sifrut ha-tsarfatit la-sifrut
            ha-anglit ba-me'a ha-18.* Tel Aviv (M.A. thesis)

ON DESCRIBING TRANSLATIONS

José Lambert & Hendrik van Gorp

1. Theoretical and Descriptive Studies

In the course of the last two decades or so, translation has gradually come to be viewed as a legitimate
object of scientific investigation. Generally speaking, the most important recent contributions to
translation studies have been made in the field of
translation theory. However, the links between the
different branches of translation studies still have
to be established more firmly. During the last ten
years, for example, Gideon Toury and a few other
scholars have repeatedly pointed out the fundamental
weakness of any translation theory which fails to
take account of the findings of systematic *descriptive*
studies (Toury 1980). In spite of this, the importance
of descriptive studies for translation theory has not
been sufficiently recognized. This explains why the
concrete study of translations and translational behaviour in particular socio-cultural contexts has
often remained isolated from current theoretical research, and why there is still, on the whole, a wide
gap between the theoretical and the descriptive approach. We should ask ourselves, therefore, how
translations are to be analyzed, in order to make our
research relevant both from a historical *and* from a
theoretical point of view. Indeed, our methodology
in this respect too often remains purely intuitive.
It is symptomatic, for instance, that the recent
Dutch study *Uitnodiging tot de vertaalwetenschap* (Invitation
to Translation Studies; Van den Broeck & Lefevere 1979)
stresses the need for descriptive studies, but omits
to specify how they should be carried out.
     Among the scholars who have been arguing for
better collaboration between historical and strictly
theoretical translation research, some have tried to
elaborate methodological schemes and principles.

Rather than discussing or summarizing them here, we shall present a comprehensive methodological framework of our own, which will enable us to study various aspects of translation within the context of a general and flexible translation theory.

2. A Hypothetical Scheme for Describing Translations

Rather than starting from any preconceived definitions or evaluation concepts, we base our research on a scheme (Lambert & Lefevere 1978) which contains the basic parameters of translational phenomena, as presented by Itamar Even-Zohar and Gideon Toury in the context of the so-called polysystem hypothesis (Even-Zohar 1978; Toury 1980). The scheme is as follows:

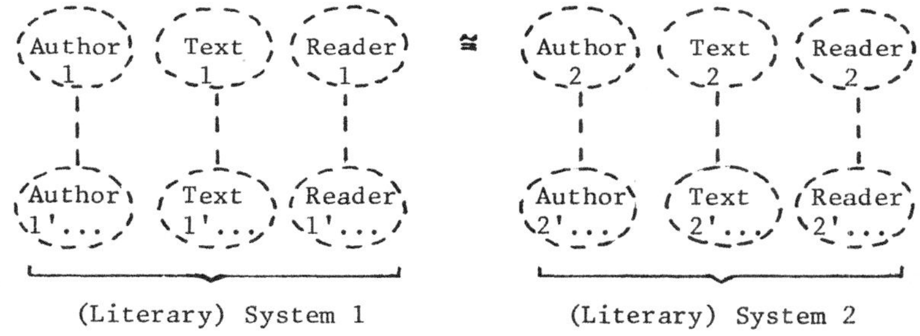

Explanation:
- Text 1: source text;
- Text 2: target text;
- Author 1 and Reader 1 belong to the system of the source text;
- Author 1 is to be situated among the authors of the source system;
- Text 1' and Reader 1' are to be situated within the source system;
- System 1 refers to the system of source text, source author and source reader (this system is not necessarily a strictly literary one, since literary systems cannot be isolated from social, religious or other systems);
- Author 2, Text 2, Reader 2 etc. are to be situated within the target system;
-  : all elements of this communication scheme are complex and dynamic.
- The symbol ≅ indicates that the link between source and target communication cannot really be predicted; it stands for an open relation, the exact nature of which will depend on the priorities of the translator's behaviour - which in turn has to be seen in function of the dominant norms of the target system.

The target system need not be restricted to the *literary* system of the target culture, since translations of literary works may also function outside literature, within a translational system. In most cases however, the target system will be (part of) the literary system of the target culture, or at least overlap with it. The exact relations between the literary systems of the target and source cultures have to be examined, which is precisely the aim of our scheme. Both source (literary) system and target (literary) system are open systems which interact with other systems.

All relations mentioned in the scheme deserve to be studied:
- T1 --- T2 (relations between individual texts, i.e. between the original and its translation)
- A1 --- A2 (relations between authors)
- R1 --- R2 (relations between readers)
- A1 --- T1 $\cong$ A2 --- T2 (authorial intentions in the source and target systems, and their correlation)
- T1 --- R1 $\cong$ T2 --- R2 (pragmatics and reception in the source and target systems, and their correlation)
- A1 --- A1', A2 --- A2' (situation of the author in respect of other authors, in both systems)
- T1 --- T1', T2 --- T2' (situation of both the original and the translation as texts in respect of other texts)
- R1 --- R1', R2 --- R2' (situation of the reader within the respective systems)
- Target System --- Literary System (translations within a given literature)
- (Literary) System 1 --- (Literary) System 2 (relations, whether in terms of conflict or harmony, between both systems).

As every translation is the result of *particular* relations between the parameters mentioned in the scheme, it will be the scholar's task to establish *which* relations are the most important ones. Among the priorities to be observed, especially the target-oriented (or 'acceptable') translations and the source-oriented (or 'adequate') translations stand out. But groups of 'acceptable' translations can still show very different characteristics regarding the T2 --- T1, T2 --- A1, or T2 --- R1 relations. From an empirical point of view it can safely be assumed that no translated text will be entirely coherent with regard to the 'adequate' versus 'acceptable' dilemma.

On the basis of our scheme, we can study such problems as:
- whether a particular translation of a contemporary

or ancient text is presented and regarded as a translation or not (it may be called, say, an adaptation or an imitation);
- the vocabulary, style, poetical and rhetorical conventions within both T2 and T1;
- translation criticism and translation theory in particular literatures at particular times;
- groups of translations and groups or 'schools' of translators;
- the role of translations in the development of a given literature (conservative versus innovative functions; exotic or non-exotic functions, etc.).

The main advantage of the scheme is that it enables us to bypass a number of deep-rooted traditional ideas concerning translational 'fidelity' and even 'quality' (is a given translation good or bad?), which are mainly source-oriented and inevitably normative. The reasons why normative comments on translation can have hardly any scientific relevance have been explained at length elsewhere (Toury 1980; Van den Broeck & Lefevere 1979; Lambert 1978), although it must be admitted that both the theoretical and practical implications of the new approach to translation description are still very confused, and in many cases the analyses still turn out to be inspired by an underlying idealistic conception of what translation ought to be.

3. Relations and Equivalence

Our scheme is a theoretical and hypothetical one: it shows which relations can play a part in the production and shaping of actual translations, and which ones may be observed in translation description. In other words, it represents a comprehensive set of *questions* (how has text 1 been translated into text 2, in relation to which other texts?...) rather than a series of theses. Being no more than a heuristic tool, the scheme obviously has no ontological status. Nevertheless, it comprises all functionally relevant aspects of a given translational activity in its historical context, including the process of translation, its textual features, its reception, and even sociological aspects like distribution and translation criticism.

It will be clear that in every concrete situation the basic aspects of the scheme should be interpreted in terms of specific priorities. The central question then becomes that of equivalence: what kind of equivalence can be observed between both communication schemes, or between the particular parameters in them? Is the translation in question target-oriented (i.e. acceptable) or source-oriented (i.e. adequate)? This basic priority is examined in terms of *dominant* norms, for there is reason to believe that no translational activity is completely coherent with respect to the dilemma 'acceptable' versus 'adequate'. While, say, the stylistic features of a given translation may be primarily target-oriented, its socio-cultural references may still be drawn from the source text. Since translation is essentially the result of selection strategies from and within communication systems, our main task will be to study the priorities - the dominant norms and models - which determine these strategies. The basic 'acceptable' versus 'adequate' dilemma will, in turn, lead to more concrete questions concerning priorities at different levels of both systems. The translation process as well as the resulting text and its reception can be studied from different points of view, either in a macro-structural or in a micro-structural way, focusing on linguistic patterns of various types, literary codes, moral, religious or other non-literary patterns, etc.

Every critical statement on translation can be situated within the limits of our scheme. There is, however, an important difference between traditional statements of this kind, including those that strive for explicitness and intersubjectivity, and the type of analysis we wish to propose; indeed, we aim to replace an atomistic approach with a functional and semiotic one.

4. Binary versus Complex Relations

Traditionally, translation criticism has been viewed in a strictly binary and one-directional way, as a straightforward confrontation between T1 and T2. In many cases it has been reduced not only to (some) linguistic aspects of the equivalence problem, but even to the particular question whether or not certain linguistic features in T2 are (appropriate) equivalents of corresponding linguistic features in T1. 'Literary' translation criticism more often than not behaves in exactly the same way, at most extending the analysis to include some literary features.

While these binary approaches undoubtedly bring important aspects of the translational problem to the fore, they fail to respect the complex nature of equivalence, if only because the translator, working in a particular translational situation, does not necessarily use T1 (or S1) as the dominant model. What's more, no translation ever accepts either T1 or S1 as its exclusive model; it will inevitably contain all kinds of interferences deriving from the target system.

Our attempt to build up a synthetic commentary may well appear utopian, since it is impossible to summarize all relationships involved in the activity of translation. We are fully aware of this. Indeed, the scholar, as well as the translator, has to establish priorities. In our working scheme, however, he can at least find the means of being systematic instead of being merely intuitive: he can avoid *a priori* judgements and convictions (*theses!*), and he can always situate the aspects and relations to be observed within a general equivalence scheme.

In principle, relations within and between S1 and S2 should be taken into account. In every analysis with systemic aims, we have to try and determine which links are dominant, and what their precise functions are. But there is no reason why we should avoid to study separately particular links, such as linguistic features within T1 and T2 (perhaps in their relationships with linguistic features within T1' and T2') or particular aspects of the links between T2 and R2 or R2'. It will be obvious, though, that in a synthetic approach the dominant norms deserve to be dealt with most systematically; when accounting for an 'acceptable' translation, for instance, it will be advisable to consider in some detail the exact state of affairs within the target literature rather than the 'differences' with the source literature. In any approach we should avoid the most glaring shortcoming characteristic of most traditional commentary: the exclusion of some - or most - of the relationships to which our scheme refers.

5. The Aims and Limits of Text Comparison

The comparison of T1 and T2, to the exclusion of other factors, has often been responsible for the reductionist approach we have been criticizing. However, it still remains a crucial point, even in a systemic analysis. We often have hardly any other material for our study of translation and literary systems, and even if we do, the different translational strategies evident in the text itself provide the most explicit information about the relations between the source and target systems, and about the translator's position in and between them. Furthermore, the translated text is an obvious document for the study of conflicts and parallels between translational theory and practice. The comparison of T1 and T2 is therefore a relevant part of translation studies - as long as it does not obscure the wider perspective.

As Gideon Toury (1980:112-113) has pointed out, any text comparison is indirect; it is always a comparison of categories selected by the scholar, in a construct which is purely hypothetical. We can never 'compare' texts by simply juxtaposing them. We need a frame of reference to examine the positive and/or negative links between T1 and T2, and to examine them from the point of view of both T1 and T2. This frame of reference cannot be identified with the 'source text'. It is, rather, a combination of categories drawn from both the source and the target text, and it could even be enriched by questions arising from the source and target systems. Such a frame of reference has no significance as a normative standard (what has or has not been translated?). Reducing the confrontation to a differential observation which refers to the source text only, would allow us merely to establish what the translation *is not*. Our reference scheme should be a hypothetical standard which allows us to characterize, not just one or two texts, but translational and textual strategies, i.e. norms and models. The differential approach will, at best, be useful as a stage in the descriptive work, in so far as it is not limited to a one-directional negative approach. In order to obtain a complex rather than a reductionist model, the relationships between S1 and S2 can be used as a general background for the text comparison (for example, is a particular prose translation of verse compatible with the function of prose in the target system?).

Our own descriptive research has given us the opportunity to elaborate a practical model for a type of textual analysis in which we try to describe and test out translational strategies. In this model (see Appendix), the student first collects information about the general macro-structural features of the translation. Is the translation identified as such (as a 'translation', or as an 'adaptation' or 'imitation'), and what do these terms mean in the given period? Is the translator's name mentioned anywhere? Can the text be recognized as a 'translated text' (linguistic interference, neologisms, socio-cultural features)? Are the general text structures of the 'adequate' type (total/partial translation?) Does the translator or the editor provide any meta-textual comment (preface, footnotes)?

A survey like this already gives us a rough idea of the overall translational strategy and the main priorities in it. Since translation is determined by selection mechanisms on various textual levels, we assume, as a working hypothesis, that a translated text which is more or less 'adequate' on the macro-structural level will generally also be more or less adequate on the micro-structural level, but that it cannot be adequate on every specific level. In the same way we assume that a translation which is 'acceptable' on the macro-level will probably also be 'acceptable' on the micro-level. Of course, we need to test out whether this hypothesis helps us to gather relevant information about the translational strategy and its priorities, or, to put it in more ordinary terms, we have to observe, in this initial stage, both the text in general and a number of concrete text fragments.

It would be naïve, however, to think that an exhaustive analysis of every textual problem is feasible. We therefore have to follow a certain order in our investigations. It might be wise to begin by looking at different fragments, and then to analyze them again from the point of view of particular textual rules. Does the translator translate words, sentences, paragraphs, metaphors, narrative sequences? He will hardly have been able to translate all these text levels to the same extent and with the same degree of subtlety. Most likely, he will have sacrificed specific text levels (e.g., lexis) to other levels (e.g., literariness). Such a microscopic analysis, which could in some instances be supported with statistical data, enables us to observe the consistency and the hierarchical structure of the translational strategy. It may also allow us to formulate hypotheses concerning the origin and position of this strategy (source text? target text? target system?). And it will be easy to draw provisional conclusions about individual fragments.

These conclusions can be used at a second stage to guide the analysis of other extracts. Does the translator add or delete paragraphs, words, images, literary features, etc. throughout the text, or only in certain passages? If the latter, how to explain the discrepancies? In order to reach a more general and panoramic view of the translational method, we can bring in fragments in which new difficulties appear, in order to check our hypothesis or so as to reconstruct in more detail the exact priorities which govern the translator's activity.

By adopting a flexible method of this type the scholar will gain an insight into text rules and translational rules; he can test them throughout the text and classify them according to specific parameters, without having to accumulate random examples.

Clearly, these rules will ultimately have to be linked with other rules or, better still, with the entire system. This will then lead to questions like:
- Does translator Y always translate according to these rules? If not, can we explain the exceptions?
- Does he write his own 'creative' work according to the same rules? If not, why?
- Does he, in his 'creative' work or in his transla- tions, behave in the same manner as his fellow translators?
- Does he show a conscious awareness of rules, norms, models? Does he theorize about them? If so, are there any conflicts between his theory and practice, or between his own theories and those of others? On which points?
- Is his work as a translator more innovatory, or less so, than his 'creative' writing?
- Are there any conflicts between the translational norms and the norms and expectations of the recept- or audience (critics, readers)?

These questions, like the whole reference scheme for comparison, could of course be further developed and diversified; they are part of an open-ended re- search programme about translation as an instrument of mediation between literary systems. The systemic approach enables us not only to comment on transla- tions with the same terminology we use for comment- ing on literary systems, but also to make general descriptive statements on all levels of both the translational and the surrounding literary system (author; translator; readers; texts; micro- and macro- levels).

While describing particular translated texts in some detail, we can point the way to large-scale macro-structural research, or formulate hypotheses to guide such research. But we can and should also do exactly the opposite. General descriptive studies - like the Louvain project on 'Literature and Trans- lation in France, 1800-1850' (see Bibliography) or other similar projects - have to be tested by con- fronting them with findings extracted from particu- lar texts and phenomena. This can be done, provided the scholar employs hypothetical schemes for all as- pects and phases of the translational problem.

6. The Implications of a Systemic Approach

One should bear in mind that nearly all these aspects of the translational problem have been and are still being discussed by scholars involved in Translation Studies. It *is* new, however, to stress the need to combine and connect them systematically, and to insist upon their *systemic* nature, both on the *intersystem-ic* and on the *intra-systemic* level. This means that every particular aspect of the translational process should be described and discussed not only in terms of the Author-Text-Reader system, but also in terms of the translational system (in so far as it is distinct from the literary system) and, perhaps, other cultural systems; this is especially the case when we are dealing with the translation of literary texts or the literary translation of texts which the source system does not regard as literary. The very use of the concept of system implies that we are aware of conflicts and parallelisms between systems and subsystems.

By focusing on norms and models the most individual translational phenomenon can be described both as individual and as collective. This is one of the essential reasons why we should avoid an exclusive preoccupation with individual translators and with individual texts or their reception. It is part of the 'atomistic' approach to examine translated texts one by one, instead of looking at a series of·texts, or a series of translational problems. When dealing with individual phenomena, we are likely to overlook their general characteristics if we confine ourselves to a single descriptive category (for example, the rhyme schemes in verse translation at a given moment; clearly, they also refer to rhyme schemes in both the source and the target literature). A systemic approach on the other hand, enables us to distinguish between individual and less individual or collective norms.

The importance of large-scale research programmes should now be obvious. We cannot properly analyze specific translations if we do not take into account other translations belonging to the same system(s), and if we do not analyze them on various micro- and macro-structural levels. It is not at all absurd to study a single translated text or a single translator, but it is absurd to disregard the fact that this translation or this translator has (positive or negative) connections with other translations and translators.

Once we have adopted this position, we can hardly go on talking simply about the analysis of translated texts, and still less about the analysis of 'a translated text'. Our object is translated literature, that is to say, translational norms, models, behaviour and systems. The specific T1 and T2 analysis should be part of a larger research programme focusing on all aspects of translation. Even the distinction between literary and non-literary translation turns out to be a purely theoretical problem, since we have to determine to what extent translations belong to a translational or to a literary system or to both.

In fact, we are convinced that the study of translated literature, if approached from such a broad, systemic angle, will contribute substantially to a more dynamic and functional approach to literature as such, for there is no doubt that the analysis of literary translations provides an important key to our understanding of literary interference and historical poetics.

APPENDIX

A Synthetic Scheme for Translation Description

1. Preliminary data:
   - title and title page (e.g. presence or absence of genre indication, author's name, translator's name,...)
   - metatexts (on title page; in preface; in footnotes - in the text or separate?)
   - general strategy (partial or complete translation?)

   These preliminary data should lead to hypotheses for further analysis on both the macro-structural and the micro-structural level.

2. Macro-level:
   - division of the text (in chapters, acts and scenes, stanzas...)
   - titles of chapters, presentation of acts and scenes,...
   - relation between types of narrative, dialogue, description; between dialogue and monologue, solo voice and chorus,...
   - internal narrative structure (episodic plot?, open ending?,...); dramatic intrigue (prologue, exposition, climax, conclusion, epilogue); poetic structure (e.g. contrast between quatrains and tercets in a sonnet)
   - authorial comment; stage directions;...

   These macro-structural data should lead to hypotheses about micro-structural strategies.

3. Micro-level (i.e. shifts on phonic, graphic, micro-syntactic, lexico-semantic, stylistic, elocutionary and modal levels):
   - selection of words
   - dominant grammatical patterns and formal literary structures (metre, rhyme,...)
   - forms of speech reproduction (direct, indirect, free indirect speech)
   - narrative, perspective and point of view
   - modality (passive or active, expression of uncertainty,

                ambiguity,...)
            - language levels (sociolect; archaic/popular/dialect;
              jargon...)
These data on micro-structural strategies should lead to a
renewed confrontation with macro-structural strategies, and
hence to their consideration in terms of the broader systemic context.

4. Systemic context:

            - oppositions between micro- and macro-levels and between
              text and theory (norms, models,...)
            - intertextual relations (other translations and
              'creative' works)
            - intersystemic relations (e.g. genre structures,
              stylistic codes...)

REFERENCES

BROECK, Raymond van den & LEFEVERE, André
1979   *Uitnodiging tot de vertaalwetenschap.* Muiderberg,
        Coutinho
D'HULST, Lieven, LAMBERT, José & BRAGT, Katrin van
1979   *Littérature et traduction en France, 1800-1850. Etat
        des travaux.* Leuven, KUL - Dept. Literatuurwetenschap
        (Preprint)
HOLMES, J.S., LAMBERT, José & BROECK, Raymond van den
1978   (Eds.) *Literature and Translation. New Perspectives in
        Literary Studies.* Leuven, Acco
LAMBERT, José & BRAGT, Katrin van
1980   *'The Vicar of Wakefield' en langue française. Tradi-
        tions et ruptures dans la littérature traduite.* Leuven,
        KUL - Dept. Literatuurwetenschap (Preprint)
LAMBERT, José & LEFEVERE, André
1977   'Traduction, traduction littéraire et littérature com-
        parée', in Paul Horguelin (ed.) *La traduction, une
        profession.* Actes du XVIIe Congrès de la FIT (Montreal,
        Conseil des traducteurs et interprètes du Canada)
TOURY, Gideon
1980   *In Search of a Theory of Translation.* Tel Aviv, Porter
        Institute for Poetics and Semiotics

SECOND THOUGHTS ON TRANSLATION CRITICISM

A Model of its Analytic Function

Raymond van den Broeck

1. The need for a systemic model

Due to recent developments in translation studies, we
know that translation criticism, if taken seriously,
is not confined to being a merely subjective concern,
a matter of taste and intuition, likes or dislikes.
The admission that value judgements do play an important part in translation practice and evaluation can
by no means counter the claim that the translation
critic is able to base his account on systematic description and intersubjective knowledge of translation
processes and products. It has been observed that objective criticism is bound to take into account the
various factors involved in this process of interlingual and intercultural communication (Reiss 1971).
It is a well-known fact that Eastern European scholars have contributed much to making translation studies more systematic and objective. More particularly
with respect to translation comparison and description, special mention should be made of the Czecho-
slovak scholars, among whom especially Jiři Levý,
František Miko, Anton Popovič and Dionýz Ďurišin
have received international attention for their work.
Nonetheless the practice of translation criticism - and here I refer to the common situation in
most Western countries - seems to have taken small
profit from their endeavours. There may, of course,
be an obvious practical reason for this. Unlike most
Eastern European countries, where translators' organizations are treated on an equal footing with
writers' organizations, and where translation criticism is not only backed by an institutionalized
training of both translators and translation theorists, but also stimulated by publication facilities,
the countries in the West do little or nothing in
order to ensure the social status of their transla-

tors. As a consequence, translation criticism (so
far as it exists) and, more particularly, the reviewing of translations, is left to a random set of pub-
licists, ranging from philologists and literary critics familiar with the source language and literature
to translators from the same or related languages.
Nearly all of them are amateurs in the field of translation studies, and hence translation criticism is
amateurish. The amateurism shows itself in various
ways. In many cases reviewers treat the translated
work as if they were dealing with an original written
in their mother tongue, without betraying even by a
single remark that it is in fact a translation.
Others spend most of their time and energy on the
original author and his work, disposing of the translator's part with commonplace statements to the effect that 'the translation reads well', or 'apart
from a few mistakes the translation is excellent',
'unfortunately the translator's wording is no match
for his author's style', and the like. Some reviewers do make an attempt at error analysis, though they
mostly leave the reader in the dark as to what criteria they actually apply when they pronounce value
judgements. Most will deal with the translated text
on the quiet assumption that it can only be a more
or less faithful replica of the original. Their approach is primarily or even totally source-oriented:
they hardly consider the translation to be a (target)
text ranking among other texts in the target system.
They almost invariably fail to pay attention to the
systemic relations of the translated text to other
texts within that system, treating it instead as if
it were an isolated phenomenon.

   To say that these practices apply to Western
countries in general may seem a blanket condemnation.
However, with the possible exception of West Germany
(which like the GDR can boast a long tradition of
translation theory and practice), they are still the
general rule. Hard data in this regard are not available, but a tentative investigation carried out by
students of the University of Amsterdam 1982-83
produced clear evidence for the hypothesis that
translation criticism in the West is seriously under-
developed.[1]

   In this paper I intend to propose a model of
translation criticism and reviewing. Two preliminary
remarks are in order. First, it is an optimum model,
based on the assumption that the critic will keep in
view both the original act of communication and that
of metacommunication. Secondly, the proposed model
is in fact incomplete, since it bears primarily on

one of the three functions of translation criticism as described by Anton Popovič (1973). Apart from the analytic function, which will be my main concern, Popovič also distinguishes a postulative and an operative function. The latter two, though no less important, will be dealt with only implicitly, i.e. as interwoven with the analytic function in the reviewer's critical activity.

In my view, translation criticism, despite the subjective element inherent in value judgements, can be an objective account if it is based, at least implicitly, on systematic description. The starting-point for this description will be a comparative analysis of the source and target texts. Furthermore, a thorough description demands that not only text structures but also systems of texts be involved in the comparison. It is only at this point that the critic's value judgement can come into operation. However, in the confrontation of his own critical standards with the norms adopted by the translator, the critic should clearly distinguish one from the other. His evaluation should take account not only of the translator's poetics but also of the translational method adopted by the translator in view of the specific target audience envisaged, and of the options and policies followed in order to attain his purpose. The final outcome of this confrontation will be the reviewer's critical account.

These consecutive - perhaps partly simultaneous - operations could be represented schematically as follows:

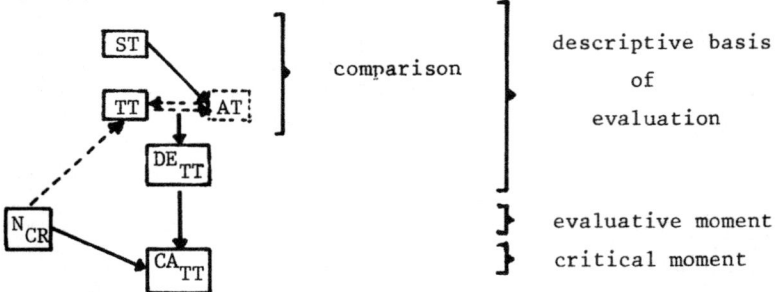

ST,TT	= source text, target text
AT	= adequate translation
DE_{TT}	= description of the target text
N_{CR}	= norm of the translation critic
CA_{TT}	= critical account of the target text (review)

2. The comparative analysis of source and target texts

The purpose of this kind of comparison is to ascertain the degree of factual equivalence between the source and target texts. By 'factual' equivalence I mean the observable (empirical) phenomenon that both the source and target texts are relatable to (at least some of) the same functionally relevant features (Catford 1965:50).

Since the comparison must be source-oriented and irreversible (the TT derives from the ST and not vice-versa), it follows that the invariant serving as a *tertium comparationis* in a comparison of this type should be ST-based. This invariant is the Adequate Translation (AT). Its nature has been described by Gideon Toury (1980:122ff).[2] In his view this intermediate construct serving as a third term in the comparison is in fact *hypothetical* in nature: the Adequate Translation is not an actual text, but a hypothetical reconstruction of the textual relations and functions of the ST. Since it comprises only such features, on various levels of description, as are functionally relevant for the structural relationships within the source text and for the structure of the text as a whole, the Adequate Translation can be regarded as the optimum (or maximum) reconstruction of all the ST elements possessing textual functions. Such elements will be termed (after Even-Zohar) 'textemes'.

The comparison of ST and TT should, of course, take into account the occurrence of shifts of expression in the translation (see Popovič 1970). In this respect the difference between obligatory and optional shifts is essential. Since obligatory shifts are rule-governed, i.e. imposed by the rules of the target linguistic and cultural system, they will not be regarded as interfering with the adequacy of the target text. Optional shifts, on the other hand, are determined by the translator's norms. As a rule, therefore, the occurrence of optional shifts will be an indication of the translator's preoccupation with creating an 'acceptable' target text, i.e. a text conforming to the norms of the target system. Of course, the translator may not only violate target norms but also break target rules. In some periods of literary history this was even the normal attitude toward translation. Thus also the non-occurrence of obligatory shifts can serve as an indication of translational norms, and is therefore essential for the description (see Popovič 1970:79).

The comparison of a target text with its source moves through three stages.

(1) A textemic analysis of the ST, leading to the formulation of the Adequate Translation, viz. the specification of the ST in terms of textemes. This analysis comprises every textual level on which linguistic and extra-linguistic elements obtain functional relevance. It includes phonic, lexical, and syntactic components, language varieties, figures of rhetoric, narrative and poetic structures, elements of text convention (text sequences, punctuation, italicizing, etc.), thematic elements, and so on. It goes without saying that certain aspects, relating to the hierarchical structuration of the various textual components and their interrelationships, should be given priority.

(2) A comparison of the TT elements corresponding to these textemes, taking into account the various shifts (or deviations) with respect to the ST. The identification of correspondences will, of course, benefit from the methods and insights of contrastive linguistics and stylistics. A general theory of expression, as proposed for example by František Miko (1970:61ff), provides a starting-point for the systematic evaluation of the shifts of expression that occur in translation.

(3) A generalizing description of the differences between the actual TT/ST equivalence and the Adequate Translation, on the basis of the comparison of the textemes. This description will state the factual degree or type of equivalence between TT and ST.

3. From text structures to systems of texts

A scientifically-based translation description is not to be confused with what is generally known as 'error analysis'. Although error analysis may be of use for translation didactics, it offers too narrow a basis for serious critical evaluation. It mostly relies on the notion of Adequate Translation not only as a *tertium comparationis* but also as a norm for judging the target text, so that every optional shift is readily considered erroneous, especially in cases where the criteria applied in the analysis do not coincide with the translator's norm.

The translation description which I wish to propose is of a different nature. It is not primarily interested in whether a translation is 'adequate', 'correct', or even 'successful'. Rather than providing answers to such questions it should deal with the 'hows', the 'whys and wherefores' of translated texts. Isolated cases are not the be-all and end-all of translation description, which should strive to detect the translator's norms and options, the con-

58

straints under which he works, and the way in which
they influence the translational process as well as
the ensuing product.

It follows that a more appropriate model of
translation description should take into account the
multiple relations between the source text and the
system of similar and/or other texts originating from
the same language, culture and tradition; between the
source and the target systems, between the target
text and its readers; between the target text and
other translations (whether or not in the same target
system) of the same source text, and so on. This complex network of relations could be represented schematically as follows:

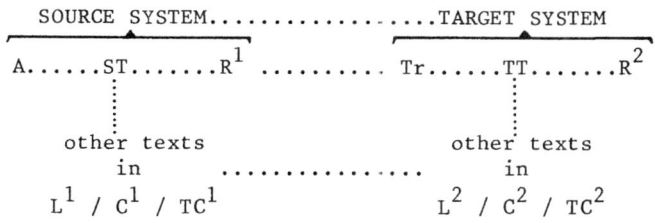

```
SOURCE SYSTEM..................TARGET SYSTEM
┌──────────────────────┐      ┌─────────────────────┐
A......ST.......R¹ .......... Tr......TT.......R²
       ⋮                              ⋮
   other texts                    other texts
      in     ...............         in
   L¹ / C¹ / TC¹                  L² / C² / TC²
```

A = author   Tr = translator
ST = source text   TT = target text
R¹ = reader of source text   R² = reader of target text

            L = natural language
            C = culture and social context
            TC = text tradition and conventions

Translation description as I understand it will thus,
in principle, regard all the relationships between a
text and the processes involved in its production and
reception as meaningful, i.e. as its proper object.
Naturally, it will have to be incorporated in a general theory of texts, of which it is more than just a
random part. Large corpora of translated texts of
different types and sorts should be submitted to comparative analysis and description, and the focus of
attention should be on how and why such texts function (or fail to function) *as texts*.

Clearly, the comparative point of view in literary studies demands a type of description that leaves
scope for the systemic relations between translated
and original literary works, between metacreativity
and the creative component, in short: the relational
function of translations. As Dionýz Ďurišin has observed:

An analysis of a translation is determined primarily by its peculiar role in the literary movement, i.e. its relational function. This basic function of translation conditions the sense of aestheticism of a given translator and modifies in many respects also that (sense of aestheticism) accepted as a norm and valid in a national literature at a certain historical moment. Hence, any 'objective' evaluation of a translation, guided solely by an abstractive translation norm and disregarding either totally or partially the above moment and related circumstances, will be incomplete, fragmentary. (Ďurišin 1974:137)

This functional approach to translation description will make use of existing or innovatory hypotheses about texts and their systemic relationships. The so-called 'polysystem theory' as elaborated by Itamar Even-Zohar, for example, has already proved to be successful with regard to the systematic study of literary translations within national literatures (see Even-Zohar 1978; Lambert 1980).

4. The critical norm confronted with the translational norm

To say that objective translation criticism should, at least implicitly, start from a descriptive basis is to admit that the translation critic's business is a scholarly occupation, requiring literary skill as well as interlinguistic and intercultural competence. It is a matter of knowledge more than of taste, of understanding more than of evaluating.

Nonetheless the critic's personal value judgement plays a distinctive role in it. This role will diminish when the translation concerned belongs to an older period and thus conforms to linguistic, aesthetic and moral standards which only historical insight and explanation can highlight. The critic's personal standards, on the other hand, may gain prominence in the case of contemporary translations. Here too, however, it is the critic's first duty to acknowledge the translator's norm as objectively as possible before (or while) confronting the reader with his own set of norms. This acknowledgement has a special bearing on the translator's view of the literary text, on the specific reading public he envisages and the ensuing degree of acceptability and/or adequacy he strives for.

With the foregoing in view the critic may or may not agree with the particular methods chosen by the translator for a particular purpose. He is entitled to doubt the effectiveness of the chosen

strategies, to criticize decisions taken with regard
to certain details. To the extent that he is himself
familiar with the functional features of the source
text, he will be a trustworthy guide in telling the
reader where target textemes balance source textemes,
and where, in the critic's view, they do not. But he
must never confuse his own initial norms with those
of the translator. All too often reviewers disregard
the variety of initial choices which translators of
literary texts have (at least in principle) at their
disposal. Translations can be either intended to
function as if they were original texts in the target
literary system, and thus acceptable to the prevailing literary taste; or they can be meant as adequate
renderings of their sources, irrespective of the
aesthetic norms of the target system; or they can
occupy a position somewhere in between these two extremes. Only if the reviewer recognizes the initial
norm adopted by the translator, will his critical
account have any objective value.

Hence it is one of the foremost tasks of translation criticism to contribute to a greater awareness
of norms among all those involved in the production
and reception of translations. In his privileged
position of a receptor who observes the total communication process (author + source text + source re-
ceptor/translator + target text + target receptor)
the critic, more than anybody else, is able to realize that translational options are not abstract or
immanent but bound to time and place. So, of course,
are his own critical norms.

Translating literature has rightly been called
a kind of critical intercourse with the literary
work; and it has been observed that every translation
implies a form of criticism of its original. The
translation critic, then, is a critic's critic, for
he brings his value judgement to bear on a phenomenon which by its very nature implies a judgement of
values.

NOTES

1. The investigation, carried out by students attending a
course of seminars on translation criticism under the direction
of James S.Holmes (General Literary Studies, University of
Amsterdam), was based on reviews published in a number of Dutch,
French, and Anglo-American periodicals, including the *New York
Review of Books*, the *TLS*, etc.
2. For reasons of economy Toury's model is presented here
in a condensed and slightly adapted form.

REFERENCES

CATFORD, J.C.
1965   A *Linguistic Theory of Translation*. London, Oxford
          University Press
ĎURIŠIN, Dionýz
1974   *Sources and Systematics of Comparative Literature*.
          Bratislava, Univerzita Komenského
EVEN-ZOHAR, Itamar
1978   'The Position of Translated Literature within the
          Literary Polysystem', in J.S.Holmes *et al.* (eds.),
          Literature and Translation (Louvain, Acco):117-127
LAMBERT, José
1980   'Production, tradition et importation: une clef pour
          la description de la littérature et de la littérature
          en traduction', *Canadian Review of Comparative Litera-
          ture*, 1980, nr 2: 246-252
MIKO, František
1970   'La théorie de l'expression et la traduction', in J.S.
          Holmes *et al.* (eds.), *The Nature of Translation* (The
          Hague/Bratislava, Mouton/Slovak Academy of Sciences):
          61-77
POPOVIČ, Anton
1970   'The Concept "Shift of Expression" in Translation
          Analysis', in J.S.Holmes *et al.* (eds.), *The Nature of
          Translation* (The Hague/Bratislava, Mouton/Slovak
          Academy of Sciences):78-87
1973   'Zum Status der Uebersetzungskritik', *Babel*, XIX, 4:
          161-165
REISS, Katharina
1971   *Möglichkeiten und Grenzen der Uebersetzungskritik*.
          Munich, Max Hueber
TOURY, Gideon
1980   *In Search of a Theory of Translation*. Tel Aviv, Porter
          Institute for Poetics and Semiotics

HOW DISTINCT ARE FORMAL AND DYNAMIC

EQUIVALENCE?

Maria Tymoczko

The arguments about 'literal versus free' and 'form versus content' are still with us in the realm of translation practice, and they affect not only naive or novice translators but editors and publishers as well.[1] Some of these distinctions have been reformed in the theoretical opposition between 'formal equivalence' versus 'dynamic equivalence', the former in Nida's words focusing "attention on the message itself, in both form and content", the latter attempting to assure that "the relationship between reception and message should be substantially the same as that which existed between the original receptors and the message" (Nida 1964:159).

Though translators are increasingly moving toward dynamic-equivalence translation (Nida 1964:162), there is still widespread predisposition toward (or perhaps nostalgia for) formal-equivalence translation. In this paper I intend to look at three reasons why formal-equivalence translations are preferred — the popular contentions that they are prima facie obvious, that they are logically direct or logically simple, and that they are somehow more objective than dynamic-equivalence translations. One thrust of all these notions is that the translator's role or input is minimized in formal-equivalence or literal translations, and that this is all to the good. Though the translator may be pictured as more than an industrious drudge with a good dictionary, the view (or hope) is perhaps that literal or formal-equivalence translations will not involve interpretation. That is, the translator's own view of the text will be severely circumscribed by the method of translation and the translator will intervene less between translation and text.

To reexamine these popular views let us consider the translation of contradictory usages: instances

in which the usage of the source language is diametrically opposed to the usage of the target language.
Nida (1964:214) observes "contradictory usages are
found in comparing any source and receptor languages".
Some contradictory usages are primarily metaphorical
in import; Nida gives the example of a Peruvian language which uses the phrase 'she left the fever'
where English says 'the fever left her' (1964:214).
But contradictory usages can also be syntactical.
The examples I should like to consider here are deceptively simple — the usage in Old Irish and English
of definite and indefinite nouns in two situations:
the introduction of a new substantive and the expression of the generic substantive.[2] The examples are
clear because they involve contradictory uses of the
definite article in the two languages, but they are
deceptively simple because determiners like the definite and indefinite articles present exceedingly complex rules and are accordingly very difficult to
model. The English articles are the despair of transformational grammar, and Bertrand Russell spent two
chapters of his *Introduction to Mathematical Philosophy* on
the implications of the definite article for philosophy and logic.

By way of a historical note I should point out
that although Modern English and Old Irish are both
Indo-European languages, the usage patterns for the
articles evolved independently in the two languages.
Indo-European did not have articles as such and in
both Irish and English the development of these features was relatively late. On the other hand, the
developments are parallel. As in the case of the
Romance languages, for example, the articles in both
English and Irish developed from old demonstratives.

In English we introduce new substantives with
the indefinite article.

(1) There was a man walking in the jungle...Suddenly
he met a lion face to face.

Thereafter the substantives are considered defined,
so the definite article is used in subsequent references: "He knew...the lion would be on him in a
minute..."[3] Sentence 1 is an example from a traditional English folktale collected in the field. It
shows the English usage of the articles found in
ordinary speech, as well as traditional oral literary form.[4] In Old Irish we find the opposite usage:
a new substantive is introduced with the definite
article:

(2) Co n-accae in fer ocond fulucht i mmedón ind feda,

64

indala lám dó cona gaisciud indi, ind lám aile oc fuiniu
in tuircc.

(3) (gloss translation) And he saw *the* man at *the*
cooking-pit in middle of the wood, one of two hands to
him with his weapons in it, the other hand at cooking
the boar. (introductory definite articles italicized)[5]

What theoretical issues are raised by the translation of such a contradictory usage? First, contradictory usages immediately show that literal or
formal-equivalence is not prima facie obvious. You
can't just sit down with the dictionary and proceed
one word at a time. In fact, a word-by-word translation of the passage won't do; the English usage generated word by word is contradictory to our own and
gives formal signals which are contradictory to those
of the source text.

(4) And he saw the man at the cooking-pit in the middle
of the wood — one of his two hands had his weapons in
it and the other hand was cooking the boar.

Sentence 4 as a translation suggests to an English
speaker that the man, the fire, and the pig are all
familiar and presumably have all appeared in the
story before; since, indeed, they do not occur in
the extant text, the reader of the translation is
disoriented — feeling that s/he should know something that s/he doesn't (perhaps because of having
forgotten the original introduction of these elements) or perhaps assuming that the text is acepha-
lous or fragmentary in some other way.
One might say that this type of disorientation
is relatively minor. The reader quickly readjusts
his/her expectations about the new items and perhaps
even learns eventually the alternative grammatical
usage of definite articles for introductory situations in literal translations from Old Irish (a fairly, dramatic way of bringing the audience to the text).
The example shows, however, that contradictory usages can be the syntactical equivalents of lexical
'false friends'; just as we generally translate a
lexical 'false friend' with a lexical equivalent
rather than its cognate, we might expect contradictory syntactic usages to be translated with the
equivalent syntactic pattern rather than word by
word. Thus, contradictory usages make it clear that
there are different levels of translation, ranging
from the word at one extreme to the entire work as
the unit of translation at the other (Nida 1964:25).
In the example we are considering, the 'tyranny of
words' gives way to grammar and opens the way for a

gradation of other translation freedoms.

As one way around the idea of a gradation of levels of translation, a proponent of literal translation might suggest that logical equivalence is the criterion to preserve in cases of contradictory usage. By reducing the source statement to its logical kernel, one can determine the corresponding formal equivalence in the target language and still remain objective. What is the same logically, one could argue, will not only be 'formally equivalent', it will be 'correct', that is, synonymous. In the case at hand, such a procedure would recognize that the logical structure behind sentence 2 is the following:

> (5) ($\exists$x) (Sx & Hx) where Sx is true of all things seen by him and Hx is true of all male humans, and
>
> ($\exists$y) (Cy & Wy & Axy) where Cy is true of all cooking-pits and Wy is true of all things in the middle of the wood and Axy is true when x is at y, and
>
> ($\exists$z) (Bz & Gxz) where Bz is true of all boars and Gxz is true when x's hand is cooking z,
>
> where the initial quantifier $\exists$x includes all three clauses in its scope.

The Irish definite article in the introductory construction is simply a way of signalling the existential quantifier. (The analysis here is somewhat simplified and reflects only the clauses with an existential quantifier. The formulation is to be read "there exists an x such that Sx and Hx, where Sx is true of all things seen...") Since English uses the indefinite article to indicate the existential quantifier, the English equivalent of the logical structure generates sentence 6.

> (6) And he saw a man at a cooking-pit in the middle of the wood. One of the man's two hands had his weapons in it and the other hand was cooking a boar.

Thus, one could justify switching levels of translation in a literal or formal-equivalence orientation when the move is required to maintain logical parity. One could justify moving beyond the tyranny of words and still claim to remain faithful to the text by appealing to the deep-structure analysis of predicate logic. No appeal to dynamic equivalence would be needed; one merely selects a formal equivalent which is logically synonymous.

The appeal to logic in this type of defense of formal-equivalence goes with the popular notion that literal and/or formal-equivalence translations are somehow more 'objective' than free and/or dynamic-equivalence translations. Proponents of the former would say that the rationale behind the translation in sentence 6 is considerably different from the procedure that would generate a translation like the following:

> (7) And he saw this man at this cooking-pit in the middle of the wood. One of the man's hands had his weapons in it and the other hand was cooking this boar.

Here the translator decides to render the Old Irish introductory definite article with an equivalent usage from informal, colloquial speech.[6] The translator might defend his/her choice by claiming that sentence 7 has the flavour of oral speech and hence is an appropriate choice for translating Old Irish oral literature. Moreover, the translator might argue that since the Old Irish article evolved from a demonstrative, it might have a residual demonstrative shading in introductory formulas; hence the choice of the English idiom with the demonstrative is apt.[7] A sceptic of dynamic-equivalence translation, however, might claim that these appeals to style, quality, and shading are much less verifiable (and hence much more subjective) than the appeal above to deep-structure logic. Thus, it might be claimed that sentence 7 is less objective than sentence 6 as a translation and accordingly should be rejected.

A second contradictory usage of Old Irish and English will offer some perspective on these arguments that formal-equivalence and literal translations are more logically direct or more objective than dynamic-equivalence translations. The second instance comes from early Irish nature poetry, where we find sentences of the following form.

> (8) Gairid caí chrúaid den:
> "is fo-chen sam saír".
> Suidigthir sıne serb
> imme-cherb caill craíb.[8]

> (9) Calls cuckoo hardy firm:
> "(is) welcome summer noble".
> Is settled of storm harshness
> which completely-cut wood of branch.

We can see from the gloss translation (sentence 9) that the singular nouns are indefinite here; they have no definite article. Using the procedures of literal translation we can generate the following, which remains on the level of the word:

(10) Hardy, firm cuckoo calls:
"Welcome, noble summer".
Harshness of storm is settled
which hacked the branchy wood.

But what does this mean? How does it preserve the content of the Old Irish sentence at all?

To get at the question of content we could, as above, again appeal to predicate logic: establish the logical significance and generate the logical equivalent in English. But in this second case the logic of the situation is far from transparent. Old Irish has no indefinite article. Thus, an indefinite noun has two possible meanings: it can indicate a definite but unknown member of a class (as with the indefinite article in English) or it can indicate generic reference, the class as a whole.[9] The first alternative can be represented in classical logical notation as

(11) $(\exists x)$ $(Cx\ \&\ Hx\ \&\ Wx)$
where Cx is true of all cuckoos
and Hx is true of all hardy, firm things
and Wx is true of all things calling welcome
to summer and where the range of discourse
is not specified
(to be read "there exists (somewhere) a hardy,
firm cuckoo welcoming summer");

or $(\exists x)$ $(Px\ \&\ Cx\ \&\ Hx\ \&\ Wx)$
where Px is true of all things in the poet's
immediate environment
and the other predicate statements have the
above values
(to be read "there exists at hand a hardy, firm
cuckoo welcoming...");

or possibly $(\exists! x)$ $(Cx\ \&\ Hx\ \&\ Wx)$
where the predicate statements have the
previous values
and we assume the poet speaks of a unique
cuckoo
(to be read "there exists a unique hardy, firm
cuckoo welcoming summer").[10]

The second possibility is that the sentence represents the universal quantifier.

(12) $(\forall x)$ $(Cx \rightarrow Hx\ \&\ Wx)$
where Cx is true of all cuckoos
and Hx is true of all hardy, firm things
and Wx is true of all things calling welcome
to summer
(to be read "all cuckoos are hardy, firm things

welcoming summer" or "everything is such that if
it is a cuckoo, it is a hardy, firm thing welcoming
summer").

*We must decide what the logical significance of the sentence
is, and to do so we will have to use criteria outside the sentence itself since the sentence generates more than one possibility.*
    This second Old Irish example is much more
complex than the first. One aspect of the problem is
that while each language has only one standard mode
for indicating a definite but previously unidentified
substantive (definite article in Old Irish, indefinite article in English), each language has multiple
possibilities for expressing the universal quantifier
using determiners such as English 'every' or 'all'.
Moreover, English can express the universal quantifier with five constructions involving the article
alone:

> (13) a. time and tide wait for no man (sg. noun,
>   ∅ article)
>   b. a fool and his money are soon parted (sg. noun
>   with indef. article)
>   c. The Child is Father of the Man (sg. noun with
>   def. article)
>   d. fools rush in where angels fear to tread (pl.
>   noun with ∅ article)
>   e. the ancients and the moderns (pl. noun with
>   def. article)[11]

    At first blush it would seem that *the* perfect
translation of the Irish sentences in example 8 would
use the English construction for the generic involving the indefinite article. Like the Irish indefinite
noun, a noun modified by the indefinite article in
English can represent both the universal quantifier
and single but unknown members of a class. That is,
a translator might be tempted to choose an English
construction with the same two logical possibilities
as the Old Irish and thus avoid deciding what the
actual logic of the sentence is. In effect some
translators have made exactly this choice and have
translated Old Irish examples of this sort with sentences like the following:

> (14) A hardy, firm cuckoo calls:
>   "Welcome, noble summer".

    This procedure would be well and good if the
Old Irish sentence were actually logically ambiguous,
but there is good reason to believe that in fact this
is not the case. The Irish seems to have only one

logical sense. On a lexical level we can cite as a parallel the way a word may have more than one meaning in general, though only a single meaning is possible in a given context. A translator choosing the English indefinite article for the translation is not necessarily being literal, s/he may simply be avoiding the decision about the logical sense of the sentence and straying into an error of meaning. To be more concrete about this point, note that the English indefinite article can range in meaning from 'one and the same' to 'any' depending on its context, and all the senses are not available in any given position. In the same way, the Irish indefinite noun has multiple meanings which occur in contrasting circumstances and are mutually exclusive depending on context.

In other words, we *must decide* what the logic of the Irish is. The logic is not given or obvious; it depends on factors outside the sentence itself; and to choose an English rendering with multiple logical possibilities may be to falsify the logical sense of the Irish sentence. In this case the logical problems posed by the text are considerably more complex than those of the first example for a literal or formal-equivalence translator. This example, in which the logic of the sentence is determined by its larger context, suggests comparison with W.V.O. Quine's doctrine of holism.[12]

To illustrate these points it will help to have a concrete example before us. The following is one of the most famous early Irish 'nature poems' — a poem which is now found in the context of a saga where it is spoken by a druid as he sets foot on Ireland's shore for the first time and claims it for his people.

(15) Am gāeth i m-muir,
    Am tond trethan,
    Am fuaim mara,
    Am dam secht ndīrend,
    Am sēig i n-aill,   5
    Am dēr grēne,
    Am cain lubai,
    Am torc ar gail,
    Am he i l-lind,
    Am loch i m-maig,   10
    Am brī a ndai
    Am brī dānae,
    Am gāi i fodb (feras feochtu),
    Am dē delbas do chind codnu.

```
Coiche nod gleith clochur slēbe?        15
Cia on co tagair aesa ēscai?
Cia du i l-laig fuiniud grēne?
Cia beir buar o thig Techrach?
Cia buar Tethrach tibi?
Cia dām, cia dē delbas faebru a ndind ailsiu?        20
Cāinte in gai--cainte gaithe?
```
                    (Macalister 1938-56:5.110-13)

A gloss translation of the first few lines illustrates the movement of the poem.

(16) I am wind in sea
     I am wave of stormy oceans
     I am sound of sea
     I am stag of seven points
     I am hawk in cliff
     I am tear of sun
     I am fairness of plants...

What is the logic of the indefinite nouns in this
poem? Do they represent the existential quantifier
or the universal quantifier? If we decide on the
former, then the poem applies to specific plants,
animals, or events in a limited environment; the
poet may, for example, be referring to distinct
shamanistic experiences in which he has taken the
role of individual natural objects, or to objects in
the immediate environment. If we decide the indefinite nouns represent the universal quantifier, the
poem is a universal statement reaching beyond the
poet's immediate spatio-temporal environment and any
specific shape-changing experiences he may have had.
    Word by word, sentence by sentence, the poem is
ambiguous; and a translator proceeding on such a
basis might be tempted to opt for the indefinite
noun in English because of its logical ambiguity, or
to imitate the Irish construction precisely and dis-
pense with the article altogether, or to vacillate
between constructions indicating the existential and
universal quantifiers. In fact, the translation history of this poem shows that translators have done
all of these things. For example, in 1916 R.A.S.
Macalister and John MacNeill translated the poem in
the following way:

(17) I am a wind on the sea.
     I am a wave of the ocean.
     I am the roar of the sea.
     I am a powerful ox.
     I am a hawk on a cliff.   5
     I am a dewdrop in sunshine.
     I am...

I am a boar for valour.
I am a salmon in pools.
I am a lake in a plain.   10
I am the strength of art.
I am a spear with spoils that wages battle.
I am a man that shapes fire for a head.

Who clears the stone-place of the mountain?
What the place in which the setting of the
          sun lies?   15
Who has sought peace without fear seven times?
Who names the waterfalls?
Who brings his cattle from the house of Tethra?
On whom do the cattle of Tethra smile?
What person, what god,   20
Forms weapons in a fort?
In a fort that nourishes satirists,
Chants a petition, divides the Ogham letters,
Separates a fleet, has sung praises,
....   25
a wise satirist.[13]

But in 1956 Macalister translated the same poem in
the following manner:

(18) I am Wind on Sea,
      I am Ocean-wave,
      I am Roar of Sea,
      I am Bull of Seven Fights,
      I am Vulture on Cliff,   5
      I am Dewdrop,
      I am Fairest of Flowers,
      I am Boar for Boldness,
      I am Salmon in Pool,
      I am Lake on Plain,   10
      I am a Mountain in a Man,
      I am a Word of Skill,
      I am the Point of a Weapon (that poureth forth
              combat),
      I am God who fashioneth Fire for a Head.

      Who smootheth the ruggedness of a mountain?   15
      Who is He who announceth the ages of the Moon?
      And who, the place where falleth the sunset?
      Who calleth the cattle from the House of Tethys?
      On whom do the cattle of Tethys smile?
      Who is the troop, who the god who fashioneth edges
              in a fortress of gangrene?   20
      Enchantments about a spear? Enchantments of Wind.
                      (Macalister 1938-56:5.111-13)

     Both these translations back away from the
logical problems raised by the poem. The earlier

translation mixes indefinite nouns with a definite
noun; thus, it gives ambiguous and seemingly contrasting syntactical signals about the logic of the
poem. On the other hand, by omitting articles entirely in most cases and by capitalizing, the later
translation suggests simultaneously that the predi-
cates are abstracts and proper nouns. But lines 11-13
("I am a Mountain in a Man/ I am a Word of Skill,/
I am the Point of a Weapon...") revert to an indefinite construction that breaks the tension established
in the opening lines. These translations can be considered literal translations or attempts at formal-
equivalence, but they are not logical.

If we look beyond the level of the sentence, we
can see internal evidence in the poem that the poet
intends a specific logical construction. The poet
seems to be speaking of universals rather than specific but previously unidentified entities. The poem
is not localized: the simultaneous evocation of the
heights of the air and the depths of the waters, of
sun and storm, argue for universality rather than
particularity. The present tense of the verb is also
telling. It indicates — along with the union of oppo-
sites built into the content — mystical, simultaneous
union with all being, where all being is symbolized
by the litany of beast, bird, fish; water and earth;
plants and elements; artifact and word. Particularized transformations are transcended in such mystical
simultaneity. By way of contrast, particularized
shapeshifting would be represented as occurring in
serial fashion and would have a temporal dimension;
we would expect the past tense in a poem indicating
specific transformations rather than the present
tense as we find here.

The literary context of the poem also reinforces
the suggestion that the deep-structure logic of this
poem involves the universal quantifier. In the tale
the druid Amairgen speaks the poem as he lands in
Ireland; he appears to be appealing to the spirit of
the land for acceptance and to be making a statement
of his (and, by extension, his people's) worthiness
to be received. In this context universals rather
than particulars are demanded; Amairgen's worth comes
from his ability to marshal the power and presence
of all wind, all waves, all sea-roar, rather than
the fleeting presence of a single gust or a single
swell. Note that the setting for this poem is likely
to be exiguous; it is probable that this poem is
older than the saga context where we find it, and
that a story-teller at some point associated the pre-
existing poem with his story. This is the case with

a good deal of early Irish poetry. The setting is nonetheless significant because the teller, as well as the original audience presumably, thought the setting logically appropriate for the poem.

The determination of the logical value of the nouns in poem 15 is reinforced by comparing the poem with other early Irish nature poems attributed to poets who are using the poems in connection with an assertion of their power. We can compare the poem above spoken by Amairgen with another nature poem attributed to a second legendary poet in another saga. In this second poem the question of indefinite nouns does not arise. As the story goes, the famous poet Athirne came to visit his pupil; the latter was able to detain the older poet by reciting the following poem.

(19) Rāthe fō foiss   fogamar:
    feidm and for cach   oenduine
    fri tóeb na llaa   lāngarit.
    Loíg brecca a broinn   osseillte
    dītnit rūadgaiss   raithnige.   5
    Rethit daim a   dumachaib
    fri dordán na   damgaire.
    Derccain dubai a   ssīthchailltib,
    slatta etha imm   ithgortu
       ōs íath domuin duinn.   10
    Draigin drissi   delgnacha
    fri toeb in lāir   lethlisse.
    Lān di meuss trumm   tendithir.
    Do-tuittet cnoi   cainmessa
       cuill robilib rath.   15

(20) Autumn — a good season for staying put:
    there's work for each and every person
    throughout the busy, short days.
    Red stalks of bracken shelter
    spotted, doe-dropped fawns.   5
    Stags race from knolls
    toward the belling of a stag-herd.
    Dark acorns in peaceful woods,
    oat stubble around grain fields
    all over the brown world.   10
    Blackthorns and spiky briars
    on the bank of a half-ruined fort.
    Firm ploughland full of heavy harvest.
    Nuts fall — a fine crop — hazels
       from forts' huge old trees.   15

In this poem about autumn, as in the earlier poem, there is no fixed spatio-temporal framework. The poem transcends any fixed scene. There is also simultaneity of perception signalled both by the present tense and by discourse about more than can be perceived by the physical eye from a single vantage point. That is, the poem has a general application rather than a specific purview. Universality in this poem, however, is indicated by plural nouns and mass nouns, while the multifaceted perspective and simultaneous perception indicate that these plural nouns bespeak universality rather than mere plurality. The plural nouns in this poem serve the same function as the indefinite nouns in poem 15; comparison of the two poems suggests both are a means of representing the universal quantifier.

Note that the literary context of the poem about autumn reinforces the proposed logical sense. We see that Athirne does not choose to depart from his pupil after hearing the poem — Athirne, thus, does not assume that the observations are restricted to the immediate environment and that he will find conditions different should he head south, for example. In the context of the tale, Athirne behaves as if the poem has universal application. Though again the setting of the poem is probably exiguous, it is a setting that indicates the medieval teller and audience took the poem as a universal statement rather than as a particularized observation.

The logical analysis of these poems also depends on consideration of the actual social roles of medieval Irish poets. The poet was considered to be a seer who could look afar in time and space with his poetic sight. The words for poet — *fili* and *éices* — etymologically both mean 'seer'. Moreover, the early Irish poet had mystical connections with nature, connections which gave him powers as an intermediary between nature and humans, as well as special knowledge.[14] We might also note that in Irish myth nature was not merely of intellectual or abstract significance; nature was originally identified with a localized earth goddess whose unified spirit or presence motivated the particularities of natural happenings. These social dimensions behind the text further suggest that poem 15 is more likely to be universal than specific, to transcend a particularized application.

As it turns out, then, to determine the logic of the individual nouns in poem 15 above, the Amairgen poem, we must assess the entire poem, as well as its literary context, the tale in which it occurs, and the literary tradition of which it is part. Moreover, the determination involves consideration of extra-literary questions, including cultural

75

factors like the role of the early Irish poet. Logically the substantives in the poem in question are not ambiguous; they are generics, expressions of the universal quantifier rather than references to single members of their several classes.

In order to indicate the logic of the individual sentences of the poem in an English translation, a translator will want to choose an English construction for the universal quantifier that clearly signals the generic. The most obvious choice is the singular noun with the definite article, the construction that Jespersen (1949:492) says "is perhaps in a strict sense the only way" of expressing the generic sense in English. The following is a translation attending to the logic of the poem.

> (21) I am the wind on the sea
> I am the wave of the stormy ocean
> I am the roar of the sea
> I am the stag of seven points
> I am the hawk on the cliff
> I am the drop of sun
> I am the beauty of plants
> I am the boar for valour
> I am the salmon in the pool
> I am the lake on the plain
> I am the hill in the rampart
> I am the hill of crafts
> I am the spear in spoils...

Paradoxically, translation 21, like translation 6 above, is again a contradictory usage to the Old Irish on the level of syntax, and again shows that the level of the word sometimes must be transcended for the sake of logic.

The significant difference here between the second contradictory usage and the first has to do with the determination of the logical sense of the original. In the second example the logic of the original is not transparent, nor can it be determined solely by the literary context of the work. To determine the logical sense of the second example we had to appeal to literary context (the mantic implications of the saga), literary tradition and genre (including poems of a similar type), and cultural practice (the role of early Irish poets). The English contradictory usage was chosen for logical reasons, but the process of determining the logic was far from simple.

This complex example of determining the logic of a sentence to be translated indicates that the popular notion that formal-equivalence translation is

more 'objective' must be reconsidered. If to determine the formal and logical sense of a sentence for
translation (particularly where contradictory usage
is a possibility), we must resort to discussions of
literary context, genre and style, the social role
of poets and poetry, and the like, how different is
this from the process of determining the dynamic impact of a text? The logical sense of sentence 8 or
poem 15 is determined by considering both formal and
cultural criteria — the process is neither more nor
less objective, neither more nor less subject to interpretation, neither more nor less likely to involve
the translator's own subjectivity, than any other
kind of translation.

The second Irish example of contradictory usage
also throws light on the relation between translation
and literary criticism. There is a tendency to hold
dynamic-equivalence translations as suspect because
they can be seen as potentially manipulating texts
to fit a particular critical view or literary theory.
By remaining literal and by sticking to formal criteria, it might be supposed that a translator can
insulate his text from the effects of critical en-
thusiasms and literary interpretations. The relation
of the English translations of Irish nature poems
such as poem 15 to critical theory illustrates that
all translations, even the most literal-seeming,
have a critical bias.

Irish nature poetry was given its modern critical definition in 1911 by Kuno Meyer when he wrote
(1911:xii-xiii):

> In Nature poetry the Gaelic muse may vie with that of
> any other nation. Indeed, these poems occupy a unique
> position in the literature of the world. To seek out
> and watch and love Nature, in its tiniest phenomena as
> in its grandest, was given to no people so early and
> so fully as to the Celt. Many hundreds of Gaelic and
> Welsh poems testify to this fact. It is a character-
> istic of these poems that in none of them do we get
> an elaborate or sustained description of any scene or
> scenery, but rather a succession of pictures and images
> which the poet, like an impressionist, calls up before
> us by light and skilful touches.[15]

Meyer here espouses the view that the poems are descriptive, though the description is not "sustained".[16]
This view has been essentially echoed for seventy
years. For example, Kenneth Jackson, whose *Studies in
Early Celtic Nature Poetry* is the most comprehensive study
of Irish nature poetry, refers throughout his book to
the poems as 'descriptive'. Thus, in discussing poem

19 above as well as three other seasonal poems that
occur in the same context, Jackson (1935:162-64) says:

> The four Irish poems (...) look very like an exercise
> upon the four seasons, not announcements of their coming
> but general descriptions of their character (...)

He continues:

> It may be that the Irish seasonal poems are the expres-
> sion of (...) gnomic awareness turned into pure nature
> description (...) Allowing for the differences of
> climate, flora and fauna, the Irish poets took stock of
> their seasons in a (...) similar way (to Hesiod), al-
> though they chose to record it as a pure description (...)

We may question, however, whether "description"
was a necessary function in medieval Ireland. The
extent to which life in early Ireland — as well as
the representation of life in early Irish literature
as a whole — had a natural setting must not be underestimated. Rural, isolated holdings meant that there
was daily contact with the weather, the change of
season, the landscape, with plants and animals. The
more life in general is set outdoors, and the more
life is a part of nature, as it was in early Ireland,
the less simple description of nature is needed for
the participants. We might conjecture that descriptive nature poetry usually represents a renewed interest and delight in nature by and for people already separating themselves from an intimate dependence on nature. Nature description is needed by
audiences whose lives are no longer entirely rural -
people separated from nature by walls, whether
the walls of town, court, or ecclesiastical
enclosure.
    Literary theory can influence interpretations
of the logic of literary works, and translation
choices can in turn obscure logical possibilities.
In the case of early Irish nature poetry, we have
seen that there are alternatives to Meyer's descriptive account of the poetry. The poems appear to be
powerfully operative, archaic mantic poetry which
may be intended as much to shape reality as to comment upon it. Moreover, the logic of translations
also can affect the target culture's view of a source
culture; thus, translations of early Irish nature
poetry that promote the descriptive account, skew
our perception of Irish poets. We come to perceive
the poets more as musicians, less as magicians and
shamans because of such translations.
    The irony in the particular case at hand is
that both Meyer and Jackson — two of the main props

of the descriptive theory of early Irish nature poetry — give logically coherent translations that are closer to mantic texts than to descriptive ones, despite their literary theories. Other translators such as Macalister, however, give translations that lock into Meyer's interpretations and obscure other alternative literary accounts. This example suggests how a literary theory could lead to 'literal' translations that confirmed the literary theory and blocked the emergence of alternative critical views.

The prevailing interpretation of Irish nature poetry is a view bolstered by the imitation of Irish syntax in English translation, as well as by our own cultural approach to nature in modern literature. What looks to be literal equivalent is a critical choice; literal translations of the Irish constructions discussed above bolster the theory of impressionistic descriptive poetry, and the theory in turn justifies the translations. But it is a choice that skirts the question of the logic of the poems — hardly an 'objective' approach to the poetry! Meyer's view can only be maintained by restricting the translation unit as well as the critical unit to the level of the sentence rather than considering larger units. The theory founders when one approaches the question of contradictory usages in the definite article from a theoretical viewpoint.

In the problematic examples I have raised we see the breakdown of the distinction between formal and dynamic equivalence. We see that these translation orientations are essentially the same in method: both are comparable in objectivity and directness, in their relation to deep-structure logic, in the nature of the evidence they call upon for determining readings. Moreover, formal equivalence can *become* dynamic equivalence. Particularly when there are two possible formal alternatives, the only way of deciding between them is on a dynamic basis. And formal equivalence *is* dynamic equivalence in the case of contradictory usages. We decide what formal equivalence is for a contradictory usage by looking at the implications of the formal structures involved to the audience; we choose a formal equivalence by considering the dynamic of the sentence with respect to both the source and receptor audiences.

This has been perhaps a somewhat technical argument to prove a point that most translation theorists probably already subscribe to: that the distinctions between literal and free, or formal equivalence and dynamic equivalence, are not so great nor so useful as they would appear to be. Moreover,

these examples show that literal and/or formal-
equivalence translations have no special claim to
being more obvious, more logically transparent, or
more objective than free or dynamic-equivalence
translations. Contradictory usages and the process
by which they are resolved can be a nice way of
demonstrating these points to any sceptics. And you
don't need Old Irish to generate examples. However,
the doubly inverted usage of the definite article
with respect to English and the relation of the
translation history of early Irish poetry to its
critical assessment, make the Old Irish examples of
contradictory usages particularly clear cases of the
theoretical issues involved.

APPENDIX: NOTES ON POEM 19

There are three manuscripts of this poem, two of which have
been edited in extenso. The earliest manuscript version, that
of the twelfth-century Book of Leinster (hereafter LL), has
been edited by R.I. Best, O.J. Bergin and M.A. O'Brien, *The
Book of Leinster, formerly Lebar na Núachongbála*, 5 vols.
(Dublin: Dublin Institute for Advanced Studies, 1954-),
2.436-39. The earliest edition of the poem and the tale in
which it is found was done by Kuno Meyer, "The Guesting of
Athirne", *Ériu* 7 (1913), 1-9; Meyer follows LL and gives major
variants from a second manuscript, Harleian 5280 (hereafter H).
A third manuscript, Royal Irish Acadamy 23.N.10 (hereafter N),
was edited by Rudolf Thurneysen in "A Third Copy of the Guesting
of Athirne", *Ériu* 7 (1914), 196-99. In addition, a more recent
edition was done by David Greene in David Greene and Frank
O'Connor, *A Golden Treasury of Irish Poetry* (London: Macmillan,
1967), pp.140-43. My edition is based on the text of LL: deviations from that manuscript are given in the apparatus below.
I have relied on earlier editions for the manuscript readings
since I have been unable to collate the manuscripts.
        The poem is composed of seven-syllable lines organized
in two stanzas of irregular length. The ends of the stanzas
are highlighted by shorter five-syllable lines. A word boundary divides the seven-syllable lines into two halves: four
syllables with a free stress pattern in the first half line
are followed by a tri-syllabic cadence. The two short lines
end in monosyllables. As with the earliest Irish poetry, there
is no rhyme here. Alliteration is used extensively, however.
There is binding alliteration linking the last word of one
line to the first word of the next. In addition each line has
two internal alliterations, often across the word boundary between the first half of the line and the cadence. The poem
also has a *dúnad:* the last syllable of the poem echoes the
first, thus bringing the poem to a proper close.

Line 1: Rāthe: LL effaced; H rathi; N raithe. *Foiss
fogamar*: LL foss fogomur; N fois fogamar. Possibly LL's reading
should be construed as an independent dative rather than the g.
sg. of the other two manuscripts. *Line 2*: 'each and every person',
literally 'every single person'. Greene's emendment for *ech
oenduini* is not necessary if we allow *feidm* to alliterate with
for. The alliteration of stressed words with unstressed words is
characteristic of seventh-century poetry; see Fergus Kelly, "A
Poem in Praise of Columb Cille", *Ériu* 24 (1973),5, and Fergus
Kelly, "Tiughraind Bhécáin", *Ériu* 26 (1975), 69. In the poem
edited by Calvert Watkins, "In essar dam do á?", *Ériu* 29 (1978),
161-65, the alliteration between unstressed and stressed words
even 'jumps' a stressed word. The presence of this type of alliteration here, like the prosody in general, is archaic.

    Line 3: fri: sic N; LL la; H rie. *Llaa*: LL llá; H laa; N
la. The form shows both the earlier spelling of *lá*, 'day', as
well as early gemination of the initial. 'Busy, short days',
literally 'full and short days' or 'fully short days'. *Duine* and
tóeb supply the binding alliteration between lines 2 and 3. The
alliteration of *t* with *d* is found in poetry of the eighth and
ninth centuries, particularly in binding alliteration; see Kelly,
"Tiughraind Bhécáin", 38-39. Hence there is no need to emend *tóeb*
to *óib* as Greene does. *Garit* may simply be an early spelling or
it may be for *garait*, the Old Irish for of the word with neutral
medial consonant; later the word is *gairit*.

    Line 4: broinn osseillte: LL broind osseilti; N broinn
oisseillti; H osselltae. There is elision of the vowel of the
preposition here, as well as below in lines 8 and 9. The nom.
pl. masc. form of the adjective in -a is attested as early as
the mid eighth century; see Thurneysen 1946:224, WB 27b16.
Binding alliteration between this line and the next is provided by the last syllable -te with *dītnit* of the following
line; it is another instance of alliteration between *t* and *d*
in the poem. Greene has again emended the line to supply *d/d*
alliteration.

    Line 5: raithnige: LL raithnigi; N raithigi. The trans-
lation inverts lines 4 and 5. 'Doe-dropped', literally 'from
a doe's belly'.

    Line 7: fri dordán: sic N; LL ri dorddan.

    Line 8: dubai: LL duba; H, N suba. If the reading *suba*
is taken, it should be translated 'pleasant' (cf. Meyer,
'sweet'). The word usually refers to strawberries, but as
Greene suggests, 'berries' is probably incorrect. Modern folk
tradition indicates a prohibition on picking most berries in
the autumn. Lugnasad, the festival opening the harvest season,
was the last day on which many berries were picked in modern
times, see Máire MacNeill, *The Festival of Lugnasa* (London:
Oxford University Press, 1962), passim. Moreover, 'pleasant'
or 'sweet' is an inappropriate epithet for acorns; their high
acid content makes them sour-tasting. The epithet 'dark', on
the other hand, is appropriate. Fallen acorns can in fact be

dark on the forest floor. Moreover, acorns have a high tannic
acid content which turns the forest floor itself dark as the
acid leeches out. (I am indebted to Dr. Mary Beth Averill for
this botanical information.) *Suba* has been preferred because
it provides internal alliteration; *dubai*, on the other hand,
provides compensatory alliteration so the line remains metri-
cally adequate. The spelling *derccain* suggests the Old Irish
nom. *derucc* rather than the later *dercu*. *Ssīthchailltib* shows
the dental inflexion for the earlier *ī* inflexion. This could
be a later scribal change, but the consonantal inflexion began
to spread at an early period; see Thurneysen 1946:204.

   Line 9: imm ithgortu: LL amm ithgortaib; H im ethgortu;
N im ethghortaibh. 'Oat stubble around grain fields', literally 'grain stalks around grain fields'. The word *ith*, here 'oat,
grain', is 'corn, grain' in general. The festival of Lugnasad,
which opened the season of autumn, marked the beginning of the
harvest of the main grain crop, the staple of life, which in
early Ireland would have been oats. The word *ith* in the context of this poem on autumn would have been specifically associated with the oat crop and would have had ritual connotations
to the audience.

   Line 10: duinn: LL, N duind. Literally, 'over the estate
of the brown world'.

   Line 11: drissi shows the earlier *i* inflexion; later the
word is inflected like an *ā* stem.

   Line 12: lethlisse: sic H; LL leithlessi; N leithlissi.
The word shows an *iā* inflexion (cf. *airlise*, 'enclosure',
Contributions to a Dictionary of the Irish Language (Dublin:
Royal Irish Academy, in progress, 1942-   ),s.v.).

   Line 13: di meuss trumm tendithir: LL do mess trum
tairnith; N do mes trumm teinnithir; H di meus trvom tindithir.
'Ploughland',literally 'land for growing grain'; ;heavy harvest',
taking *mess* in a general sense of 'fruits' rather than the
specific 'acorns'. The association of *mess* with nuts in particular, however, reinforces the image in the last two lines of
the poem. H preserves the earlier *di* for later *do* and also
shows *u* quality in the spelling of the noun.

   Lines 14-15: These are the most problematical lines of
the poem. LL reads *tuittit cnoi* (N tuitit cnae) *cuill cainmessa*
(N caínmesa) *do robilib rath* (N do roibhilibh rathi). The late
verb form is inconsistent with the linguistic level of the
rest of the poem, and there is no binding alliteration between
the last two lines. I have followed Greene's suggestion in
moving *cuill* to the last line and emending the verb to the
earlier *do-tuittet*; this solves both problems. *Robilib* stands
as an independent dative. Note that for metrical reasons the
translation keeps 'hazels' in line 14. These last two lines
are rich in significance. Hazel trees had supernatural and
magical associations; hazel nuts, in particular, figure in
some stories as the source of supernatural knowledge. Hazel
nut mead was a delicacy. Here the hazel nuts drop from *robili*

'huge ceremonial trees'. The *bile* was the tree planted near the inauguration site of each tribe, a tree which represented the vigour and life and growth of the tribe. Thus, the image in the poem is multidimensional: nature at its most bountiful sheds natural and supernatural gifts in a form which displays and embodies the well-being of all the people.

In his edition Meyer dates the language of these poems and their prose setting as "early Middle Irish, probably of the eleventh century". Greene does not date the language of the poems *per se*. He notes they "are strung together in a thin eleventh-century tale with which they seem to have little to do. They may well be textbook pieces intended to illustrate for students the technique of archaic Irish verse" (p.140).

Properly all the seasonal poems in *The Guesting of Athirne* should be dated as a group, and that is beyond the scope of this paper. In the poem on autumn edited here, however, there is nothing except the verb form *tuittit* that necessitates so late a date as the eleventh century. To be sure, the poem was copied by a Middle Irish scribe and there are Middle Irish spellings. Nonetheless, if we accept Greene's emendation of the last two lines, the language of the poem stands as Old Irish. The later forms (*-gaiss* for earlier *-gass* and the dental inflexion of *caill*) might well be scribal alterations; even if not, similar forms are found in the glosses by 850. I would suggest 850 as a *terminus ad quem* for this poem. There are many signs that point to an earlier dating: the Old Irish vocabulary (*fri, di, fó*); early spellings (*rāthi, -garit, rethit, llaa, ōs, imm*); the early inflexion of *drissi* and possibly *derccain* as well; traces of gemination in *llaa* and *ssīthchailltib*, and of the u-quality in *meuss trumm*.

The best argument for an early date, however, is the metrics. It seems easier to surmise that the poem is archaic than that it is archaising. The cadenced metres were not in general use after the Old Irish period, and even in Old Irish their use is very restricted. The pattern of *t/d* alliteration which occurs three times in the fifteen-line poem suggests an eighth-century date at the earliest, while the alliteration of an unstressed word with a stressed word in line 2 suggests that the poem is still influenced by some metrical standards typical of seventh-century poetry. These two factors, in conjunction with the linguistic evidence discussed above, seem to point to an early eighth-century date.

NOTES

1. An earlier version of this paper was presented to the translation section of the Tenth Congress of the International Comparative Literature Association, New York City, August 23, 1982. My thanks to A.Thomas Tymoczko for advice on the logical notation in the paper and other helpful suggestions.

2. I am assuming in this paper that Old Irish is the

source language and English the target language.

3. Katharine M.Briggs and Ruth L.Tongue, eds., *Folktales of England* (London: Routledge & Kegan Paul, 1965), pp.144.

4. Jespersen (1949:480) notes that in modern written literature the traditional usage has been abandoned: "Nowadays the technique in which the author carefully introduces the person or thing he wants to tell the reader about is not very common. Instead he simply uses the definite article (or a name, or even a pronoun) at once and then the reader must try in what follows to find out about the person or thing in question."

5. John Strachan, ed., *Stories from the Táin* (1944; rept. ed. Dublin: Royal Irish Academy, 1964), p.5. For the Irish usage see Thurneysen 1946:296.

6. For examples of this construction from English folk literature see Briggs, pp.125, 132. The construction is discussed in H.A.Gleason, Jr., *Linguistics and English Grammar* (New York: Holt, Rinehart and Winston, 1965), p.348.

7. There are, for example, English constructions where the demonstrative sense continues to cling to the definite article. See Jespersen 1949:410-11.

8. The quatrain is adapted from James Carney's "Three Old Irish Accentual Poems", *Ériu* 22 (1971), 41.

9. Thurneysen 1946:296. Jespersen 1949:420 observes that in English grammar "the term 'indefinite article' is not very felicitous, as this article actually refers to a definite item, even if it is not made known which member of the class is mentioned".

10. The first formulation assumes but does not specify that the range of discourse is the poet's immediate environment, thus allowing the possibility of changing the range of discourse without changing the logical formulation. The second builds this specification into the logical notation. The discussion here relies on classical logical symbolism; more recent discussions of these issues by such people as Montague are beyond the scope of this paper.

The grammatical complexities of the Irish here are also significant. In the absence of an indefinite article, to stress 'there is a unique x' Irish generally uses *oen*, 'one'; we might compare *oen* with the English indefinite article which is a continuation of the Old English *an*, 'one'. The absence of *oen* in the sentence in question mitigates against, but does not strictly rule out, the third formulation here.

11. Otto Jespersen, *A Modern English Grammar*, vol.2, 4th ed. (Heidelberg: Carl Winter, 1936), pp.131-35.

The number of possible constructions for the generic has to do with the effacement of the significance of definite/indefinite and number in such references. Cf. Randolph Quirk, Sidney Greenbaum, Geoffrey Leech, and Jan Svartvik, *A Grammar of Contemporary English* (New York and London: Seminar Press, 1972), p.147, "...in the noun, the distinctions that are important for count nouns with specific reference between defi-

nite and indefinite and between singular and plural disappear
with generic reference. This is so because generic reference
is used to denote what is normal or typical for members of a
class. Consequently, the distinctions of number and definite-
ness are neutralized since they are no longer relevant for the
generic concept." They note, however, that the definite form
implies existence (p.148).

Jespersen 1949:424, in exploring the connotations of the
various generic constructions, notes that "with *a* the sb refers to all members (or any member) of the class or species it
denotes, but only as a representative of the members. It does
not denote the class or species in itself. I propose the term
all-representative use. The meaning of *a* here approaches that
of *any*." In his discussion of the plural constructions he observes (1949:442) "The term toto-generic in connexion with
plurals should not be taken to mean 'denoting the genus' in a
strict sense such as the sg with the def. article...The plural
has rather a general than a generic sense. It rather denotes
all members of the genus than the genus as a whole." On p.492
he continues "...plurals may denote all members of the species,
but they do not denote the species itself...". Cf. pp.420,438.

12. Technically, the logic of the first example also extends beyond the sentence itself. It depends on knowing that
the man, cooking-pit, and boar have never been mentioned previously in the text; thus, it depends on a considerable portion
of the literary work.

13. R.A.S. Macalister and John MacNeill, eds. and trans.,
*Leabhar Gabhála, The Book of Conquests of Ireland; The recen-
sion of Micheál Ó Cléirigh* (Dublin: Hodges, Figgis, 1916), pp.
262-67. Lines 4 and 9 of translation 17 differ slightly from
translation 18 below because of textual differences in the
Ó Cléirigh manuscript; line 10 of the text above is also missing in Ó Cléirigh. In addition the radical differences between
the two translations in the second stanza are also due to
textual differences; the text of this stanza, however, is not
pertinent to the argument in this paper.

14. For a more extensive discussion of the social functions of early Irish poets, see Maria Tymoczko, "'Cétamon':
Vision in Early Irish Seasonal Poetry", *Éire-Ireland* 18 (1983),
4.17-39.

15. Note that Meyer pioneered the edition and translation
of many Irish nature poems. Surprisingly, as we will see below,
his translations are generally logically clear even when the
logical sense is inconsistent with his critical views.

16. See B.K.Martin, "Medieval Irish Nature Poetry",
Parergon, 21 (1978), 19-32, and the references cited there for
various readings of Irish nature poetry. Martin surveys various
critical views all of which see description in the poetry —
from Gray and others who see "Gothic wildness and fervour" in
early Irish nature poetry, to the late Romantics who found in
the poetry sensitivity and love of nature, to Meyer's theory

of impressionism.

REFERENCES

JACKSON, Kenneth
1935   *Studies in Early Celtic Nature Poetry*. Cambridge,
         Cambridge University Press
JESPERSEN, Otto
1949   *A Modern English Grammar*. Vol. 7. Copenhagen,
         Munksgaard
MACALISTER, R.A.S.
1938-56 (ed. & transl.) *Lebor Gabála Érenn, The Book of the
         Taking of Ireland*. 5 vols. Dublin, Irish Texts Society
MEYER, Kuno
1911   (transl.) *Selections from Ancient Irish Poetry*.
         New York, Dutton
NIDA, Eugene
1964   *Toward a Science of Translating*. Leiden, Brill
THURNEYSEN, Rudolf
1946   *A Grammar of Old Irish*. Reprint 1961. Dublin, Dublin
         Institute for Advanced Studies

WAYS THROUGH THE LABYRINTH

Strategies and Methods for Translating Theatre Texts

Susan Bassnett-McGuire

The translator of theatre texts faces a problem unlike that involved in any other type of translation
process. The principal difficulty resides in the
nature of the text itself, for whilst interlingual
translation involves the transfer of a given written
text from the source language (SL) to the target language (TL), all kinds of factors other than the linguistic are involved in the case of theatre texts.
Leaving aside for the moment those texts written as
plays but designated as strictly literary (e.g the
'plays' of Byron and Shelley, where performance is
expressly discounted by the authors), a theatre text
exists in a dialectical relationship with the performance of that text. The two texts - written and performed - are coexistent and inseparable, and it is
in this relationship that the paradox for the translator lies. The translator is effectively being
asked to accomplish the impossible - to treat a written text that is part of a larger complex of sign
systems, involving paralinguistic and kinesic features,
as if it were a literary text, created solely for the
page, to be read off that page.
Discussing the problem of reading a theatre
text, Anne Ubersfeld points out:

> Le texte du théâtre est le seul texte littéraire qui ne
> puisse absolument pas se lire dans la suite diachronique
> d'une lecture, et qui ne se livre que dans une épaisseur
> de signes *synchroniques*, c'est-à-dire étagés dans l'es-
> pace, spatialisés. (Ubersfeld 1978:153)

> (A theatre text is the only kind of literary text that
> quite categorically cannot be read in the diachronic
> sequence of ordinary reading, and that only yields it-
> self up to a density of synchronic signs which are
> arranged hierarchically in space, spatialized.)

A major obstacle in the development of theatre studies has been the continued emphasis on the verbal text to the exclusion of the other sign systems involved in the creation of theatre. This has resulted in an imbalance, where the verbal text is prioritised and becomes the high status text to the detriment of all the other systems. As a result, certain texts, such as the plays of Shakespeare, for example, are perceived as absolutes and performance is expected to adhere to a notion of 'fidelity' to that written text. The fact that the written text may have been set down following a performance or series of performances becomes irrelevant. Once it is written, the play acquires a solidity and prominence and, in the case of Shakespeare, is then treated as a literary text and read as such. It has now become almost impossible for the English-language director to be freed from the tyranny of the written Shakespearean text which becomes a straight-jacket preventing mobility. There is an apocryphal tale of an East European director who, on leaving a British production of a Shakespeare play, remarked: "That's wonderful. Everything remains to be done. All they played was the text." A fitting comment on Anglo-Saxon textual imperialism.

Tadeusz Kowzan defines five categories of expression in the making of a performance which correspond to five semiological systems:

(1) The spoken text (for which there may or may not be a written script)
(2) Bodily expression
(3) The actor's external appearance (gestures, physical features, etc.)
(4) The playing space (involving size of venue, props, lighting effects, etc.)
(5) Non-spoken sound. (Kowzan 1975:52-80)

Kowzan goes on to divide these five categories into thirteen distinct sub-sections, but constantly stresses the non-hierarchical nature of the different sign systems. The written text in his opinion is merely one component among several, and a performance may involve as few or as many of the different systems as are thought necessary.

Kowzan's early structuralist redefinition of the position of the verbal text in the creation of theatre heralded the start of a series of attempts to explain the relationship between the written and the performed and to establish a grammar of performance. Fundamental to all these attempts was the idea that the written text contained a series of clues

for performance that could be isolated and defined.
So some favoured a model following the notion of deep
structure, where the performance text could be extracted from the written by analysing the implicit
in the utterances of the characters in the play (e.g.
Pagnini 1970), whilst another line of approach attempted to unravel patterns of gestural structures
in the language. Paola Gulli Pugliatti devised the
notion of the *latent sign*, arguing that the units of
articulation of a dramatic text "should not be seen
as units of the linguistic text *translatable* into stage
practice" but rather as "a linguistic transcription
of a stage potentiality which is the motive force of
the written text" (Pugliatti 1976:146). A slightly
different approach was favoured by Franco Ruffini,
who argued that the written text was not *actual* performance but *positive* performance, by which he means
that the staging of a written text results in the
merging of the two texts, with the performance text
being "submerged" into the script of the play
(Ruffini 1978:85).

All the debates on the nature of the relationship between the written and the performance text
were characterised by one interesting feature – the
dimension of interlingual translation is completely
absent from the discussions. Yet the problem facing
the translator of a theatre text must be fundamental
to the debate: whether a performance text is latent
or embedded or positively existent in the written
text, the translator carries the responsibility of
transferring not only the linguistic but a series of
other codes as well.

The strategies of translators have obviously
varied widely at different points in time, but it is
possible to distinguish some basic categories. One
issue on which there seems to be general consensus
of agreement is the fact that the theatre text is
time-bound in a way that distinguishes it from prose
or poetry. Because of its nature, since the theatre
text is composed of *dialogue* and *stage directions* (songs
can be read as part of the dialogue), the problem of
form merges with the question of speech rhythms. In
the case of a verse drama, for example, the translator may take care to foreground metrical features,
but in the case of naturalist dialogue, the translator will opt for naturalistic speech rhythms in the
TL which will inevitably belong to a particular time.
There is therefore a special need for the continued
retranslation or updating of theatre texts, where
patterns of speech are in a continuous process of
change. The dialogue of plays from the 1950s can

seem as archaic as that of plays from the 1890s today. This problem of speech rhythm, syntax and collo-
quialisms is particular to texts with dialogue and
the translator needs to be aware of minute changes
of register, tone, and style, all of which are bound
to an explicit context in both SL and TL systems.

Translation strategies

(1) <u>Treating the theatre text as a literary work</u>.
This is probably the most common form of theatre
translation. The text is treated as if it were a literary work, and the translator pays attention to distinctive features of dialogue on the page. No allow-
ances are made for patterns of intonation and other
paralinguistic features and often implicit in this
type of translation is the notion of 'fidelity to
the original'. This kind of translation is particularly common where complete works of a given playwright are undertaken, and where the commission is
for publication rather than for stage production.

(2) <u>Using the SL cultural context as frame text</u>.
This type of translation has become increasingly popular in the past decade, particularly in the English-
speaking world. It involves the utilization of TL
stereotypical images of the SL culture to provide a
comic frame. So in the case of British productions
of De Filippo in the 1970s, and equally in the case
of Dario Fo's plays in English, the frame text is
provided by a comic set of signs denoting Italian-
icity. Hence in the National Theatre production of
Filomena Maturano, the text was played with mock-Italian
accents and much of the text was rendered in 'Anglo-
Italian' jargon. The result of this type of translation is to create a massive ideological shift: the
frame tells British audiences that the play is primarily 'about' comic foreigners, and so when Dario
Fo's *Accidental Death of an Anarchist* was performed in
English, it had become a farce about the absurdities
of Italians and their forces of authority, rather
than being a savage satire on the corruption of the
police and systems of power.

(3) <u>Translating 'performability'</u>. This very
vexed term is frequently used by translators of
theatre texts who claim to have taken into account
the performance dimension by reproducing linguistic-
ally the 'performability' of the text. Claims for
'performability' are widely made, although the concept is never defined. What it seems to imply is an
attempt in the TL to create fluent speech rhythms
and so produce a text that TL actors can speak with-

out too much difficulty (at least in the opinion of the translator). Features of 'performability' include substituting regional accents in the SL with regional accents in the TL, trying to create equivalent registers in the TL and omitting passages that are deemed to be too closely bound to the SL cultural and linguistic context.

(4) <u>Creating SL verse drama in alternative forms</u>. In this type of translation the principal criterion is the verse form. Racine's alexandrines have been variously rendered in English in blank verse, herioc couplets and free verse in attempts to foreground metrical patterns in the SL text whilst declining to use a verse form that does not transfer happily into English. Likewise, translators of Greek tragedy have used a wide range of verse forms. The danger of foregrounding form are all too obvious - frequently attempts to create translated verse drama result in texts that are obscure, if not downright meaningless, where the dynamics of the SL text no longer come across.

(5) <u>Co-operative translation</u>. Of all the strategies listed here, the cooperative produces probably the best results. It involves the collaboration of at least two people on the making of the TL text - either an SL and a TL native speaker, or someone with knowledge of the SL who works together with the director and/or actors who are to present the work. This method parallels the way in which theatre spectacle is created collaboratively, and the translator becomes someone who produces a basic *scenario* that is then worked on by the company. This type of translation avoids the notion of 'performability' as a quality that can be added to the written text and involves the translator simultaneously in the written and oral versions of the text. This type of translation strategy lies at the opposite pole from strategy 1 above.

The advantage of stategy 5 is that it involves the translation process with a set of problems related to the performance of a theatre text: the problem posed by differing theatre conventions of SL and TL cultures and the problems of different styles of performance. So, for example, the tradition of the actor's use of space and time in England, Italy and Germany (both East and West) is quite different. A performance of a Shakespeare play, to take a random example, in a major theatre in those three languages, is vastly different: the English version would almost certainly be played in a shorter time than either of the others and the German one would almost certainly be the longest. The reason for this distinction lies

not in the language but in the acting styles. British
classical acting requires the actor to physicalise
the text, to reinforce possible textual obscurities
with kinesic signs, to push forward through the language of the text, even at times *against* the text.
The German tradition, which is more intensely intellectual, tends to the opposite extreme - the text
acquires a weightiness that the spatial context reinforces and it is the text that carries the actor
forward rather than the reverse. The Italian tradition of virtuosity on the part of the individual
actor creates yet another type of performance style:
the text of the play becomes the actor's instrument
and the performance of that play is an orchestration
of many different instruments playing together.

Acting conventions and audience expectations are
components in the making of performance that are as
significant as conventions of the written text. The
theatre of a given society will inevitably comprise
a set of culturally determined codes that are performance conventions but are also present in the
written text - the use of hyperbole in Renaissance
English theatre, of irony in French and English
eighteenth-century comedy, of stychomythia in the
Greek theatre, of 'purple passages' in Ibsen and
alienation devices in Brecht. The problem for the
translator arises when these codes cease to have
functional significance in the TL theatre. Again and
again we see contemporary productions of Greek tragedy in which the role of the chorus is minimalised by
cutting the number of lines and/or by reducing the
chorus to a single individual to conform to contemporary criteria of stage naturalism. Or the ironic
counterpoint of stychomythia is heightened and transformed into a naturalistic exchange, since western
audiences today are unused to the tonal shifts of
Greek theatre and directors/translators are motivated
by the need to clarify a convention that has ceased
to have meaning.

In his article 'Mother Courage's Cucumbers'
André Lefevere discusses English translations of
Brecht and notes the extent of the ideological shift
that has taken place with the transfer of Marxist
texts into an anti-Marxist TL system (Lefevere 1982).
He might also have noted that Brecht's plays were
written with the idea of a state-subsidised theatre
in a society where arts education was a plank in the
rebuilding of a country devastated by years of Nazi
rule and then by further years of war. The transfer
of those plays into a theatre context governed by a
market economy adds yet another dimension to the

ideological shifts that take place in translation.

Because of the multiplicity of factors involved in theatre translation, it has become a commonplace to suggest that it is an impossible task. Translators have frequently tried to fudge issues further, by declaring that they have produced a 'version' or 'adaptation' of a text, or even, as Charles Marovitz described his *Hedda Gabler*, a 'collage'. None of these terms goes any way towards dealing with the issues, since all imply some kind of ideal SL text towards which translators have the responsibility of being 'faithful'. The distinction between a 'version' of an SL text and an 'adaptation' of that text seems to me to be a complete red herring. It is time the misleading use of these terms were set aside.

In an essay entitled 'Illustrators, Actors and Translators' published in 1908, Luigi Pirandello, arch-believer in the pre-eminent role of the writer in the creation of theatre, argued that illustrators of books, actors and translators share a common difficulty inherent in their work. All three, in his view, falsify the original text, they reinterpret and in so doing rewrite it, recreate it. He condemns this as a distortion, but accepts that there is no alternative to this paradox. The illustration reflects the creative process of the illustrator at work on the text of the novel, the actor brings his interpretation to the character created by the playwright and the translator brings his own style and interpretation to the work of the SL author. Faithfulness is therefore an impossible concept and can only exist if the interpretative processes are not undertaken at all.

Pirandello starts by attacking what he perceives as deformations of an original, but ends up by suggesting that creative interpretation must have *carte blanche* in order to develop. Looking at the way in which two directors approached *King Lear*, the value of interpretative freedom is all too plain. The Italian director Giorgio Strehler approaches the play through images from his own cultural context - a key literary referent is Dante's *Divina commedia*, in which the protagonist descends through Hell and returns out again, thanks to God and his faithful guide, to begin the ascent of Mount Purgatory. Strehler's key contextual referent is the liberation of Italy from Fascist rule and the ravages of war. In contrast, the film-director Grigori Kosintsev reads Shakespeare through Dostoyevsky, with the torments of Raskolnikov, the agony over the meaningfulness of life and death, and refers back to images of the

destruction of Stalingrad and the prison camps for
his inspiration. Reading *King Lear* through such images
serves as a starting-point for the creation of an
authentic TL text that is both a translation of an
original written by a Renaissance Englishman but is
also a uniquely Italian or Russian work in its own
right.

Discussing the staging of a written text, Patrice
Pavis (1976) plays on words: *mis en scène - mis en signe*.
The performance text involves a range of sign systems
that harmonize with the written, extending that written text into space. Petr Bogatyrev stresses that
the linguistic code is merely one of many and notes
that

> ...le discours théâtral qui doit être le signe de la
> situation sociale d'un personnage, est accompagné par
> les gestes de l'acteur, complété par son costume, le
> décor, etc.; qui sont également les signes d'une
> situation sociale. (Bogatyrev 1971 (1938):523)
>
> (...theatrical speech, which should be the sign of a
> character's social position is accompanied by the actor's
> gestures, completed by his costume, the setting, etc.,
> all of which are equally signs of a given social position.)

So the written text is one code, one system in a complex set of codes that interact together in performance. The translator therefore has to work on a text
that is, as Anne Ubersfeld defines it, *troué*, not complete in itself. And in creating a text for performance in the TL, the translator necessarily encounters an entirely different set of constraints in
terms of TL conventions of stage production.

In addition to the fundamental problem of translating a text that is part of a dialectical relationship with other systems, the translator of theatre
texts has further difficulties to tackle. Dramatic
dialogue is conventionalised and is based, as Keir
Elam succinctly puts it, on "an *I* addressing a *you*
here and *now*" (Elam 1980:139). In other words, what
lies at the origin of dramatic discourse is the
deixis, ?¬d Alessandro Serpieri goes so far as to
argue tl ⸚ it is the verbal index that is the foun-
ding semiotic unit of dramatic representation:

> In the theatre (...) meaning is entrusted *in primis* to
> the deixis, which regulates the articulation of the
> speech acts. Even rhetoric, like syntax, grammar, etc.
> are dependent, in the theatre, on the deixis, which
> subsumes and unites the meaning borne by the images,
> by the various genres of language (prose, poetry), by
> the various linguistic modes of the characters, by

intonation, by rhythm, by proxemic relations, by the
kinesics of the movements, etc. (Serpieri 1978; cf.
Elam 1980:140)

Serpieri's theory, discussed in monolingual terms
only so far, may yet help in the locating of a key
for the translator searching for the magic doorway
that will lead through the labyrinth of multiple
codes. For a radical alteration of the deictic system
of the SL text is bound to alter the dynamics of the
text in all kinds of unexpected ways. Let us consider
an episode from Strehler's *Lear*, translated by Angelo
Dallagiacoma and Luigi Lunari. In Act I, scene 1,
Lear has rejected Cordelia who, he feels, has not
adequately expressed in words her love for him. Her
two suitors, Burgundy and France, are now being asked
if they will take her, and this extract begins with
Burgundy's refusal.

BURGUNDY:
Pardon *me*, Royal Sir;
Election makes not up in such conditions.
LEAR:
Then leave *her*, sir; for by the power that made *me*,
I tell *you* all *her* wealth. (To France). For *you*, great King,
I would not from *your* love make such a stray
To match *you* where *I* hate; therefore beseech *you*
T'avert *your* liking a more worthier way
Than on a wretch whom Nature is asham'd
Almost t'acknowledge *hers*.
FRANCE:
                    This is most strange,
That *she*, whom even but now was *your* best object,
The argument of *your* praise, balm of *your* age,
The best, the dearest, should in this trice of time
Commit a thing so monstruous, to dismantle
So many folds of favour. Sure, *her* offence
Must be of such unnatural degree
That monsters it, or *your* fore-vouched affection
Fall into taint; which to believe of *her*
Must be a faith that reason without miracle
Should never plan in *me*.
CORDELIA:
                    I yet beseech *your* Majesty
(If for *I* want that glib and oily art
To speak and purpose not, since what *I* well intend,
I'll do't before *I* speak), that *you* make known
It is no vicious blot, myrther or foulness,
No unchaste action, or dishonour'd step,
That hath depriv'd *me* of *your* grace and favour,
But even for want of that for which *I* am richer,

A still-soliciting eye, and such a tongue
That *I* am glad *I* have not, though not to have it
Hath lost *me* in *your* liking.
LEAR:

Better *thou*
Hadst not been born than not t'have pleased *me* better.

In this passage the units of deixis are italicized
to show the way in which they are foregrounded in the
speeches of the various characters. Lear refers to
Cordelia as *her*, thus marking her new status as hated
object rather than as a loved and named individual
(previously in the scene he has referred to her both
by name and by epithets of love, "our joy"). When he
addresses her directly, it is with the distancing
pronoun *thou*. In contrast, France's speech puts the
onus of responsibility onto Lear, emphasizing through
the use of the pronoun *your* the bond that has previously existed between father and daughter and implying that Lear is somehow to blame for its breakdown. His speech ends with the emphatic, independent
me. Cordelia takes up the first-person pronoun. Her
speech is full of *I* statements, reinforcing her position and insisting on her principles. These deictic
units are all perfectly in keeping with the characters that use them, and conform also to the context
of the scene. If there is such a thing as 'gestural
language', then it must surely lie in the interweav-
ing of these units.
    In the Italian version, the units are changed:

BORGOGNA:

Perdonate*mi* sire. Ma a queste condizioni la scelta non si pone.	Forgive me sire, but there can be no choice in such conditions.

LEAR:

Allora è no.	Then it's no.
Poichè per l'onnipotenza che *mi* ha creato	Because through the Almighty who created me,
vi ho detto tutto ciò che *essa* possiede.	I have told you all she has.
(Borgogna esce; Lear si rivolge a Francia)	(Exit B; Lear turns to F.)
Quanto a *voi*, nobile re,	As for you, noble sir,
non vorrei demeritar*mi* tanto il *vostro* affetto	I would not wish to lose your great affection
da unir*vi* all'oggetto del *mio* odio.	By joining you to the object of my hate.
Vi esorto dunque a volgere la *vostra* attenzione	I therefore urge you to turn your attention
a scelte più degne di questo miserabile niente,	to more worthy choices than this wretched nothing

che la natura stessa si vergogna	whom nature herself is
di riconoscere.	ashamed to acknowledge.

FRANCIA:

È molto strano che la *vostra*	It is very strange that your
figlia prediletta	favourite daughter
fino a ieri argomento di ogni	who until yesterday was the
vostra lode	subject of all your praises
balsamo della *vostra* vecchiaia	balm of your old age
la migliore	the best
la più cara	the dearest
abbia potuto in questo batter	should in a wink have
d'occhio commettere non so she	committed an act of such
cosa di tanto orribile	horror
da perdere l'amplissimo manto del	that she has lost the wide
vostro favore.	mantle of your favour.
Certo deve trattarsi di un delitto	It must indeed be a crime so
tanto fuor di misura	far beyond measure
da parere mostruoso.	as to appear monstrous.
O si deve dubitare del *vostro*	Or is your ancient, much
antico a decantato affetto?	vaunted love to be doubted?

CORDELIA:

Vi supplico maestà	I beseech your Majesty
– se di tutto ciò che accade	– if of all that occurs
è causa solo il *mio* non saper	the sole cause is my not
dire	knowing how to say
quel che non sento –	that which I do not feel –
rendete noto almeno che	at least make it known that
non fu nè una infamia nè un	it was no infamy nor crime,
delitto,	
nè che fu azione turpe o	nor foul nor dishonourable
disonorevole	deed
a privar*mi* del *vostro* favore;	that lost me your favour;
ma solo quel che *mi* manca:	but merely that which I do
	not have:
uno sguardo da mendico	a beggar's glance
e una lingua che sono lieta di	and a tongue I am thankful
non possedere.	not to possess.

LEAR:

Meglio per *te* non essere nata	Better that you had never
	been born
che aver*mi* tanto poco compiaciuto.	than to have pleased me so
	little

(Strehler 1973)

In this Italian translation the deictic units are different. This is partially due to the system of Italian verbs which contain the personal pronoun in the endings of the stem, but it is not the only cause. The impersonal construction has been used more frequently by France and Cordelia, and these two characters are consequently changed. Whereas Lear in Italian uses the *you* and *she* pronoun systems of the English, all the affirmative pronouns are absent from France's speech, which concludes on a direct question to Lear instead of on a statement of intent. France's only pronoun is *vostro/a*, and as a result his speech is transformed into an attack on Lear, a confrontation that is not only out of keeping with the character but is also out of keeping with the protocol of the context.

In much the same way, Cordelia's speech is a plea to her father for the restoration of her good name rather than an affirmation of her unchanging position. Where the English text begins with *I yet beseech your Majesty*, the Italian has *Vi supplico maestà*. The gestus is totally different, and the effect is produced through changes in the linguistic code that involve non-translation of the deictic units in the line.

Some years ago, in an early article on problems of theatre translation (Bassnett-McGuire 1978), I suggested that there might be a gestural language distinguishable within the written text. This theory was based on work in theatre practice, where directors and actors distinguish physical signs to follow from off the printed page. I raised the question as to how this gestural language might be discernible, suggesting that it might exist in a manner similar to the Stanislavskian sub-text that is decoded by the actor and encoded into gestural form. Now, with hindsight, the idea of gestural patterning in a text appears to be a loose and woolly concept: it may be all very well for monolingual actors to speculate on the gestus of a text, but where interlingual translation is involved other solutions must be sought. It now seems to me that if indeed there is a gestural language in a text, then there is a way of deciphering it and therefore of translating it, and so far one of the most hopeful lines of enquiry seems to be that of the deictic units. Since these units determine the interaction between the characters on stage, they also determine characterization and, ultimately, feed into the other codes of performance. By analysing the way in which the deixis operates in the SL text, it will become apparent whether those units can be viable in the TL, what they signify by their presence and equally by their absence, what happens to the dynamics of the scene when they are altered.

The strategy of collaborative translation may suggest ways of tackling this problem. The native SL speaker and the native TL speaker may have an instinctive sense of deixis in a given scene. In the case of the Barker-Rheinfrank translation of Brecht's *Die Tage*

der Commune (*The Days of the Commune*) deictic shifts mark
a series of transformations of register as illustrated in the following passage:

Babette: Wenn die Commune weniger zahlt als das Kaiserreich,
              brauchen *wir* sie nicht. Und Jean hat gekämpft, um
              gerade diese Ausbeutung nich mehr ertragen zu müssen,
              sagt er.
Philippe: An seiner Hose bescheisst ihr seine eigene Mutter
              und seine Freundin. *Ihr* müsst sofort...
Geneviève: *Wir*? Was ist mit *euch*?
Philippe: Gut. *Wir* müssen...
Geneviève: Das ist besser.
Philippe: Also, was müssen *wir*?
Langevin: (nach einer Pause zu Babette und Philippe): Wenn
              sie zusperren, oder wenn sie den festgelegten Lohn
              nich zahlen, werden *wir* ihre Betriebe konfiszieren
              und *selber* weiterführen. Ueberhaupt müssen *wir* in
              den Fabriken und Werkstätten die kollektive Arbeit
              organisieren.
Babette: Woher soll man das wissen?
Geneviève: *Ich* versuche, Schulen zu organisieren, in denen die
              Kinder es lernen. Da muss man anfangen. Aber wie soll
              man anfangen, wenn sie Türen und Schränke verschlos-
              sen haben?
Philippe: (belehrend): Zumindest die können *wir* aufbrechen,
              denke *ich*. (Er geht an eine Tür, holt sein Taschen-
              messer heraus und macht sich am Schloss zu schaffen).
Langevin: Was, *du* bist ein Bäcker und doch bereit, auch
              Schlosserarbeit zu tun. Kinder, *ich* sehe Lichter für
              die Commune. Das nächste wird vielleicht sein, dass
              der daneben auch noch das Regieren lernt.

              (Philippe hat die Tür geöffnet. Alle lachen.)
              Erwartet nicht mehr von der Commune als von *euch*
              selber.   (Brecht s.d.)

The significance of the pronoun system in this passage is the juxtaposition of *wir*, which symbolizes
collective action, with *sie*, the enemy, the other side.
Philippe begins with the formal pronoun *Ihr*, but is
corrected by the women and learns to use *wir*. At the
end of the scene, Langevin addresses Philippe with
the comradely, personal *du* form, thus signifying that
he has become part of the group and has been accepted.
The Barker-Rheinfrank translation follows the German
text closely, but makes some significant alterations:

Babette: If *we're* going to get less pay under the Commune
              than *we* did under the Empire, then *we* don't want it.
              And Jean says that he fought for the Commune so that
              he could be free from being exploited.

Philippe: How his mother and his girlfriend are being cheated
              over his army trousers. *You've* got to...
Genevieve: *Us?* And what about *you?*
Philippe: All right *we've* got to...
Genevieve: That's better.
Philippe: Right then, what have *we* got to do?
Langevin: (After a pause to Philippe and Babette): If they
              shut up shop or don't pay fixed wage rates we'll
              confiscate and run the shops *ourselves*. The factories
              and workshops are being organised as labour collect-
              ives in any case.
Babette: How are *we* going to understand all this?
Genevieve: *I'm* trying to organize the schools so that the chil-
              dren can start to learn it there. That's where *we*
              have to start. But how can *we* begin when *we* can't
              open the doors and cupboards?
Phillipe: (teaching her): Well at least *we* can break those
              open, *I* think. (He takes a pocket knife out of his
              pocket and gets to work on the lock).
Langevin: What's this, a baker turning his hand to the lock-
              smith's trade. Children, things are looking up for
              the Commune. Next thing *we* know he'll be learning
              the job of governing.

              (Philippe has opened the door. All laugh.)
              Never expect more of the Commune than *you* expect of
              yourselves. (Brecht 1978)

The impersonal construction in English is used formally and has strong upper-class connotations, quite out
of keeping with the discourse of this play. The translators have therefore substituted a *we* form in several places where the German impersonal is used and,
although this does not in any way diminish the growing sense of solidarity which is the keynote of this
scene, it does reduce the levels of complexity present
in the SL text. The deictic shifts mark changes of
position, changes of class allegiance in the SL,
whereas in the TL text that solidarity is established
from the beginning. The translators have omitted the
du address in Langevin's speech, replacing it with an
impersonal construction so that Philippe is no longer
addressed directly. In spite of the closeness of tone
between the SL and TL, these shifts in the deixis do
mark a significant change in language value. It is
perhaps not too far-fetched to see implicit in this
simplification of the discourse a reflection of the
greater sophistication of German political language
and of Brecht's own position. The Barker-Rheinfrank
translation does not attempt to alter the political
position of the SL author, unlike many English translations (cf. Lefevere 1982), but nevertheless an

analysis of the text as a whole shows that significant changes do occur. Their version instinctively
picks up on the register of working-class socialist
discourse in English which is characterised by a
uniformity of tone rather than by a variety of tones
and levels. It is perhaps worth speculating on the
relative lack of success of English versions of Brecht
by considering the way in which complex concepts expressed through a variety of forms, of which the
deictic units are only one example, become thinned
out and simplified in English, diminishing the impact of the play.

In the limited space of this paper I have chosen
to emphasize the significance of deictic units, but
it would be far too simplistic to suggest that 'faithful' adherence to the deictic units of the SL text
in translation could solve the problems of the translation of written theatre language. As can be seen
from the two examples offered, what is crucial about
the deictic units is not their presence per se but
their function in the text. The changes in the Italian version of Cordelia's speech do actually alter
the characterization and create a very different
gestural understructure which, I feel, also implies
an ideological shift. In this case I feel unhappy
about the changes, because the Italian Cordelia is
made into a supplicant, a victim from the outset,
rather than a warrior queen on a par with her sisters
in all but cruelty as the English text depicts her.
In the case of the shifts in the Brecht passage, what
appears to be reflected is the different level of
political sophistication in the German and English
working classes, an extra-contextual factor which
nevertheless impinges on the translators' text.

Translating for the theatre is an activity that
involves an awareness of multiple codes, both in and
around the written text. At times, the way forward
may be through close, almost literal adherence to
the SL text, whilst at other times there may have to
be a process of intersemiotic translation, wherein
a function of the SL text or a system working within
it is substituted in the TL text - as in the case of
jokes, puns, obscenities, topical satire, etc. Because of this multiplicity, any notion of there being
a 'right' way to translate becomes a nonsense, as
does the whole question of defining 'translation' as
distinct from 'version' or 'adaptation'. What is
more problematic is the notion of 'performability',
the implicit, undefined and undefinable quality of a
theatre text that so many translators latch on to as
a justification for their various linguistic strate-

gies. It seems to me that the time has come to set aside 'performability' as a criterion for translating too, and to focus more closely on the linguistic structures of the text itself. For, after all, it is only within the written that the performable can be encoded and there are infinte performance decodings possible in any playtext. The written text, *troué* though it may be, is the raw material on which the translator has to work and it is with the written text, rather than with a hypothetical performance, that the translator must begin.

REFERENCES

BASSNETT-McGUIRE, Susan
1978   'Translating Spatial Poetry: an Examination of Theatre
        Texts in Performance', in J.S.Holmes *et al.* (eds.),
        Literature and Translation (Leuven, Acco):161-176
BOGATYREV, Petr
1971   'Les signes du théâtre', *Poétique*, 8:517-30 (original-
        ly in *Slovo a Slovesnost*, 1938)
BRECHT, Bertolt
s.d.   *Die Tage der Commune*. Berliner Ensemble acting script,
        unpublished
1978   *The Days of the Commune*. Transl. Clive Barker & Arno
        Rheinfrank. London, Methuen
ELAM, Keir
1980   *The Semiotics of Theatre and Drama*. London, Methuen
KOWZAN, Tadeusz
1975   *Littérature et spectacle*. The Hague, Mouton
LEFEVERE, André
1982   'Mother Courage's Cucumbers: Text, System and Refrac-
        tion in a Theory of Literature', *Modern Language
        Studies*, Fall 1982:3-20
PAGNINI, Marcello
1970   'Per una semiologia del teatro classico', *Strumenti
        critici*, 12:122-140
PAVIS, Patrice
1976   *Problèmes de sémiologie théâtrale*. Montreal, Les
        presses de l'Université de Québec
PUGLIATTI, Paola Gulli
1976   *I segni latenti: Scrittura come virtualità in King
        Lear*. Messina/Florence, D'Anna
RUFFINI, Franco
1978   *Semiotica del testo*. Rome, Bulzoni
SERPIERI, Alessandro
1977   'Ipotesi teorica de segmentazione del testo teatrale',
        Strumenti critici, 32-33:90-137
STREHLER, Giorgio
1973   *Il Re Lear di Shakespeare*. Verona, Bertani
UBERSFELD, Anne
1978   *Lire le théâtre*. Paris, Editions sociales

IMAGES OF TRANSLATION

Metaphor and Imagery in the Renaissance Discourse on Translation

Theo Hermans

In the Renaissance conception of literature, translation and imitation stand in a paradoxical relation
to each other. They are often discussed together and
regarded as closely related or complementary activities, but on other occasions they are felt to be
miles apart. Especially in the seventeenth century
we may find them described in similar terms, sometimes by means of the same images, analogies and
metaphors, but even at the level of their respective
metalanguages they may touch at one point, perhaps
partly overlap, but they rarely if ever merge completely.
    Broadly speaking, the view among Renaissance
writers, translators and critics alike seems to be
that, in so far as translation and imitation are considered in conjunction, translation is, at best, a
particular and restricted form of imitation - whereby both forms still contrast unfavourably with 'invention' - and, at worst, a mechanical and merely
utilitarian exercise of no literary merit whatsoever.
Even when translation and imitation are associated
with each other, translation almost invariably
emerges as the less deserving of the two. The main
reasons for this appear to be, first, that the ultimate goal of 'total' translation, which would repro-
duce the source text faithfully and completely in all
its aspects across the language barrier, is unattain-
able; secondly, that the translator's freedom of
movement is severely restricted, so that he finds
himself in a subordinate and even subservient position with regard to his model; and thirdly, that,
whatever its relative value, the translated text necessarily remains a copy of an original work and is
thus by definition inferior to that original, the
more so since translation denies itself the emulative
impulse which could act as a challenge, pitting the

translator against the original author.

The paradoxical relationship between translation and imitation may be illustrated with reference to some treatises and handbooks on the art of poetry from mid-sixteenth-century France.

In the chapter on translation in his *Art poétique* of 1545, Jacques Peletier du Mans calls translation "the truest kind of imitation," but he goes on to describe the translator as one who, in rhetorical terms, "subjects himself" not only to someone else's *inventio* but also to the *dispositio* and, as far as he can, to the *elocutio* of the original author's work.[1] At the end of the chapter he conjures up the chimera of a 'total' translation of Virgil, which would render the Latin word for word and sentence for sentence while preserving all the elegance of the original text, only to conclude that "it cannot be done."[2] Thomas Sebillet's *Art poétique françoys* (1548) paints a more optimistic picture. Reflecting the marked upturn in translation activity in France from around 1530 onwards (see Guillerm 1980:6), Sebillet can claim that "Translation is nowadays very much favoured by Poets of esteem and by learned readers," and in a typically favourable comparison he likens the translator to one who "extracts the hidden treasure from the bowels of the earth in order to put it to common use."[3]

Barely a year later, however, translation is cut down to size by Du Bellay's *Deffence et illustration de la langue francoyse* (1549). While he concedes a limited role for literal translation as an instrument for the dissemination of knowledge (Du Bellay ed. 1948:34,59, 192), he resolutely denies that translation can play a part in the growth of literature or the enrichment of the vernacular (*ibid.*:32,38). Du Bellay rejects translation of literature because of its inability to transfer intact "that energy, and - what shall I call it - that spirit, which the Romans would have termed *genius*" and which apparently resides in works of art. The translator, then, is like a painter who can depict a person's body but not his soul[4] - an image, incidentally, which Dryden will repeat with minor variations nearly 150 years later in his criticism of the word-for-word translations of Holyday and Stapylton.[5] In place of translation, Du Bellay advocates imitation, significantly changing the metaphors in his exposition as well: the French poets should do as the Romans did, "imitating the best Greek writers, transforming themselves into them, devouring them and, having digested them well, converting them into blood and nourishment."[6]

The provenance and context of this 'digestive' imagery is easy to trace. Du Bellay took it, directly or indirectly, from Seneca. The image itself is part of a series of 'transformative' analogies and metaphors commonly used both in the ancient Roman and in the Renaissance discourse on imitation. Thanks to a number of modern studies on the principles and the metalanguage of Renaissance imitation (see, among others, Gmelin 1932, Von Stackelberg 1956, and especially Pigman 1980), we know that among the variants of the 'transformative' cluster of analogies are apian, simian and filial metaphors, and that apart from this class of images we can distinguish a series of 'dissimulative' metaphors and analogies, in which the need to conceal or disguise the relation between the imitation and the model is emphasized, and an 'eristic' series, which employs images of strife, struggle and competition with the model, but also includes, in a weaker version, the notion of following in someone's footsteps. As G.W.Pigman (1980:9) has pointed out, these images, analogies and metaphors are not just incidental ornaments; on the contrary, they carry the burden of the argument, and as such they are at the heart of the concept of imitation as the various writers and theoreticians see it.

As far as the images, metaphors and analogies of the Renaissance discourse on translation are concerned, everything remains to be done in the task of collating and interpreting them, although there have been isolated attempts to describe particular aspects of the Renaissance theory of translation from this angle (see, for example, Guillerm 1980, and occasional remarks in Zuber 1963 and 1968, and Steiner 1970). As in the case of imitation, the images appear to be highly functional, and they form an integral and essential part of the Renaissance theory of translation. They bear on the very possibility of translation as well as on the relation between the translation and its original and between the translator and his audience. The existence of a rich and international stock of metaphors in the Renaissance texts on translation is obvious at a glance, and has indeed been pointed out more than once. Its relevance should be equally obvious. When, towards the middle of the seventeenth century, the norms of literary translation change considerably as the so-called 'new way of translating' comes into vogue in France and England, the shift is signalled by a change in the metaphorical apparatus in translators' prefaces and critical statements. On the other hand, the division of labour between translation and imitation in the sixteenth and seventeenth centuries, and the changing attitudes towards it, are also reflected in the distribution of the images and metaphors used to discuss both activities. Peletier's metaphors of submission and of digging up valuable treasures, for example, are commonplace in the six- teenth-century discourse on translation, but they are not normally part of the metalanguage of imitation, while Du Bellay's images of digestion and transforma- tion are not normally found in statements on transla- tion, at least not in the sixteenth century.

The material for an investigation into these images and metaphors, then, is extracted not from the translations themselves, but entirely from the con- temporary discourse on translation, i.e. from meta- texts. These include prefaces and dedications, lauda- tory poems, and more or less occasional statements in various handbooks, critical works, and letters. In order to put the account in the following pages into perspective, two cautionary remarks need to be made. The first involves a question of interpretation. Whereas handbooks, critical works and letters will, on the whole, contain fairly 'neutral' statements which can often be accepted at face value, laudatory poems, prefaces and dedications are governed to a considerable degree by rhetorical conventions. Being stereotyped forms, they will frequently exaggerate their conventional postures, topoi and formulae. In prefaces, and even more so in dedications, the ex- pected stance is one of modesty, even self-deprecia- tion. The translator will consequently understate his own abilities and achievement in order to high- light the difficulty of the task, the excellence of the model and/or the erudition of his patron (see Leiner 1965). The opposite applies to congratulatory poems, which are given to overstatement and hyperbole (Curtius 1953:163-4) and, in their fulsome praise, invariably upgrade the translator's achievement and projected self-image. As we shall see, the different images used in these two contrasting conventions are of some interest.

The second remark concerns the fact that a sys- tematic investigation of the kind attempted here is hampered by the lack of specialist bibliographies (in each of the languages covered: English, French, Dutch and German) and of modern scholarly editions of many of the relevant texts. Exhaustiveness is therefore out of the question. The absence of tho- rough bibliographies (giving details of such things as prefaces, dedications, dedicatees, laudatory poems and their authors, etc.) and of modern editions of translated literature is no doubt symptomatic of the

peripheral position of translation studies in the
scholarly study of literature generally.

*

Although in the course of their theoretical reflections the Renaissance translators frequently refer
to the brief comments on translation made by Cicero
and Horace (whereby the latter's one and a half lines
relating to "fidus interpres" were usually taken out
of context and misunderstood), for our present purposes Quintilian's more extensive comments on imitation provide a more convenient starting-point. In
Book X of the *Institutio oratoria*, Quintilian, having
stated the ineluctable pre-eminence of invention over
imitation, discusses the practice of imitation in
terms of "following in the tracks of others" and
"treading in the forerunner's footsteps", but in the
same breath he stresses the need to compete with the
model, for "the man whose aim is to prove himself
better than another, even if he does not surpass him,
may hope to equal him," whereas "the mere follower
must always lag behind" (Quintilian ed. 1922,iv:79).
In any case, he goes on, imitation in the absolute
sense is both impossible and futile: not even nature
can produce an exact likeness of something else, and
"whatever is like another object must necessarily be
inferior to the object of its imitation, just as the
shadow is inferior to the substance (and) the portrait
to the features which it portrays" (*ibid.* :79-81).
It is, of course, the idea of contest ("contendere
potius quam sequi") which gives imitation its emulative edge. It is this aspect which 'Longinus', with
a passing reference to Hesiod, will treat in terms of
wrestling with a stronger opponent, a struggle that
leads to inevitable but honourable defeat (*On the
Sublime*, chapter 13); Dryden will copy the image almost
verbatim in the preface to his *Troilus and Cressida* (1679).[7]
In the Renaissance literature on imitation, the
'footsteps' topos, derived from Quintilian, is used
in a number of ways. In its strongest formulation,
the aspect of emulation is indicated by metaphors
denoting contest and competition, and goes hand in
hand with the 'wrestling' image. Another variant -
which for obvious reasons has no equivalent in the
discourse on translation - is found in Petrarch, who
makes avoiding the footsteps of his predecessors a
central principle of his conception of imitation
(Pigman 1980:21). In its weakest form the *vestigia*
topos appears simply as following an admired model
at a respectful distance.

For the Renaissance translators, the 'footsteps'
metaphor proves useful in a variety of ways as well.
In its strictest application, to follow an author
step by step usually means translating word for word.
Although in the early Renaissance, for example in
Germany, strict word-for-word translation was sometimes seen as a commendable imitation of Latin style
(see Schwarz 1944:369), most later translators are
prepared to follow their source text only so closely
as the 'propriety' or the 'nature' of the target language will allow. The metaphor can then still be used
to indicate the strictest possible adherence to the
model, without any 'deviation' from its meaning. The
French translator Etienne de Courcelles employs the
image in this sense in a letter of 1628 to Hugo
Grotius: "I was so afraid of weakening your argument
by straying from your words that I followed them
closely throughout, as far as the propriety of our
language permitted it."[8] In the preface to his Dutch
translation of Grotius' play *Sofompaneas* (1635), Joost
van den Vondel adopts a more lenient, middle-of-the-
road approach: "We have not wanted to follow too
closely on the heels of the Latin, nor to stray too
far from our distinguished predecessor (voorganger),"
and he leaves it to Grotius to judge whether he has
successfully steered this middle course.[9] In this
somewhat freer approach the natural image is that of
following at a certain distance, and the more liberal translators frequently criticize their stricter
colleagues for treading upon their authors' heels,
i.e. doing them an injustice by adhering too closely
to their every word. "I do not affect to follow my
author so close as to tread upon his heels," one W.L.
notes in the preface to his version of Virgil's
Eclogues (Amos 1920:146), and Dryden in his 'Discourse
Concerning ... Satire' (1692) comments on Holyday and
Stapylton in the same terms:

> We have followed our authors at greater distance, tho'
> not step by step, as they have done. For oftentimes they
> have gone so close that they have trod on the heels of
> Juvenal and Persius, and hurt them by their too near
> approach. A noble author would not be pursued too close
> by a translator. (Dryden ed. 1962,ii:153)

However, the footsteps metaphor is not just used by
translators to describe their policy in translating,
but also to express the hierarchical relationship between the source and target texts. The sense of hierarchy is already present in Quintilian's statements
on imitation as the relation of front runner to follower. In the case of translation the metaphor should

be seen - and often occurs - in conjunction with a host of other images and direct pronouncements denoting subordination and qualitative inferiority.

The position of power and authority which the source text holds vis-à-vis the target text is probably the most obvious. 'Following' in this context implies not only dependence in the logical and chronological sense (the translated text being derived from the source text), but also a relation of stronger versus weaker, of free versus confined, of owner or master versus servant or slave. To translate is to accept wilful confinement and restriction of one's liberty of movement in order to follow in someone else's tracks. "We might have written more sweetly had we not wanted to tie ourselves more closely to the text," the young Vondel observes in the preface to his Dutch translation of Du Bartas in 1620.[10] In the address 'To the Reader' which prefaces his version of Theophrastus' *Characters* (1616), John Healey points out that "to be too servile or too licentious, are alike amisse in a Translater," for one "darkneth the beautie of the worke" and the other "implieth a secret disabling, as if the Original might be bettered"; but, he concludes, "if there were a necessity to erre in either, I had rather be too strict than any whit too bold" (Lathrop 1933:264).

This sense of the translator's restricted freedom is accepted, later in the century, even by the freer translators such as Nicolas Perrot d'Ablancourt and John Denham (though not by Cowley), but it is again more strongly emphasized by Dryden when he feels he has to stake out his own position with regard to the 'libertine' translators of the school of Denham and Cowley. In his preface to Ovid's *Epistles* (1680) Dryden stresses that the translator's freedom concerns matters of phrasing only, it does not extend to matters of substance ("I suppose he may stretch his Chain to such a Latitude, but by innovation of thoughts, methinks he breaks it", Dryden ed. 1962,i: 272), and in the dedication of his *Aeneid* (1697) he puts it even more strongly: "But slaves we are, and labour on another man's plantation; we dress the vineyard, but the wine is the owner's" (*ibid.*,ii:250).

Being no more than a labourer who works for a master, the translator takes no credit for his work, as translation does not confer ownership of intellectual property. As early as 1529 Richard Hyrd explains in the prologue to his translation of Juan Vives' *Instruction of a Christian Woman* that if there is anything good in the book it is entirely due to Vives, who wrote it, and to Thomas More, who checked the trans-

109

lation (Nugent 1956:75). The 'Epistle to the Reader' in John Stradling's translation of Justus Lipsius' *Two Books of Constance* (1595) invites us to give thanks to God, to Lipsius and to Stradling's patron, in that order (Vanderheyden 1979:161). While these translators may be excluding themselves out of sheer conventional modesty, the *Art poétique* (1545) of Peletier du Mans, a book of a different kind, states in the same vein that a translator can never lay claim to the title of author, and that it is the translator's name which lives on through that of his author, not vice versa (ed.1930:106). There is an unmistakable note of resentment - or is it a rhetorical *captatio benevolentiae*? - in Hugues Salel's prefatory poem to his version of the first ten books of the *Iliad* (1545), when he states that translation is "a difficult task that brings much labour and little honour, for whatever the perfect translator may achieve, the honour always goes to the original writer."[11] This also applies to Etienne Pasquier's rather sour remark in 1594 about translation being "a wretched, thankless and slavish labour."[12] Examples of this kind could be multiplied (see Guillerm 1980:8-10).

It is very unusual to see the relation of power between source text and target text turned upside down in statements made by translators themselves. One such exception is Philemon Holland's preface to his version of Pliny (1601), which resorts to military imagery in its call to the English people to

> ...endeavour by all means to triumph now over the Romans
> in subduing their literature under the dent of the
> English pen, in requitall of the conquest sometime over
> this Island, atchieved by the edge of their sword
> (Matthiessen 1931:179)

On the whole, though, it is only the laudatory poems which emphatically invert the hierarchy between original and translation. According to Ben Jonson's two epigrams (1609) on Clement Edmonds, it is the translator who has made Caesar's name immortal, not the other way round (Jonson ed.1963:54-55); and Thomas Stanley's commendatory poem on Edward Sherburne's translation of Seneca's *Medea* (1648) declares that Sherburne deserves "a double wreath: for all that we/ Unto the poet owe, he owes to thee" (Stanley ed.1962: 64). Around the same time the Dutchman Isaac Vos uses some elaborate military imagery in his complimentary verses on Lion de Fuyter's Dutch version of Lope de Vega's *Carpio, or the Confused Court* (1647), describing how the translator has brought back "in triumph" Spain's most valuable treasure, and concluding:

```
          ... be content, Lope,
To follow with quick strides
Your conqueror, who will share with you
The praise for the Confused Court.
Be glad, Vega, who are his captive
By law of arms, that he is prepared
To share with you that which is wholly his.13
```

Similarly, in his congratulatory lines on Dryden's
translation of Persius (1693), Congreve exclaims that
Persius was "dead in himself, in you alone he lives",
and "To you, we, all this following Treasure owe"
(Kinsley & Kinsley 1971:206). Clearly, though, the
fact itself that the translator's subordination to
the original author is so insistently turned on its
head in these complimentary poems suggests that the
sense of hierarchy is very much present in the translators' minds.

The property relation to which Dryden referred
(above) - that of master to servant, of owner to
hired labourer or slave - also occurs in a different
form, in the figure of the translator showing off
with borrowed feathers, under false pretences. In
the preface to his translation of Du Bartas (1620),
Vondel typifies the translator as a magpie among
peacocks, trying unsuccessfully to don peacock feathers (ed.1927-40,ii:229) - the image itself is familiar from sixteenth-century emblem books and derives
from Ovid. Vondel's compatriot Constantijn Huygens
puts it in characteristically ambivalent fashion when
in the introductory poem to his Dutch version of a
number of English epigrams (1650) he admits that he
is offering only "borrowed enjoyment", but quickly
adds that "even borrowed goods are good goods" since
they come from "noble spirits";14 the rest of the poem
then turns into a clever defence of the role of the
translator as mediator.

The subordination to the model is, obviously,
most strongly felt by the literal translators. For
those who advocate a somewhat freer approach, this
abject submission becomes something they resent and
reject, in terms which stress the opposition between
a certain degree of liberty on the one hand and total
subservience, enchainment and superstitious servility
on the other. As early as 1540 Etienne Dolet's Maniere
de Bien Traduire d'Une Langue en Aultre lists as the third
of its five rules that "in translating one should not
become so subservient as to translate word for word,"15
and in the preface to Persius his Satires (1616) Barten
Holyday proudly announces:

I have not herein bound my selfe with a ferularie super-

stition to the letter: but with the ancient libertie of
a Translator, have used a moderate paraphrase (...): yet
so, that with all conventient possibilities, I stick unto his Wordes. (Kitagaki 1981:162-3)

In the same year Malherbe explains in the preface to
his French translation of Pliny that, rather than adhering to "the servitude of translating word for
word" he has taken the liberty of adding and omitting
in order to clear up obscurities in the source text
and to avoid offending the delicate stylistic sensibilities of his audience.[16]

Malherbe clearly points the way to the more
libertine conception of translation that would quickly gain ground in France and England in the following
decades. In the preface to his first published translation, the *Octavius* of Minucius Felix (1637), Perrot
d'Ablancourt, the leading exponent and theoretician
of the 'belles infidèles', denounces the "Judaic
superstition of tying oneself to the words" of the
source text rather than communicating what the words
are meant to express.[17] When a few years later, in
the preface to his *Annals* of Tacitus (1640), he asserts
- perhaps unexpectedly - that apart from a few omissions dictated by "les delicatesses de nostre Langue"
he has

> everywhere else followed (Tacitus) step by step, and
> rather as a slave than as a companion, although I could
> perhaps have taken more liberty, for I am not transla-
> ting a passage, but a Book[18]

there is every reason to believe that he is giving an
ironic twist to a stock metaphor, for in the same
paragraph he again denounces the "overscrupulous
translators" - a condemnation he regularly repeats
in subsequent prefaces (for example in 1654 and 1662;
D'Ablancourt ed. 1972:188,202).

The advocates of the 'new way' in England leave
no doubt about their rejection of the traditional
servility of the translator. In his well-known poem
on Richard Fanshawe's version of the *Pastor Fido* (1648),
John Denham puts it squarely: "That servile path thou
nobly dost decline / Of tracing word by word and line
by line" - yet, although he dismisses the "narrowness"
and "slavish brains" of the stricter translators, he
still accepts that a degree of confinement and restriction are the translator's inescapable condition:
"Yet after all (lest we should think it thine) / Thy
spirit to his circle dost confine" (Steiner 1975:63-
4). The 'free' translator's newly-won freedom, in
other words, is largely a matter of broadening the

unit of translation from the individual word or line
or sentence to larger wholes, but it does not affect
the essential hierarchy of power and ownership that
exists between author and translator. Just as the
lack of *inventio* in the translator's product puts him
in a secondary position with regard to the original
writers among his contemporaries, so it is the pre-
eminence and authority of the original author's *inventio*
which forces even the most libertine translator into
some form of submission. Perhaps the only exception
in this respect is Abraham Cowley's defiant preface
to his *Pindarique Odes* (1656). He too rejects the work
of the stricter translators as "a vile and unworthy
kinde of Servitude," but goes on to claim absolute
freedom of action:

> I have in these two Odes of Pindar taken, left out, and
> added what I please; nor make it so much my aim to let
> the Reader know precisely what he spoke, as what was
> his way and manner of speaking. (Steiner 1975:67)

Cowley, however, is indifferent to whether his version is called translation or imitation. His method,
and the 'competitive' metaphors in the preface to the
Pindarique Odes ("resolving ... to shoot beyond the
Mark"), point to an emulative urge normally absent
from the discourse on translation proper.

*

As was indicated above, the 'footsteps' metaphor and
its variants can be used to express not only the
translator's subordination to his model, but also
the perception of a qualitative difference between
the translated text and its source text. In this respect, too, there is a whole series of associated
images and analogies suggesting the inferiority of
the translation, and the deficient talents of the
translator, in comparison with the original text and
its author.

   In contrast with Cowley's assertion that rather
than endeavouring to produce a copy of the source
text one should aim to go beyond it ("for men resolving in no case to shoot beyond the Mark, it is a
thousand to one if they shoot not short of it"), the
more conventional translator is fully prepared to admit his weakness and hence the futility of contesting
the original author's superiority. In the prologue
to his translation of Sophocles' *Electra* (1537),
Lazare de Baïf concedes that he is not sufficiently
well versed in either the source or the target language to be able to compete with Sophocles (he was in

fact working from Erasmus' Latin version of the play),
and so he is content to be "no more than his simple
faithful translator."[19] Vondel repeatedly uses simi-
les, mostly derived from Ovid, which all imply that
the translator is bound to come to grief if he were
to challenge his model's superiority: the translator
is like Phaeton, who wanted to drive the chariot of
the sun and was struck down (1620); if he wants to
compete with David's psalms, he will suffer Lucifer's
fate (1640); if he hopes to outdo Sophocles, he is
like Pan challenging Apollo and will end up growing
donkey's ears like Midas (1668; Vondel ed. 1927-40,
ii:229-30; iv; 53; x:548). In a number of similar
images Vondel expresses the translator's inferior
powers in terms of limping behind the model, or in
the opposition between soaring high and flying low,
as in the dedicatory poem accompanying his translation
of Ovid's *Metamorphoses* (1671): "We have tried, sail-
ing low to the ground, and in the shadow of (Ovid)
who soars on high like an eagle, to follow him at a
distance, in the Dutch way";[20] further Vondelian analogies include that of the inexperienced choirboy
and the lead singer (1616), or the original song and
its faint echo (1660; *ibid*., i:477; vi:86). Huygens
speaks in the same vein of being happy merely to
"stammer after" John Donne (ed.1892-99,vi:338).

There are several other clusters of metaphors
and analogies emphasizing the inferior quality of
the translated work. G. de la Pinelière's dedication
of his translation of Seneca's *Hippolytus* (1635) refers
to "offering false pearls and pieces of crystal in
place of diamonds."[21] The preface to Nicholas Haward's
version of Eutropius (1564) says that those unable
to read the original language "must needes contente
them selves to wade only in the troubled streames of
Translators: for that they are not able to attayne
to the well spryng it selfe" (Jones 1953:19). Among
the more common images are those describing a translation as the reverse side of a tapestry or carpet,
and translating as exchanging the sumptuous garb of
the original for a rough and homespun garment. In the
prologue to his *Electra* (1537) Lazare de Baïf refers
explicitly to the story of Themistocles (as told by
Plutarch), who did not want to speak to the Persian
King through an interpreter because, he said, a translation was no better than the reverse side of a tapestry, and De Baif duly concludes that "in my translation I cannot show you anything but the reverse
side of Sophocles' triumphant and excellent tapestry."[22] The image is subsequently used in the same
sense by, among others, Cervantes (*Don Quixote*, Part

Two,1615), James Howell and his French translator
Baudoin (*Dendrologie*, 1641; cf. Zuber 1968:87), the
Frenchman E.B. (in a translation of Cicero, 1644;
ibid.:86) and in an epigram on translation by Huygens
(1622; ed.1892-9,vii:8)

The 'garment' metaphor, which is attested dozens
of times, is not necessarily disparaging in itself
(see below), but becomes a vehicle for expressing the
inferiority of the translated text through the opposition of 'rich' versus 'poor' garment. The opposition occurs in some ingenious variations: a "playne
and homespun English cote" in contrast with an original "richely clad in Romayne vesture" (Arthur Golding,
1564), "Velvet" versus "our Countrie cloth" (Thomas
Wilson, 1570), "newlie arraied with course English
cloth" (Abraham Fleming, 1581), and, even more colour-
ful: "their rich and sumptuous French garments,"
"robes of Salomon" and "riche mans purple" as opposed
to "poore and base English weeds," "the rags of Frus"
and "Lazarus patches" (Joshua Sylvester, 1592; Jones
1953:19-22).

Vondel further refers to his translations in
terms of a pale star which derives its light from the
sun (1616), candlelight compared to sunlight (1635),
and reflected light in contrast with direct light
(1660; ed.1927-40,i:477; vi:86). As these examples
show, the metaphors often serve the dual purpose of
stressing the derivative nature of the translated
text as well as its qualitative inferiority. On only
one occasion does Vondel turn the image into a cautious justification of translation, by pointing out
that even a faint light will shine in the darkness
(*ibid.*,i:477). Huygens, on the other hand, is more determined in his revaluation of such metaphors, arguing in a poem of 1650 that the weaknesses of the
translation highlight the excellencies of the original just as a painting needs the contrasts between
light and dark, and that shaded light is beneficial
to those who are dazzled by bright sunlight - meaning,
presumably, readers unfamiliar with the original lan-
guage.23

The contrast between the source and target texts
in terms of body (or substance) and shadow provides
yet another image for underlining both the derivative
and inferior quality of the translated work. The passage in Quintilian's *Institutio oratoria* still echoes in
John Florio's address to the reader in his translation of Montaigne (1603): his version, he admits,
falls short of the quality of the source text "as
much as artes nature is short of natures art, a picture of a body, a shadow of a substance" (Matthiessen

1931:117). As late as 1700 the dialogue between
'Eumenes' and 'Philenor' prefaced to the anonymous
translation of Lucian's *Charon* speaks of translation
being only "a Shadow and Resemblance of the Original
Piece" (Kitagaki 1981:300). Huygens describes translations as "shadows of beautiful bodies" in 1625 and
1630 (ed.1892-9,i:285; ed.1910-7,i:289), but in a
poem of 1633, which may be counted as one of the most
elegant statements on translation in the seventeenth
century, he again manages a witty revaluation. In
successive stanzas he explores the various aspects
of the simile, arguing that although shadows are like
the night, they are still daughters of light; although
they are distorted shapes, something of the original
form still remains visible; although they are dark
and obscure, it is a poor reader who cannot see through
them; although they are lacking in warmth, their cool-
ness is only superficial and, like pepper corns, they
are hot inside; although they are mere 'nothings',
they are 'embodied nothings', and like daydreams, feed
on reality.[24] The purpose of Huygens' argumentation
is clearly to counteract, if only to a limited extent,
the negative import of the 'shadow' metaphor by focusing on the relative value and use of translation:
for all its deficiencies, it can retain the most essential characteristics of the model from which it
derives. Huygens' play with metaphors encapsulates
his moderate attitude towards translation generally,
a mixture of scepticism and appreciation, inasmuch as
he is prepared to argue that limited value need not
mean absence of any value whatever.

It is, again, only in the hyperbolic language
of the laudatory poems that the view of translation
as second-hand and second-best, as derivative and
inferior in quality, is negated and the relationship
between translation and original inverted. Translation then comes out on top, and the source text is
assigned second place. The commendatory poem by a
certain I.Knight on Barten Holyday's *Persius* (1616)
puts it bluntly, with an interesting variant on the
'following in the author's footsteps' metaphor:

> How truly with thine author thou dost pace,
> How hand in hand ye go (...)
> He might be thought to have translated thee,
> But that he's darker, not so strong; wherein
> Thy greater art more clearly may be seen (Kitagaki 1981:163)

Other poems, too, suggest that the translation is so
good that the source text seems to be derived from it
instead of the other way round. Thus Jonson's epigram
on Joshua Sylvester's version of Du Bartas (1605):

Bartas doth wish thy *English* now were his
(...)
As his will now be the *translation* thought,
Thine the *originall*   (*ibid.*:118)

Huygens' poem on Jacob Westerbaen's Dutch translation
of the *Aeneid* (1660) holds that if Virgil were alive
today he would want to translate Westerbaen's text
into Latin, which would produce an even better result
than the original *Aeneid* (ed.1892-9,vi:288). James
Wright's verses on Dryden's *Aeneid* (1697) also claim
that "we know not which to call/ The Imitation, which
th'Originall", for "such (is) the Majesty of your
Impress/ You seem the very Author you translate" -
to which he adds in the next stanza that "were (Virgil) now alive with us, (...) Himself cou'd write no
otherwise than thus" (Kinsley & Kinsley 1971:222-3).
Obviously, compliments of this kind should always be
seen in their rhetorical context: their point is precisely that they present a deliberate inversion of
the relation between translation and original as it
is commonly perceived in critical treatises and in
the translators' own comments.

*

Huygens' cautious revaluation of translation (in the
poem of 1633, above) opens the way for a very different set of images and metaphors bearing on the justification of translation. On the whole, the translators and theoreticians use two lines of defence:
first, by pointing out that, in spite of its apparent
shortcomings, translation is rendering useful serv-
ices to the large number of people who do not read
foreign languages; and secondly, by continually re-
stating that, in spite of the odds being stacked
heavily against it, translation is, after all, possible.

The first argument, that translation serves the
common good, implies a direct appeal by the translator to his audience, and as such it offers a positive
counterweight to the subordination and qualitative
inferiority of the translation vis-à-vis its source
text. The emphasis, consequently, is on the useful,
even essential role of translation in the dissemination of knowledge: it is translation that opens doors,
that brings light and enlightenment for all, and not
just for the select few; in other words, translation
performs a public function. The strength of the argument obviously lies in the steadily growing size of
the market for translations in the sixteenth and
seventeenth centuries. In the early Renaissance the

defenders of writing in the vernacular and the defenders of translating into the vernacular both refer to
the biblical saying that "no man lyghteth a candle
to cover it with a bushell" (for instance, Thomas
Elyot in 1541 and Thomas Phaer in 1544; Jones 1953:
49). Some translators go so far as to claim that not
to translate amounts to withholding something valuable from the people. As early as 1475 the German
translator Heinrich Stainhöwel says that he has en-
gaged in translation so that those without Latin
"should not be deprived of something so good" (Vanderheyden 1980:147). Observing the scarcity of Dutch
translations from the Latin in 1541, the Flemish publisher Jan Gymnick, in the preface to an anonymous
translation of Livy, thinks it disgraceful that "so
many costly and profitable treasures have been with-
held, indeed stolen from the common man" (*ibid.*: 142).

Even those who justify their work in less emotional language make the same point over and over
again. The metaphors are those of providing access,
unlocking, uncovering, removing obstacles, bringing
into view. Nicholas Grimald's statement, in the preface to his version of Cicero (1556), is as representative as any:

> ... chiefly for our unlatined people I have made this
> latine writer, english: and have now brought into light,
> that from them so longe was hidden: and have caused an
> auncient wryting to become, in maner, newe agayne: and
> a boke, used but of fewe, to wax common to a great meany:
> so that our men, understanding, what a treasure is
> amonge them (...) may, in all pointes of good demeanour,
> becomme pereless (Vanderheyden 1980:144)

William Painter's dedication of his *Second Tome of the
Palace of Pleasure* (1567) puts it in more general terms:
translators, he says,

> ... imploye those paines, that no Science lurke in
> corner, that no knowledge be shut up in cloisters, that
> no Historie remain under the maske and unknowne attire
> of other tongues. (Jones 1953:44)

But the preface to the Authorized Version of the
Bible (1611) is even more emphatic and lyrical:

> Translation it is that openeth the window, to let in the
> light; that breaketh the shell, that we may eat the ker-
> nel; that putteth aside the curtaine, that we may looke
> into the most Holy place; that remooveth the cover of
> the well, that wee may come by the water (Pollard 1911:349)

In many cases, moreover, the point is given additional emphasis by referring to the 'rich treasures'

118

which the translator delivers to all, so that he can be cast as a discoverer returning from distant shores or a digger for gold. Sebillet's *Art poétique* (above) spoke of the translator as one who "extracts the hidden treasure from the bowels of the earth in order to put it to common use." Ben Jonson's complimentary poem on Chapman combines the image of the valuable treasure with that of the translator as discoverer (Jonson ed.1963:369), and one T.G., writing in Holyday's *Persius* (1616), is equally metaphorical:

> What lay imprisoned, and confin'd alone
> Only to deeper apprehension;
> Thy more benigne, sublim'd, transcendent wit
> Hath reacht, and conquer'd, and imparted it.
>
> (Steiner 1970:61)

The latter two poems are laudatory pieces, and in this case their imagery is a direct continuation of that found in critical handbooks and the translators' own prefaces. Their role, in this context, is simply to confirm, at best to intensify, the translators' own self-defence.

*

A fairly large number of prefaces and dedications describe the translation in question as a 'jewel in a rough casket', the casket being the language of the translation, the jewel representing the content. The image can serve several purposes. It can be used as a justification for translating, in line with the image of the treasure worth having and now being offered to all. It is also used, as will be seen below, to express the possibility of translation *per se*: only the casket is changed, the jewel is preserved intact. When it occurs in the specific form of a 'jewel in a *rough* casket', it may be associated with the 'rough garment' metaphor, for both imply the admission of a certain loss incurred in the translation process, with the proviso that the loss is no more than superficial and does not affect the content. The address to the reader in Abraham Fleming's translation of Aelian's *Register of Histories* (1576) makes the point in a very fulsome manner: the book

> ... is like unto an inestimable Iuell, or precious pearle, which although yt be inclosed in a homly wodden box, and shut up in a simple casket, little or nothing worth in comparison, yet it is never a whit the lesse in vallue notwithstanding, but reserveth his price undiminished. (...) Open this base boxe, and lifte upp the lydd of this course casket, wherein so riche and

costely a Iuell is inclosed. (Lathrop 1933:79-80)

The 'garment' and the 'jewel' metaphors are combined in Arthur Golding's preface to his *Histories of Trogus Pompeius* (1564), which first contrasts the "playne and homespun English cote" with the original "Romayne vesture" and goes on to claim that

> ... the valewe and estimacion of Thistory, is no more abased thereby, then should the vertue of a precious stone, by setting it in brasse or yron, or by carying it in a closur of Leather.   (Jones 1953:20)

In both these cases, and in other similar statements, the implication is that translation is a matter of changing merely the outward form, not the substance of the source text, and that the loss is therefore negligible.

The underlying idea, the view of language in which form and substance, words and meaning, signifier and sifnified can be separated, finds expression in a series of metaphorical oppositions revolving around the notions of 'outside' versus 'inside' or 'perceptible' versus 'imperceptible', such as body and soul, matter and spirit, garment and body, casket and jewel, husk and kernel, the vessel and the liquid contained in it, a chest and its contents. The strength of this conception of language, and the particular form in which it appears in the metatexts of Renaissance translation, may possibly be explained with reference to the tradition of biblical interpretation and of Medieval allegorical reading, but such ramifications would lead us far afield. The fact that some of the metaphorical oppositions just mentioned can also have slightly different applications - for example, 'garment' as verse form (Harington) or as metre (Chapman) - need not concern us here either. The point at issue is that the conception of language in terms of 'outside' versus 'inside' implies the possibility of translation by isolating 'form' from 'meaning' and granting priority to the latter. This is indeed how Erasmus sees it:

> Language consists of two parts, namely words and meaning which are like body and soul. If both of them can be rendered I do not object to word-for-word translation. If they cannot, it would be preposterous for a translator to keep the words and to deviate from the meaning.
> (Schwarz 1955:155)

Charles Estienne's preface to his translation of Terence's *Andria* (1542) describes the translator as "one who renders the meaning, the expression, the spirit of a given matter without constraint of language."[25] As late as 1654 a poem by Huygens sums up just about all the stock metaphors for the opposition between 'poor outside' and 'rich inside' (body/soul, skin/body, casket/jewel, husk/kernel) in order to demonstrate that translation is able to preserve the essence undiminished, and that it is the rich inside, not the rough and worthless outside that matters (Huygens ed.1892-9,v:122-3).

From an early stage onwards, however, this unproblematic notion of translatability is countered by an awareness that the idiomatic structures of individual languages do not always match and that these formal differences may hamper the transference of the 'spiritual' content. A typical metaphor presents translation as pouring something from one vessel into another. Its origin may lie in the Latin term 'transfundere', which is used, among others, by Juan Vives early in the sixteenth century (Vanderheyden 1980: 133). Interestingly, it is rarely used without suggesting that this 'decanting' can be done without spilling or loss of quality to the content. John Healey's 'To the Reader' prefaced to his translation of Theophrastus (1616) admits that "by powring it out of the Latin into the vulgar, the great disproportion of Languages and abilities considered, it cannot but (by my unskilfulnesse) it hath taken some wind" (Lathrop 1933:264). In the dedication of his *Electra* translation (1639), Vondel complains that the constraints of rhyme and metre have meant that the content has suffered, since "pouring something from one language into another through a narrow bottle-neck cannot be done without spilling."[26] James Howell also uses the image in connection with translation (Steiner 1975:146), and his French translator Baudoin explains that translating is like decanting wine: some bouquet and quality is inevitably lost.[27] Sir Richard Fanshawe employs the image in the same sense in the dedication of his translation of the *Pastor Fido* (Fanshawe ed.1964:4).

When John Denham subsequently uses it, in the preface to his *Destruction of Troy* (1656), he strikes a somewhat different note, for to him

> Poesie is of so subtile a spirit, that in pouring out of one Language into another, it will all evaporate; and if a new spirit be not added in the transfusion, there will remain nothing but a *Caput mortuum*, there being certain Graces and Happinesses peculiar to every Language, which gives life and energy to the words (...).
>
> (Steiner 1975:65)

Here the metaphor has become problematic, for Denham
makes it clear that because of the "certain Graces
and Happinesses peculiar to every Language" poetry
will evaporate completely if simply poured from one
language into another without some compensatory effort on the translator's part. The metaphor also
opens up a rather new perspective, in that it osten-
sibly derives from the world of alchemy. 'Caput mortuum' is the term used by alchemists for the residue
after a process of distillation, and its symbol is a
skull (Crosland 1962:228). The implication is, presumably, that translating poetry is not so much a matter of pouring a liquid, but a complex and delicate
process requiring a certain artistic input by the
translator and resulting in a product of a different
nature from what it was before. Denham does not enlarge on what he means by "Poesie", but one is reminded of Du Bellay's open-ended catalogue of formal
and conceptual attributes that together make up artistic quality, which he finally sums up in the Latin
term 'genius'.28

Clearly, the view that 'poetry', as an artistic
quality, is composed of both formal and conceptual
properties undercuts the simple dichotomies implied
in the 'inside' versus 'outside' metaphors of language. The increasingly problematical nature of literary translation as the libertine translators of the
mid-seventeenth century see it, is exactly captured
in the way Denham bends a metaphor, originally intended to express the possibility of translation, to
focus instead on the threatened loss of the essential
'poetic spirit' in the transfer. For the French translators of the 'belles infidèles' school, the 'garment'
metaphor becomes problematic in the same way and because of a similar perception of the indissolubility
of form and content, of a writer's stylistic "tour"
and his "pensée" (see Zuber 1963:291). It is then also in this context that we have to see the repeated
insistence with which Dryden uses the word 'genius'
when he speaks of translation in his prefaces and
essays: translating poetry is a matter of preserving
the 'genius' of the original, and consequently the
translator should possess a 'genius' akin to that of
his author.

The shift in the approach to the translation of
literature in particular is anticipated in Chapman's
prefaces to his translation of Homer (1610-1616).
Just as the "sense and elegancie" of different languages is bound up with their different linguistic
forms, so too are the poet's "spirit" and his "art"
inseparable from the particular form in which they

are expressed; hence his advice to translators to

> ... aspire
> As well to reach the spirit that was spent
> In his example as with arte to pierce
> His Grammar, and etymologie of words   (Spingarn 1908:77)

Hence also his firm rejection both of "word-for-word traductions" which sacrifice the "free grace" of the original, and of taking "more licence from the words that may expresse / Their full compression" (*ibid.*:77, 78). The only proper solution is to strive "With Poesie to open Poesie" (*ibid.*), in other words, to attempt to produce an equivalent poetic effect.

It is this notion of equivalent poetic effect that will appeal to certain translators in England and France a few decades later. Denham praises it in Richard Fanshawe's *Pastor Fido* (1648), when he contrasts Fanshawe with the literal translators: "They but preserve the Ashes, thou the Flame,/ True to his sense, but truer to his fame" (Steiner 1975:64). In the preface to his *Destruction of Troy* he puts it even more directly when he says of the translator that "it is not his business alone to translate Language into Language, but Poesie into Poesie" (*ibid.*:65) - the echo from Chapman is too obvious to be missed, Cowley's endeavour to render Pindar's "way and manner of speaking" rather than "precisely what he spoke" (*ibid.*:67) puts the emphasis squarely on poetic style and eloquence rather than on content. In France, D'Ablancourt's preface to his first translation, the *Octavius* of Minucius Felix (1637), makes a very similar point in claiming that "Two works resemble each other more if they are both eloquent than if one is eloquent and the other is not," and in the same paragraph he unwittingly echoes Chapman in observing that different languages have different "beauties and graces", so that a compensatory effort is required on the translator's part.[29] The preface to the second part of his Tacitus translation (1644) repeats that "the way to arrive at the greatness of the original is not by following it step by step, but seeking out the beauties of the (target) language in the way the original author sought out the beauties of his language."[30]

The changed conception of the priorities of translation, and the agreement between the advocates of the 'new way of translating' in France and England, is also apparent from some of their metaphors. Just as, for example, Denham speaks of an unpoetic translation as a *"Caput mortuum"*, D'Ablancourt repeatedly refers to a translation which lacks eloquence as a "carcass" (Minucius Felix, 1637; Thucydides, 1662;

123

D'Ablancourt ed.1972:111,202). In the preface to
Sylvae (1685), Dryden too remarks that "a good poet
is no more like himself in a dull translation than
his carcass would be to his living body" (Dryden ed.
1962,ii:20).

It is in metaphors like these that the new attitude towards translation crystallizes. In addition,
they show the extent to which these 'libertine' translators have moved away from the traditional discourse
on translation and towards imitation. Instead of -
and sometimes in addition to - the conventional images of subordination and inferiority, the translators and theoreticians who adopt the new approach
either devise new metaphors with a different slant,
suggesting a direct personal relationship between
translator and author, or they turn towards the traditional metaphors of imitation. Cowley's bold re-
solve to "shoot beyond the Mark," for example, clearly belongs in the sphere of the eristic metaphors of
imitation. In Chapman's view of the translator's task
the close familiarity with the author's artistic per-
sonality is very much in evidence: the translator
should be susceptible to all the qualities of the
source text, and through spiritual affinity with his
author and a process of internalization he should assess the writer's "true sense and height" and then
set out in search of an equivalent poetic expression.

No doubt Chapman would have approved of Marie
de Gournay's attitude - and imagery - when she observes in 1623 that to translate is

> ... to engender a Work anew (...). Engender, I say, be-
> cause (the ancient writers) have to be decomposed by
> profound and penetrating reflection, in order to be re-
> constituted by a similar process; just as meat must be
> decomposed in our stomachs in order to form our bodies.[31]

The 'digestive' analogy, like Du Bellay's metaphor in
his *Deffence et illustration*, comes straight out of the
sphere of imitation. Chapman would probably also have
agreed with G.Colletet's statement, in a speech to
the French Academy in 1636, that we should write

> ... in such a way that we are not a mere Echo of the
> words (of the Ancients); we should conceive things in
> the same spirit in which they would have conceived them,
> and search in our language, as they did in theirs, for
> terms capable of an exalted and magnificent expression.[32]

and with the advice of Franciscus Junius (François
du Jon) in 1637 that we should not "ape the outward
ornaments, but express above all the inner force of
the (original) work" (Warners 1957:85). The point is

however, that both Colletet and Junius are referring not to translation, but to imitation; both are actually rehearsing Quintilian's remark that "imitation (...) should not be confined merely to words" (ed. 1922:89).

In this view, the translator's wish to absorb in its entirety the 'spirit' of the original work makes for a sense of respectful admiration and a close person-to-person relationship rather than the submissiveness of the traditional translators. Consequently, the translator casts himself as a caring friend, a companion, a host, concerned for his author's well-being. Roscommon's *Essay on Translated Verse* (1684) tells the translator to

> ... chuse an Author as you chuse a Friend:
> United by this Sympathetick Bond,
> You grow familiar, intimate and fond   (Steiner 1975:77)

D'Ablancourt's emphasis on 'eloquence' in the translated text is invariably justified in terms of the need to preserve the original author's integrity, in a very personal sense. Guez de Balzac's comment on D'Ablancourt's version of Xenophon, in a letter to Conrart dated 25 April 1648, fully captures the new spirit:

> How grateful I am to him (*i.e.* D'Ablancourt) for the services rendered in Paris tc the good people of Athens! These are not the marks of inferiority or tasks performed out of servility; they are acts of courtesy, acts of pure hospitality![33]

It is also this personal relationship, the notion of spiritual affinity and the translator's sense of responsibility as if to a respected friend, that prompts the translator to update his model, making the author speak as he would have spoken had he lived in the translator's day and age. In his *Discours sur Malherbe* (1630), Antoine Godeau states that the best translators in France have always written

> as if they were animated by the spirit of those they explain to us (...) and they make them speak with such charm as if they had never breathed any other air but that of the Louvre.[34]

John Denham likewise holds in 1656 that "if Virgil must needs speak English, it were fit he should speak not only as a man of this Nation, but as a man of this Age" (Steiner 1975:65). Interestingly, Dryden's changing view of translation and imitation is reflected in his statements on this point. In the preface to Ovid's *Epistles* (1680) he refers to Cowley's practice as 'imitation' rather than 'translation' because of the latter's endeavour "to write, as he supposes that author would have done, had he lived in our age and in our country" (Dryden ed.1962,i:270). In the 'Discourse Concerning ... Satire' (1692), which criticizes the literal versions of Holyday and Stapylton, he says that he and his fellow translators "endeavoured to make (Juvenal) speak that kind of English which he would have spoken had he lived in England, and had written to this age" (*ibid.*,ii:154). Finally, in the dedication of his *Aeneid* (1697) – in which he "thought fit to steer betwixt the two extremes of paraphrase and literal translation" – he has tried "to make Virgil speak such English as he would himself have spoken, if he had been born in England, and in this present age" (*ibid.*: 247).

Considering the extent to which the libertine translators had in previous decades been moving in the direction of imitation, however, the shifts in Dryden's position are less surprising than they may seem. As early as 1648 Edward Sherburne's preface to his *Medea* is undecided whether to call the version a translation or a paraphrase (Steiner 1970:70). Cowley is equally indifferent to whether his *Pindarique Odes* should be termed 'translation' or 'imitation' (Steiner 1975:67). D'Ablancourt declares in the preface to his version of Lucian (1654) that it "is not properly Translation, but it is better than Translation,"[35] and in a letter written shortly afterwards to the much stricter translator François Cassandre he repeats that his work "cannot properly bear the name of translation, but there is no other."[36]

The close bond between translator and author as suggested in the 'digestive' images, the close personal relationship and the endeavour to write as the author would have done had he lived here and now, ultimately results in the total identification of the translator with his author. The necessary empathy between them, and the translator's absorption of his model, becomes total identity. The supreme image for this transformation is the Pythagorean notion – occasionally acknowledged as such – of the migration of souls, or metempsychosis. Chapman describes his sense of spiritual communion with Homer in the allegorical poem 'Euthymiae Raptus' (1609), in which the poet tells the translator that

> ... thou didst inherit
> My true sense (for the time then) in my spirit;
> And I, invisiblie, went prompting thee,
> To these fayre Greenes, where thou didst english me
>   (Kitagaki 1981:132)

But only the later translators and theoreticians take the idea to its logical conclusion. In the preface to his translation of Thucydides (1662), D'Ablancourt observes daringly that

> ... this is not so much a portrait of Thucydides, as Thucydides himself, who has passed into another body as if by a kind of Metempsychosis, and from being Greek has become French.[37]

And Roscommon's *Essay on Translated Verse* (1684) tells us that the "Sympathetick Bond" between translator and author should be such that in the end the translator is "No Longer his Interpreter, but He" (Steiner 1975: 77).

It is at this stage, finally, that the discourse of the 'libertine' translators meets that of the laudatory poems on translation generally. For again and again the complimentary verses praise translators for having rendered their authors so well that the success of the operation must be attributable to some miraculous migration of souls, or at least a unique affinity. As early as 1577 Ronsard's poem on Amadis Jamyn's *Iliade* argues that just as Homer was filled with Jupiter's spirit in writing his epic, so Homer's soul has passed into Jamyn, and now "You are both one, in one body united / Heaven is your common father."[38] Needless to say, a translation produced in such circumstances reads like an original. The poem by T.G. on Barten Holyday's *Persius* (1616) claims that Holyday has written

> As if thou didst consult with th'Authors Ghost;
> Such height, such sacred indignation
> As seemes a Persius, no translation.   (Steiner 1970:61)

Similarly, Ben Jonson's epigram on Henry Savile's translation of Tacitus (1591) begins with the lines:

> If, my religion safe, I durst embrace
> That stranger doctrine of *Pythagoras*,
> I should beleeve, the soule of *Tacitus*
> In thee, most weighty *Savile*, liv'd to us
> (Jonson ed.1963:42)

Two Dutch poems on two separate translations of Du Bartas, finally, make exactly the same point. J.J. Starter, writing on Zacharias Heyns' version (1621), also refers explicitly to Pythagoras' notion of metempsychosis, for only by assuming that "Du Bartas' soul has passed into our Heyns" can he comprehend the latter's astounding achievement.[39] And Anna Roemers Visscher, praising Baron Wessel van Boetselaer's translation (1622), exclaims:

Du Bartas lives! he writes! he calls me his friend,
O noble Baron, his spirit resides in you (...)
You are Du Bartas, or he was the same as you.[40]

The irony of these poems is, of course, that they
were written independently of each other, for different translators, both of whom could apparently pride
themselves on possession of the French poet's soul.

As we saw, the rhetoric of the complimentary
poem is such that it consistently inverts the images
of subordination and inferiority pertaining to the
traditional metalanguage of translation, and upgrades
the judgements on the use and value of translation.
It is a measure of the distance travelled by the
'libertine' school of translators - and of their
amazing self-confidence - that their views on the
translation of literary texts eventually led them by
a different route to an almost identical position.
Thinking the complex nature of literary language and
literary translation through to its conclusion, that
is, they arrived at a point which for the stricter
practitioners of the genre existed only in the hyperbolic and unworldly language of the laudatory mode.

NOTES

1. "La plus vraie espèce d'Imitation, c'est de traduire.
Car imiter n'est autre chose que vouloir faire ce que fait un
autre: Ainsi que fait le Traducteur qui s'asservit non seule-
ment à l'Invention d'autrui, mais aussi à la Disposition: et
encore a l'Elocution tant qu'il peut (...)" Peletier ed.1930:
105   (I have modernized Peletier's eccentric spelling, T.H.)
2. "Et qui pourrait traduire tout Virgile en vers français, phrase pour phrase et mot pour mot: ce serait une louange
inestimable (...) Puis, pensez quelle grandeur ce serait de
voir une seconde Langue répondre à toute l'élégance de la
première: et encore avoir la sienne propre. Mais comme j'ai
dit, il ne se peut faire." *Ibid.*:110-111
3. "Pourtant t'averty-ie que la Version ou Traduction est
auiourdhuy le Poëme plus frequent et mieux receu des estimez
Poëtes et des doctes lecteurs (...). Et luy (*i.e.* the translator) est deue la mesme gloire qu'emporte celuy qui par son
labeur et longue peine tire des entrailles de la terre le tre-
sor caché, pour le faire commun à l'usage de tous les hommes".
Sebillet ed.1972:73.
4. "... ceste energie, et ne scay quel esprit, (...) que
les Latins appelleroient *genius*. Toutes les quelles choses se
peuvent autant exprimer en traduisant, comme un peintre peut
representer l'ame avecques le cors de celuy qu'il entreprent
apres le naturel." Du Bellay ed.1948:40-41.
5. "We lose (the author's) spirit, when we think to take
his body. The grosser part remains with us, but the soul is

flown away in some noble expression, or some delicate turn of words or thought. Thus Holyday, who made this way his choice, seized the meaning of Juvenal; but the poetry has always escaped him." ('A Discourse Concerning ... Satire') Dryden ed. 1962,ii:153.

6. "Immitant les meilleurs auteurs Grecz, se transformant en eux, les devorant, et apres les avoir bien digerez, les convertissant en sang et nourriture..." Du Bellay ed.1948:42.

7. "We ought not to regard a good imitation as a theft, but as a beautiful idea of him who undertakes to imitate (...); for he enters into the lists like a new wrestler, to dispute the prize with the former champion. This sort of emulation, says Hesiod, is honourable (...) - when we combat for victory with a hero, and are not without glory even in our overthrow." Dryden ed.1962,i:242.

8. "Je sai bien que je n'ai point esgalé l'élégance de vostre stile latin; mais j'ai eu tellement peur d'affoiblir vos argumens en m'esloignant de vos paroles, que je les ai suivi (*sic*) de près par tout, autant que la propriété de nostre langue l'a peu permettre." Zuber 1968:261.

9. "Wy hebben het Latijn niet al te dicht willen op de hielen volgen, noch oock te verre van onzen treffelijcken voorganger afwijcken. Maer of wy hier in de rechte maete houden, dat zal het Groote Vernuft (...) kunnen oordeelen." Vondel ed. 1927-40,iii:435.

10. "... dat wy zoetelijcker hadden mogen vloeijen zoo wy ons niet naeuwer aenden texst wilden binden..." Vondel ed.1927-40,ii:229.

11. "   ...c'est une peine
Qui grand travail et peu d'honeur ameine
(Car quoy que face ung parfaict traducteur,
Tousjours l'honeur retourne a l'inventeur)"
                              Weinberg 1950:128.

12. "... un labeur misérable, ingrat et esclave." Zuber 1968:24.

13. "Nu *Lopes* zijt te vreen
En volght met fluxe schreen
Uw' winnaar, die met uw' het lof
Sal delen, van 't *verwarde Hof.*
O! vega uw' verblijt
Die sijn gevanghen zijt
Door krijghs-recht, dat hy rechtevoort
Uw' deelt, 't geen hem heel toebehoort" De Fuyter 1647.

14. "'Tis een' geleende vreughd / Daer ik u op onthael; maer leengoed is oock goed goed, (...) dit's een leen van edel' menschen geesten." Huygens ed.1892-9,iv:206.

15. "Le tiers poinct est qu'en traduisant il ne se fault pas asservir jusques à là que l'on rende mot pour mot." Weinberg 1950:81-82.

16. "Si, en quelques autres lieux, j'ai ajouté et retranché quelque chose, (...) j'ai fait le premier pour éclaircir des

obscurités qui eussent donné de la peine à des gens qui n'en
veulent point; et le second pour ne tomber en des répétitions
ou autres impertinences dont sans doute un esprit délicat se
fût offensé (...); mais je n'ai pas voulu faire les grotesques
qu'il est impossible d'éviter quand on se restreint à la servitude de traduire mot à mot." Ladborough 1938-9:85.

17. "Ce seroit une superstition Judaïque de s'attacher aux
mots et de quitter le dessein pour lequel on les employe.
D'ailleurs ce ne sont pas les paroles d'un Dieu, pour avoir
tant de peur de les perdre." D'Ablancourt ed.1972:111.

18. "Par tout ailleurs je l'ay suivy pas à pas, et plutost
en esclave qu'en compagnon; quoy que peut-estre je me pûsse
donner plus de liberté; puisque je ne traduis pas un passage,
mais un Livre, de qui toutes les parties doivent estre unies
ensemble, et comme fonduës en une mesme corps." D'Ablancourt
ed.1972:120-121.

19. "Car de moy je ne suys que son simple truchement fidele
pour certain autant qui m'a esté possible, mais non suffisament
exercité en l'un et l'aultre langaige pour me debvoir paragon-
ner à luy." Weinberg 1950;75.

20. "Het luste ons hem, die als een arent opgaet streven,
    In zyne schaduw, laegh langs d'aerde, naer te zweven,
    Van ver te volgen, op een' Nederduitschen trant"
                          Vondel ed.1927-40,vii:377.

21. "... ie n'auray peut-estre donné à nostre Reine que de
fausses perles et de petits morceaux de cristal au lieu de
diamants..." Leiner 1965:455.

22. "Mais, Sire, (...) ayez s'il vous plaist souvenance de
ce que Themistocles dist au roy des Perses, lequel vouloit parler à luy des affaires de la guerre par truchement et inter-
prete. Auquel fist response (luy monstrant l'envers d'une tapis-
serie) que telle estoit l'interpretation d'un langaige comme
l'envers d'un tapiz.(...) Semblablement vous, Sire, ayez estime
que par la mienne translation je n'ay pouvoir de vous monstrer
aultre chose que l'envers de la triumphante et excellente tapis-
serie de Sophocles." Weinberg 1950:74.

23. "'Tswart geeft het wit syn lyf, de doncker maeckt het
                                    klaer.
    En wat waer Maneschijn, wanneer 'tgeen nacht en waer?
    Of, dunckt u 'tHollandsch swart het Engelsch witt te
                                    decken,
    Noch komt u 'tswart te baet. 'Khebb lamper-doeck sien
                                    trecken
    Voor ooghen die 'tgeweld van somer-sonne-schijn
    Niet uijt en konden staen."   Huygens ed.1982-9,iv:207.

24. "'T vertaelde scheelt soo veel van 't Onvertaelde dicht,
    Als lijf en schaduwen: en schaduwen zijn nachten.
    Maer uw' bescheidenheid en maghse niet verachten;
    Tzijn edel' Iofferen, 'tzijn dochteren van 'tlicht.

En schaduwen zijn scheef, als 'taansicht inde Maen:
Soo dese dichten oock: maer, magh ick 'tselver seggen,
Gelyck aen schaduwen die lamm ter aerde leggen,
Men sieter noch wat trecks van 'trechte wesen aen.

En schaduwen zijn swart en duijster in te sien:
Soo dese dichten oock: Maer 'tzijn gemeene ooghen
Die door het swacke swart van schad'wen niet en moghen:
Wat schaduw soud' den dagh aen Tessels oogh verbien?

En schaduwen zijn koel, en op haer heetste lauw:
Soo dese dichten oock: maer 'tkoel en is maer korst-
                                          koelt':
'tvier schuylt'er in, gelijck't in 's minnaers koele
                                          borst woelt,
En peper is niet heet voor datme'r 'tvier uyt knauw'.

En schaduwen zijn, niet; dat's droomen bij den dagh:
Soo dese dichten oock: maer 'tzijn gelijfde Nietten:
En slaet ghij 'tvoetsel gae daer uijt mijn' droomen
                                          schieten,
'K hadd pitt en mergh geslockt eer ickse droomd' en
                     sagh." Huygens ed.1892-9,ii:267-8. "

25. "...ung traducteur, tel que les Graecz appelloient
paraphraste (c'est-à-dire, qui rend le sens, la phrase, et
l'esprit d'une matiere sans contrainte du langaige)." Weinberg
1950:90.

26. "Rijm en maet, waer aen de vertolcker gebonden staet,
verhindert oock menighmael, dat de vertaelder niet zoo wel en
volmaecktelijck naspreeckt, 't geen zoo wel en heerlijck vóór-
gesproken word; en yet van d'eene tael in d'ander, door eenen
engen hals te gieten, gaet zonder plengen niet te werck."
Vondel ed.1927-40,iii:642-3.

27. "... comme du vin que l'on tire de son premier vaisseau;
d'où si on le verse dans des bouteilles, quelque soin qu'on y
apporte, il ne laisse pas de s'affoiblir, à cause que ses
esprits s'evaporent, et se dissipent insensiblement." Zuber
1968:88.

28. "... à cause de ceste divinité d'invention qu'ilz (i.e.
the poets) on plus que les autres, de ceste grandeur de style,
magnificence de motz, gravité de sentences, audace et variété
de figures, et mil' autres lumieres de poësie: bref ceste energie, et ne scay quel esprit, qui est en leurs ecriz, que les
Latins appelleroient *genius*." Du Bellay ed.1948:40.

29. "Et du reste je croy que deux ouvrages sont plus sem-
blables quand ils sont tout deux eloquens, que quand l'un est
éloquent et qu l'autre ne l'est point.(...) Et apres tout ce
n'est rendre un Autheur qu'à demy, que de luy retrancher son
eloquence. Comme il a esté agreable en sa langue, il faut qu'il
le soit encore en la nostre, et d'autant que les beautez et les
graces sont differentes, nous ne devons point craindre de luy
donner celles de nostre pays, puis que nous luy ravissons les

siennes." D'Ablancourt ed.1972:110-1.
     30. "... le moyen d'arriver à la gloire de son original,
n'est pas de le suivre pas à pas, mais de chercher les beautez
de la langue, comme il a fait celles de la sienne." D'Ablancourt ed.1972:128.
     31. "... engendrer une OEuvre de nouveau(...). Engendrer,
dis-je, parce qu'(...) il faut deffaire (the original author)
par une cogitation profonde et penetrante, afin de le refaire
par une autre pareille: tout ainsi qu'il faut que la viande
meure et se defface en nostre estomac, pour en composer nostre
substance." Zuber 1963:292.
     32. "... de telle facon, que l'on ne soit pas le simple
Echo de leurs paroles; il faut concevoir les choses du mesme
air qu'ils les eussent conceuës; et rechercher dans la langue,
comme ils faisoient dans la leur, des termes capables d'une
haute et magnifique expression." Zuber 1968:75.
     33. "Que je luy scay bon gré des offices qu'il rend à Paris
aux honnetes gens d'Athenes! Ce me sont pas des marques d'infé-
riorité ny des debvoirs de subjetion; ce sont des effets de
courtoisie; ce sont des actes de pure hospitalité!" Zuber 1963:
282.
     34. "... comme s'ils estoient animez de l'esprit de ceux
qu'ils nous expliquent (...) et (les) font parler aussy agre-
ablement que s'ils n'avoient jamais respiré un autre air que
celuy du Louvre." Zuber 1968:49.
     35. "Cependant, cela n'est pas proprement de la Traduction;
mais cela vaut mieux que la Traduction." D'Ablancourt ed.1972:
186.
     36. "Je ne prétens donc point qu'elle (i.e. the translation
of Lucian) vous serve de modèle, elle n'est pas assez exacte pour
cela, et ne peut porter le nom de traduction qu'improprement, et
parce qu'on ne peut lui en donner d'autre." Hennebert 1861:180.
     37. "Car ce n'est pas tant icy le portrait de Thucydide,
que Thucydide luy mesme, qui est passé dans un autre corps
comme par une espece de Metempsycose, et de Grec est devenu
François." D'Ablancourt ed.1972:202.
     38. "En toy (i.e. Homer) Jupiter transformé
        Composa l'oeuvrage estimé
        De l'Iliade et l'Odissee,
        Et tu as ton ame passee
        En Jamyn pour interpreter
        Les vers qu'en toy fit Jupiter (...)
        Tous deux en un corps n'estes qu'un,
        Le ciel vous est pere commun"   Carrington 1974:128.
     39. "Wie sou dit wonderwerck my andersins verklaren,
        Als dat sijn siel sou sijn in onsen HEYNS gevaren?
        En dat hy in hem werckt, en dat hy in hem sweeft
        In Nederland, als hy in Vranckrijck heeft geleeft? (...)
        O bondigh Nederland! hoe seer sijt ghy verbonden
        Aen d'Hemel, mits hy u heeft BARTAS Geest gesonden,
        Bekleed in 't Edel lijf van ZACHARIAS HEYNS." Starter ed.
                                            1864:298-9.
132

40. "Du Bartas leeft! hy schrijft! hy noemt my sijn vrien-
                                                        dinne
        O edel Heer Baron, in u soo rust sijn geest:
        Want sonder die en wast niet moog'lijck aen te halen
        Sijn Boeck in suyver duytsch soo aerdigh te vertalen,
        Ghy zijt het selfs, of hy haeft u gelijck geweest."
                                Roemars Visscher ed.1881,ii:109.

REFERENCES

AMOS, Flora Ross
1920   *Early Theories of Translation*. New York, Columbia UP
ABLANCOURT, Nicolas Perrot d'
ed.1972 *Lettres et préfaces critiques*. Ed. Roger Zuber. Paris,
        Didier
BELLAY, Joachim du
ed.1948 *La deffense et illustration de la langue francoyse*. Ed.
        Henri Chamard. Paris, Didier
CARRINGTON, Samuel M.
1974   'Amadis Jamyn, Translator of Homer', *Kentucky Romance
        Quarterly*, xxi, Supplement nr.2 (*French Renaissance
        Studies in Honor of Isidore Silver*):123-36
CROSLAND, Maurice
1962   *Historical Studies in the Language of Chemistry*. London,
        Heinemann
CURTIUS, Ernst Robert
1953   *European Literature and the Latin Middle Ages*. London,
        Routledge & Kegan Paul
DRYDEN, John
ed.1962 *Of Dramatic Poesy and other critical essays*. Ed.
        G.Watson. 2 vols. London/New York, Dent/Dutton
FANSHAWE, Richard
ed.1964 *A Critical Edition of Sir Richard Fanshawe's 1647 Trans-
        lation of Giovanni Battista Guarini's 'Il Pastor Fido'*.
        Ed. W.F.Staton & W.E.Simeone. Oxford, Clarendon Press
FUYTER, Lion de
1647   *Lope de Vega Carpioos Verwerde-Hof. Gerijmt in Neder-
        duytse vaarzen door L. D. Fuyter*. Amsterdam, Johannes
        Jacot
GMELIN, H.
1932   'Das Prinzip der Imitatio in den romanischen Litera-
        turen der Renaissance', *Romanische Forschungen*, xlvi:
        83-360
GUILLERM, Luce
1980   'L'auteur, les modèles et le pouvoir ou la topique de
        la traduction au XVIe siècle en France', *Revue des
        sciences humaines*, lii, nr 180:5-31
HENNEBERT, Frederic
1864   *Histoire des traductions françaises d'auteurs grecs et
        latins pendant le XVIe et le XVIIe siècle*. Brussels,
        Th.Lesigne

HUYGENS, Constantijn
ed.1982-9 *De gedichten van Constantijn Huygens, naar zijn hand-
        schrift uitgegeven.* Ed. J.A.Worp. 9 vols. Groningen,
        J.B.Wolters
ed.1911-7 *De briefwisseling van Constantijn Huygens (1608-1687).*
        Ed. J.A.Worp. 6 vols. 's-Gravenhage, M.Nijhoff
JONES, Richard Foster
1953   *The Triumph of the English Language. A Survey of Opin-
        ions Concerning the Vernacular from the Introduction of
        Printing to the Restoration.* London, G.Cumberlege/
        Oxford UP
JONSON, Ben
ed.1963 *The Complete Poetry.* Ed. W.B.Hunter. New York, New York
        UP
KINSLEY, James & KINSLEY, Helen
1971   (eds.) *Dryden. The Critical Heritage.* London, Routledge
        & Kegan Paul
KITAGAKI, Muneharu
1981   *Principles and Problems of Translation in Seventeenth-
        Century England.* Kyoto, Yamagushi Shoten
LADBOROUGH, R.W.
1938-9 'Translation from the Ancients in seventeenth-century
        France', *Journal of the Warburg Institute,* ii:85-104
LATHROP, Henry Burrowes
1933   *Translation from the Classics into English from Caxton
        to Chapman 1477-1620.* Madison, Wisconsin UP
LEINER, Wolfgang
1965   *Der Widmungsbrief in der französischen Literatur (1580-
        1715).* Heidelberg, Carl Winter
MATTHIESSEN, F.O.
1931   *Translation. An Elizabethan Art.* Cambridge, Harvard UP
NUGENT, Elisabeth M.
1956   (ed.) *The Thought and Culture of the English Renaissance.
        An Anthology of Tudor Prose 1481-1555.* Cambridge,
        Cambridge UP
O'SULLIVAN, Maurice J.
1980   'Running Division on the Groundwork: Dryden's Theory of
        Translation', *Neophilologus,* lxiv:144-59
PELETIER DU MANS, Jacques
ed.1930 *Art poétique.* Ed. A.Boulanger. Paris, Belles lettres
PIGMAN, G.W.
1980   'Versions of Imitation in the Renaissance', *Renaissance
        Quarterly,* xxxiii,1:1-32
POLLARD, Alfred
1911   *Records of the English Bible. The Documents Relating to
        the Translation and Publication of the Bible in English,
        1525-1611.* London etc., H.Frowde/Oxford UP
QUINTILIAN
ed.1922 *The Institutio Oratoria of Quintilian in four volumes.*
        With an English Translation by H.E.Butler. London/New
        York, Heinemann/Putnam's Sons

ROEMERS VISSCHER, Anna
ed.1881 *Alle de gedichten*. Ed. Nicolaas Beets. 2 vols. Utrecht,
J.L.Beijers
SCHWARZ, Werner
1944 'Translation into German in the Fifteenth Century',
Modern Language Review, xxxix:368-73
SEBILLET, Thomas
ed.1972 *Art poetique françoys*. Geneve, Slatkine Reprints
SPINGARN, J.E.
1908 (ed.) *Critical Essays of the Seventeenth Century*.
3 vols. Oxford, Clarendon
STACKELBERG, Jürgen von
1956 'Das Bienengleichnis. Ein Beitrag zur Geschichte der
literarischen *Imitatio*', *Romanische Forschungen*, lxviii:
271-93
STANLEY, Thomas
ed.1962 *The Poems and Translations*. Ed. G.M.Crump. Oxford,
Clarendon
STARTER, J.J.
ed.1864 *J.J.Starters Friesche Lusthof*.... Ed. J.van Vloten.
Utrecht, L.E.Bosch
STEINER, T.R.
1970 'Precursors to Dryden: English and French Theories of
Translation in the Seventeenth Century', *Comparative
Literature Studies*, vii:50-80
1975 *English Translation Theory 1650-1800*. Assen/Amsterdam,
Van Gorcum
VANDERHEYDEN, J.F.
1979 'Verkenningen in vroeger vertaalwerk 1450-1600. "Ghe-
nuechlijck ende oock profijtelijck"', *Verslagen en
mededelingen, KANTL*, 1979 nr 2:149-83
1980 'Verkenningen in vroeger vertaalwerk 1450-1600. De
"translatio doctrinae sapientiaeque"', *Verslagen en
mededelingen, KANTL*, 1980 nr 1:129-57
VONDEL, Joost van den
ed.1927-40 *De werken van Vondel*. Ed. J.F.M.Sterck *et al*. 10 vols.
Amsterdam, Wereldbibliotheek
WARNERS, J.D.P.
1957 'Translatio - Imitatio - Emulatio'(part 2), *De nieuwe
taalgids*, il:82-88
WEINBERG, Bernard
1950 (ed.) *Critical Prefaces of the French Renaissance*.
Evanston (Ill.), Northwestern UP
ZUBER, Roger
1963 'La création littéraire au dix-septième siècle: l'avis
des théoriciens de la traduction', *Revue des sciences
humaines*, 1963:277-94
1968 *Les 'Belles Infidèles' et la formation du goût classique.
Perrot d'Ablancourt et Guez de Balzac*. Paris, A.Colin

TRANSLATION AND LITERARY GENRE

The European Picaresque Novel in the 17th and 18th Centuries

Hendrik van Gorp

1. Object and Method

In a recent study devoted to picaresque literature, Harry Sieber wrote that

> ... the translations of Spanish picaresque novels are the key to an understanding of the European history of the genre. Translators were 'readers' who not only injected their own tastes and attitudes in their translations, but also assessed and attempted to include the sensibilities of a wider 'invisible' reading public   (Sieber 1977:59).

I wish to enlarge on this observation with the help of some important translations dating from the seventeenth century and the first decades of the eighteenth century. These early translations were instrumental in orienting and directing subsequent versions and thus contributed substantially to the development of the picaresque genre in several national literatures of Western Europe.

In the first instance, then, we are dealing with 'genetic relations' ('the term is Ďurišin's) between original works and translations. The nature of these relations is often described in a foreword in which the translator explains his position with regard to the original version or to other translations. More important, however, are questions bearing on the position of translations within the national literatures concerned and the 'typological relations' (Ďurišin) between translations and originals. Accordingly, I shall not attempt an exhaustive description of the large number of translations of picaresque novels that have appeared since the end of the sixteenth century, but a typological comparison of the Spanish *novela picaresca* with several 'pilot translations' of the seventeenth and early eighteenth centuries.

As the point of departure for such a comparison
I shall use a kind of blueprint of the Spanish picaresque novel, as outlined in my recent study of the
genre (Van Gorp 1978). This blueprint will serve as
an initial *tertium comparationis*, underlining both the
typical structure of the picaresque novel as a story
with an open ending, and the cultural and ideological tensions between the picaro and his society. As
far as the translations are concerned, my observations relate to the 'matricial norms' (Toury 1978:87)
of individual versions, taking into account literary
as well as socio-cultural factors. The conclusions
that can be drawn from this inquiry remain, obviously,
limited in scope. Nevertheless, in so far as they are
based on various essential 'textemes', they offer a
clear picture of a common type of translation. By
proceeding in this way, that is, treating a particular genre during a particular period, it will be possible to illustrate some aspects of the part played
by translations in the spread of a particular genre
from one literature to another.

The Spanish *novela picaresca* is usually defined
in terms of a number of formal and thematic characteristics (Van Gorp 1977; Miller 1967; Guillén 1962).
As far as the plot is concerned the typical picaresque
novel presents an episodic story-line, in which events
are largely determined by chance: "anything can happen
to anyone at any time" (Miller 1967:37). The motifs
which steer the plot are mostly of a materialistic
nature, although they also touch on the Spanish concept of 'honour'. They are held together by the central theme of disenchantment and disillusion. As for
the relation between the picaro and the world around
him: the narrator-protagonist is a lonely figure, a
man of poor origin, badly treated even by his social
equals, and generally leading a somewhat shady existence. The world he is confronted with is peopled by
a series of stereotyped lords and masters and by representatives of all walks of life. The relation between the picaro and his antagonists, often marked
by dishonesty on both sides, embodies the central
theme of disillusionment and underlines the highly
critical view of society typical of the picaresque
novel.

These summarily sketched characteristics are
common to a large number of novels published in Spain
between 1600 and 1645, following on the spectacular
success of *La vida de Guzmán de Alfarache* (1599-1604) by
Mateo Alemán. It was Alemán's novel which led to renewed interest in the anonymous *La vida de Lazarillo de
Tórmes* of 1554, which may be regarded as the prototype

of the picaresque genre. In what follows I shall refer to the most important translations of these two
texts and of *La vida del Buscón llamado don Pablo* (1626)
by Francisco Quevedo, another typical example of the
genre.

2. Translations in Western Europe

The catalogue of translations of the picaresque novels
just mentioned reveals a high proportion of French
versions. Indeed, most English, German and Dutch
translations can be traced back directly to French
sources. The crucial role played by these French
texts can be explained by political and cultural factors. During the sixteenth and early seventeenth centuries the international prestige of Habsburg Spain
was very great, while on the cultural front the country could boast influential prose writers such as
Montemayor, Montalvo (*Amadís de Gaula*,1508), Cervantes
and others. Spain's neighbour France was in a state
of political and religious turmoil. Towards the middle of the seventeenth century, France became the
dominant political and cultural power on the Conti-
nent. The fact that, as a consequence of this, the
flow of translations from Spain to France would be
reversed, need not concern us here.

In the course of the seventeenth century, then,
France began to act as an intermediary between Spain
and countries like England, Germany and the Low
Countries. Direct contacts between Spain on one side
and Germany and England on the other were relatively
rare in any case. For a time, the Low Countries did
have close contact with Spain (even engaging in close
combat on occasion), but here too the French influence became predominant in the latter half of the
seventeenth century.

However, the fact that so many translations in
England, Germany and the Netherlands are based on
French versions is not always immediately apparent
from their title pages, which more often than not
present the book in question simply as 'translated
from the Spanish'. A clear example of such a doubtful
reference is the novel *Don Diego de Noche* by Salas Bar-
badillo, author of several picaresque stories. In a
French translation of 1636 it was attributed to
Quevedo, probably in order to stimulate the sale of
the book. The subsequent Dutch, English and German
versions all attribute the novel to Quevedo. In many
other cases, too, the central position of French translations is indisputable. We shall have to take this
into account when we look at the evolution of the
translations.

Broadly speaking, three successive phases can
be distinguished in the method of translating (Lambert 1965); they are connected with the changes in
national prestige indicated above.

The earliest translations are explicitly philological: they are 'lexical' translations, offering
an 'adequate' or source-oriented type of equivalence.
Often produced hurriedly at the behest of friends,
these translations are intended primarily to inform
the reader by means of a diverting story about the
manners and customs of the Spaniards. The extended
title of the French version cf *Lazarillo de Tormes* speaks
for itself: *L'Histoire plaisante et facétieuse du Lazare de
Tormes Espagnol. En laquelle on peult recongnoistre bonne par-
tie des moeurs, vie et conditions des Espagnols* (1561). The
title of the Dutch version (1579), based on the French,
is in the same vein.

Around 1620 the translations become noticeably
freer and move to an 'acceptable' or target-oriented
type of equivalence, reflecting the growing self-
confidence and assertiveness of French culture at the
time. The translators apply French cultural and social
norms and take their bearings from the leading writers
of their own country. Although at first the greater
freedom manifests itself at the level of language and
style only, soon the development of the story is a-
dapted to current target norms too. The initial situation undergoes little change, but the plot is accom-
modated in such a way that amorous adventures over-
shadow social criticism and the protagonist's material
needs. Conspicuous are the changes made to the endings
of a number of novels. In line with the fashion
in 'regular' novels of the period, translations are
given a 'happy ending' incompatible with the element
of disillusion and the typical 'open ending' of the
original *novela picaresca*.

Towards the end of the seventeenth century the
method of translation becomes even more free, so
that we can speak of adaptations rather than translations. Let us now trace that evolution by considering
some pilot translations of the three most important
novels (*Lazarillo de Tormes*, *Guzmán de Alfarache*, *La vida del
Buscón*). I propose to look first at the narrative
structure and the ending of the novels in translation,
and then at the figure of the picaro.

In the first phase of the translation of *La vida
de Lazarillo de Tormes* (1554), roughly from 1560 to 1620,
when we are still dealing with 'adequate' translations,
the reader's attention is drawn directly to the amusing character of the story, as the titles indicate:
L'Histoire plaisante et facétieuse du Lazare de Tormes Espagnol

(1561); *Histoire plaisante, facétieuse, et récréative du Lazare de Tormes Espagnol* (1594); *The pleasant history of Lazarillo de Tormes a Spaniarde* (1576); *The most pleasant and delectable history of Lazarillo de Tormes, a Spanyard* (1596). The German translators speak of 'abentheuerliche Possen' ('farcical adventures'; 1617) and 'wunderliche Bossen' ('strange and amusing adventures'; 1624)(see Laurenti 1968:34ff.). The second phase starts with the publication in Spain of the rather more whimsical sequel to *Lazarillo de Tormes* by Juan de Luna in 1620. Partly in imitation of the *Segunda Parte* the accent in the translations gradually shifts to the amorous adventures of the picaro; in France this shift coincides with the emergence of the so-called 'belles infidèles'. That phase eventually gives rise to a series of adaptations starting with an "imitation en vers" (1653), in which the episodes about the love perils of Lazarillo's mother and his wife's liaison with the archpriest are rather coarse. The phase ends with the "traduction nouvelle" by the Abbé de Charnés (1678) which, in conformity with the norms of novel writing, concludes with the death of Lazarillo. In an edition published as late as 1797 this translation was announced as "Augmentée de plusieurs choses qui avoient été négligées dans les autres impressions", so much so that subsequent translators at last felt inclined to go back to the "véritable original espagnol".

The versions of *La vida del pícaro Guzmán de Alfarache* (1599-1604) show a similar though not identical evolution. The French translation of the first part by Chappuys, as early as 1600, is clearly written in haste and follows the original almost word for word. The first part of Chapelain's *Le Gueux, ou la vie de Guzman d'Alfarache* (1619) may also be termed a lexical translation, though it is evident that the translator was not at all afraid to intervene. He played with the idea of deleting a number of fragments which he considered undesirable, but refrained from doing so: "Si j'osais tailler à ma fantaisie, cette clause et beaucoup d'autres qui t'auront ennuyé sauteraient". In the second part, however, he took the decisive step: "J'ai été réduit à changer, omettre et suppléer quantité de choses".

The move proved successful, and the trend reached its climax in the 'belle infidèle' by Gabriel Brémond (1695), who, as he put it, 'planed' and polished the text. In his preface he remarked: "Ce n'est pas une petite affaire, que d'un habit à l'Espagnole, en faire un à la Française, et surtout d'un habit vieux". As late as 1732 Alain-René Lesage used this translation as an example for his own *Histoire de Guzman d'Alfa-*

rache, nouvellement traduite et purgée de moralités superflues.
He too observes in his lengthy foreword that "Aleman
a (...) trop chargé de moralités son Guzman d'Alfarache". Consequently he dropped the "air dogmatique"
of the story, which in his opinion would not appeal
to the French reader. Moreover, he says, his friends
told him he would do the French public a favour by
providing "une traduction de Guzman d'Alfarache, purgée de moralités superflues" (see also his title!).
For this reason he feels justified in shortening and
even dropping a number of episodes which in his view
drew the reader's attention away from the principal
character. In this respect he is in full agreement
with Brémond, whom he cannot but praise:

> J'avoue qu'elles (i.e. les choses qui y sont ajoutées
> par ce Traducteur) son ingénieusement imaginées, et
> qu'il a répandu partout un goût galant. Je dirai même
> encore à sa gloire, que sa traduction en général, est
> fort égayée et remplie d'expressions (...) heureuses.

Since Lesage does not want to be outdone by Brémond
in any way, he makes the moral tension of the story
give way to even more adventure.

The increasingly free versions by Chapelain,
Brémond and Lesage thus do not just aim at turning
the original texts into stylistically more elegant
pieces of writing. They also affect the structure of
the novel by omitting the moralizing passages and
even complete chapters, and accentuating the adventurous aspects of the story. As in the case of *Lazarillo*
the shift is clearly perceptible in the way the novel
is brought to a conclusion. Chapelain translates
rather literally: "Je mis fin à toutes mes disgrâces
..." ("Aquí di punto y fin a estas desgracias"), without however mentioning the failures which according
to the Spanish original await the protagonist: "la
que después gasté todo el restanto della (vida) verás
en la tercera y última parte..." Lesage concludes his
translation as follows: "Telles sont, Lecteur, mon
cher ami, les aventures qui me sont arrivées jusqu'à
présent". The term "disgrâce" is replaced by "aventures"! The preceding sentence once more accentuates
very clearly the hero's gallant character: insertions
such as "généreux sentiment" and "au service du Roi"
amount to a hymn of praise to Guzmán. The vagabond
has changed into a respectable "gentilhomme".

In the case of the translations of Quevedo's
Vida del Buscón llamado Don Pablos (1626), the situation
is somewhat different, but no less clear. Here, the
French version by De Geneste (*L'aventurier Buscon*, 1633)
acquired a virtual monopoly in France as well as

abroad. The first phase is missing: Quevedo's novel
was published in 1626, by which time the 'belles infidèles' were beginning to make an impact in France.
De Geneste tells us nothing about the way he approached his task, but his publisher Billaine informs the
reader that the Spanish text "a esté façonnée à la
Françoise d'une main qui l'a merveilleusement bien
embellie". However, the translator's interventions
are not limited to stylistic embellishment, but, again,
affect the structure of the novel as well. The protagonist is now an "Aventurier Buscon" who finds hap-
piness in the end, whereas the original Pablos had to
escape to India, where his situation was to become
even worse ("Y fuéme peor, como vuestra merced verá
en la segunda parte, pues nunca mejora su estado
quien muda solamenta de lugar, y no de vida y costum-
bres"), the French Buscon succeeds in getting married
to the lovely Roselle, "une jeune bourgeoise (...)
douée d'une parfaite beauté", who is, moreover, the
"fille unique d'une maison extrêmement riche".

In the so-called "nouvelle traduction" by Raclot
(1699), which finds its origin in the version of 1633,
the tone of the narrator-protagonist's concluding
words has become totally different from that of
Quevedo's: "Voilà, cher Lecteur, le succès et l'heur-
euse issuë de mes aventures de même que l'état présent de mes contentements". The vicissitudes of fortune still sound weakly in "...mais comme il n'y a
personne qui se puisse vanter d'être heureux avant
sa mort, je ne sçay si parmi tant d'excès de bonne
fortune, il ne m'arrivera pas quelque desastre (...)
et que ma fin ne soit pareille au commencement...".
Nonetheless the French Buscon is at that moment the
happiest man in the world, taking his leave from the
reader with a fond wish: "Veüille le Ciel me le (*i.e.*
le bonheur) conserver long-temps dans la compagnie
de mon aimable Roselle".

The ending of the French Buscon can be found in
most of the translations of Quevedo's novel in France
as well as in the Netherlands (1642 and 1699), Germany (1671 and 1704) and England (1657). This seems
fairly typical of the way in which a foreign genre
is affected by a powerful aesthetic code, in this
case the classicist code of seventeenth-century France.
Like many others, Sieur du Plaisir insists in his
Sentiments sur les Lettres (1683) that a story "should always have a conclusion". Charles Sorel, author of
L'Histoire comique de Francion (1623), is of the same
opinion. In his *Bibliothèque Françoise* (1664), a work
written in later life and offering comments on the
literary production of his time, he is critical of

Le Page disgracié (1643) by Tristan l'Hermite (regarded by several critics as a picaresque story), because it consists of two parts "without a conclusion", and of the *Romant comique* (1651) by Scarron because the author did not really complete it at all: "On doit avoir regret que l'Autheur n'a point fait la Conclusion..." (p.178). Given this context, we need not be surprised that De Geneste adapted his translation to the prevailing literary taste of the moment.

The changes in the narrative structure and especially in the concluding passages of *L'Aventurier Buscon* contributed in their turn to the rise of a literary genre that was at least partly new. The protagonist of the anonymous *De Haagsche Lichtmis* (The Libertine from The Hague, 1679), one of the best-known examples of picaresque literature in Dutch, marries, as did the French Buscon, the daughter of a clothier and becomes a well-to-do middle-class man. And *Gil Blas de Santillane* (1715-35) by Lesage, the outstanding example of the European picaresque novel in the eighteenth century, is certainly the culmination of this desire for a stable and socially respectable existence. As a matter of fact, the happy ending becomes a typical feature of the adventurous picaresque novel of this period. *De vermakelyken Avanturier* (The Amusing Adventurer, 1695) by the Dutchman Nicolaas Heinsius Jr. provides a poignant illustration of this. Towards the end of the novel the protagonist marries a rich girl, and all seems well. In imitation of the 'romanists', Heinsius writes, he should now have concluded his story with the marriage of Mirandor and Clarice. But he does not. On the contrary, he chooses a characteristic picaresque ending: Clarice's brother, her mother and she herself die one after the other. Mirandor returns to his native country, but he will not stay there for long, as is apparent from the final address to the reader:

> This, dear Reader, is what I thought proper to acquaint you with of my Adventures. As my Sedentary Life begins already to grow irksome to me, I don't know but I may be again destined to travel the World, and be the Sport of Fortune. If that misfortune should happen, perhaps I may appear again upon the stage, and find new subjects to entertain you, unless Death (...) should come and put a stop to it.

This open ending sounds as a last echo of that of the Spanish *novela picaresca*, a genre Heinsius was indeed familiar with. At the same time *De vermakelyken Avanturier* is a good example of the new type of hybrid picaresque-adventurous novel which in the early eighteenth

century found its way into the French as well as into
the German and Dutch language areas, while in England
it became part of the successful new tradition of
Defoe's *Robinson Crusoe* (1719).

The stress on the more adventurous element of
the plot and on the 'bourgeois' conclusion reflects
a changed view of the figure of the protagonist as
well. The Spanish picaro was a socially marginal person of low birth. This fact represented an important
aspect of the *novela picaresca*, and nearly every Spanish
picaresque novel starts with the description of the
environment and origin of the protagonist. The parodic character of this description is relevant to the
central theme of 'honour': the picaro's simple parents
are ironically described as if they were noblemen.
The first sentence of *Lazarillo de Tormes* is typical:
"Well, first of all Your Grace should know that my
name is Lázaro de Tormes, son of Tomé Gonzáles and
Antona Pérez, who lived in Tejares, a village near
Salamanca...". The genealogy of Pablos in Quevedo's
Buscón is an even more vivid example. He calls himself
the son of Clemente Pablo and of Aldonza Saturno de
Rebollo, the daughter of Octavio de Rebollo Codillo
and grand-daughter of Lépido Ziuraconte. In De Geneste's translation, however, Pablos, or better Pablo,
is simply the son of Isidor and Roquille, but he is
given a rather more likeable appearance than in the
original version: "...d'ailleurs j'estois assez complaisant à tous ceux qui m'envisageoint (...) la
nature m'avait donné un visage et une taille que
chacun trouvait passablement agréable". In the 'nouvelle traduction' by Raclot the attribute "assez
complaisant" is strengthened to "extrêmement complaisant"!

Through a series of similar lexical shifts the
original Pablos is gradually transformed into a for-
tune-hunter, as the Spanish 'buscón' (= a clever
thief) becomes the French 'busquer fortune'. The new
protagonist is portrayed as an adventurer, comparable
to the hero in a chivalric romance. His success in
Europe is complete and culminates in the character
of Gil Blas de Santillane. It is interesting to note
that in the second half of the eighteenth century the
Spanish writer José Francisco de Isla, who wanted to
reintroduce the adventures of Gil Blas in Spain,
"volées à l'Espagne et adoptées en France par Mr.
Lesage" (1783), also transformed Gil Blas' mother
from a 'bourgeoise' into a farmer's wife (Molho 1968:
119). De Isla changed the conclusion of the novel as
well, making of the gentleman-hero a lonely hermit.

As I pointed out above, the motif of descent is

related to the central theme of the picaresque novel.
In the translations and adaptations this motif
acquires a different functior. Although the Spanish
concept of honour has nothing to do with material
gain, the French versions do relate money and property to honour. Lesage clearly took his cue from the
translations of De Charnés (*Lazarillo*), Brémond (*Guzmán*)
and De Geneste-Raclot (*Buscón*) when he provided Gil
Blas with a comfortable position in the end. Similar
mercantile motifs are present in Dutch (*De Haagsche
Lichtmis* and *De Vermakelyken Avanturier*) and in English
works (Defoe's *Moll Flanders* and Smollett's *Roderick Random*; Smollett was himself a translator and imitator
of Lesage).

3. The religious and political background

The shifts that are apparent in the French translations of Spanish picaresque novels have their origin
in cultural factors (the aesthetic code of French
classicism in the seventeenth century) and in social
factors (the picaro, now moving in a foreign society,
becomes an adventurer). But religious and political
factors played an important part as well, especially
in countries where the contacts with Spain were rather strained. This was certainly not the case in
France. In the sixteenth and early seventeenth century the French reading public took a lively interest
in everything that happened in Spain. The translators
usually remained neutral in matters of politics and
religion and principally charged themselves with the
transference of information. In other countries, however, ideological factors played a more important
role in the translational strategy. In the Dutch language area, for example, political and religious circumstances (the Eighty Years' War, 1568-1648) left
their mark on many translations from the Spanish.
The Dutch translator of *Guzmán de Alfarache* (1655) felt
obliged to appeal to the goodwill of his deeply anti-
Spanish reader: "Ick bidt U, haet hem (*i.e.* Guzman)
niet om dat hy een Spangiaert is, de namen der Natien
gheven niet..." ("I pray you, do not hate him because
he is a Spaniard; the names of the nations are not
important"). In the first Dutch translation of *Lazarillo* (1669) a number of slighting comments on Spaniards generally were inserted (Vles 1926:57-58). The
translator, who otherwise remains fairly formal, suddenly turns into a vigorous stylist in the bantering
episode of the papal preacher, a change of tone that
can only be explained in terms of the anti-Catholic
feeling of the period.

In England, too, the unexpected success of De

Luna's second part of *Lazarillo* is probably due to religious and political factors. De Luna, who had fled Spain for religious reasons, lived in England for a time. The translation of his *Lazarillo II* was reprinted six times in a period of fifty years, a remarkable contrast with the rather cool reception in other countries.

In the German language area the influence of political and religious factors is no less conspicuous. In Southern Germany in particular, the translators were by no means anti-Spanish; on the contrary, many used the situations described in the Spanish texts as a means to propagate the Counter-Reformation in their own country. The first important translation of the *Lazarillo* (1617) had its origin in the Spanish *Lazarillo castigado* (1573), one of the most typical imitations 'a lo divino' from the period of the Inquisition. The German version became a moralizing exemplary tale, siding with the Church in political and religious matters. The priests and the clergymen whom the Spanish *Lazarillo* encounters are replaced by representatives of the lower aristocracy. In the translation of De Luna's *Segunda Parte* ("Aus dem Frantzösischen in das Teutsche übergesetzt" by P.Küefuss, 1653), the wanderings of the 'converso' at the beginning of the story acquire a spiritual significance: the protagonist says farewell to the world, and at the end of the story he opts for a life of solitary contemplation (see Rötzer 1972).

A similar spiritualization of the picaresque theme of disenchantment may be found in the adaptation of *Guzmán de Alfarache* by the Jesuit Aegidius Albertinus, whose *Der Landstörtzer Gusman von Alfarache* (1615) is a milestone in the German narrative tradition. The first part is a fairly free translation of Alemán followed by the apocryphal sequel by Juan Martí. In contrast to what happens later in Lesage's *Gil Blas*, the story seems to have been chosen precisely on account of its moralizing tendencies, and some even more didactic comments were added to it ("theils gemehrt und gebessert"). This adaptation became the German prototype of a hybrid of the picaresque novel and the 'Bildungsroman'. Ignoring the *Segunda Parte* by Alemán, Albertinus wrote a second part himself, which, true to his religious vision, ends with the picaro's conversion: left to his fate, the hero decides to do penance in solitude. In a third part (1626) written by Martinus Freudenhold, Guzman goes on a pilgrimage to the Holy Land. Clearly, a Protestant counterblast was to be expected and a *Guzmannus reformatus* was duly published in Cologne in 1658. An element of spiritu-

alization is also present in Grimmelshausen's *Simpli-
cissimus* (1669), which many critics consider to be a
kind of picaresque Bildungsroman. Needless to say,
the socio-political situation in Germany during the
first half of the seventeenth century, which saw the
horrors of the Thirty Years' War, created a fertile
breeding-ground for a literature in the picaresque
tradition.

4. Conclusion

The West European translations of the Spanish pica-
reque novel in the seventeenth and early eighteenth
centuries are at first fairly literal versions, later
changing to freer translations and adaptations in
which aesthetic, ideological and religious factors
play an important part. This can be deduced not only
from the prefaces by the respective translators, but
also from the way the texts themselves are manipulated: a narrative structure adapted to current norms,
and concluded by a happy ending; a gentleman-picaro
with bourgeois airs, and, principally in Germany, a
political and religious reinterpretation. France
clearly led the way in this respect and often acted
as mediator.

A large number of these translations also contributed substantially to the establishment of models
for imitation in the various vernaculars and thus
profoundly influenced the national literatures in
question. An obvious illustration is De Geneste's
translation of Quevedo's *Vida del Buscón* and the English,
Dutch and German versions based on it. The result was
a tradition of hybrid picaresque adventure novels
such as Nicolaas Heinsius' *De vermakelyken Avanturier*,
Lesage's *Gil Blas de Santillane* and Smollett's *Roderick
Random* clearly influenced by Lesage.

On the other hand, the adaptation of the Spanish
Guzmán by Aegidius Albertinus is the starting-point of
a tradition in German narrative in which picaresque
and didactic elements are combined, together with
influences from Defoe's *Robinson Crusoe* (the so-called
'Robinsonaden'). Ultimately, though, the development
of the genre in Germany is also determined by systemic rules. In the seventeenth century the Germany literary system as a whole was less strictly codified
than the French, especially in the case of a 'lower'
genre like the novel; moreover, it was very much in
a formative stage, and hence open to impulses from
abroad. In German literature of the period, the novel,
as a genre, still has a mainly didactic function,
whereas in the more developed French system enter-
tainment was the novel's principal function, because

147

for doctrine and moralizing other sub-genres were available.

Be that as it may, the examples will have made it clear that the evolution of literature, especially of a literary genre, is not just a national, intra-literary concatenation of cause and effect or a question of action and reaction in formal matters. Aesthetic norms as well as social, ideological, religious and other factors, which manifest themselves clearly in translations, can play an essential role.

REFERENCES

ĎURIŠIN, Dionýz
1972   Vergleichende Literaturforschung. Berlin, Akademie-Verlag
GORP, Hendrik van
1977   'Picareske vertelstructuren?', in W.J.M.Bronzwaer et al.
       (eds.), Tekstboek algemene literatuurwetenschap (Baarn,
       Ambo):208-229
1978   Inleiding tot de picareske verhaalkunst. Groningen, Wolters
GUILLÉN, Claudio
1962   'Towards a Definition of the Picaresque', in Proceedinas
       of the Third Congress of the International Comparative
       Literature Association (The Hague, Mouton):252-266
LAMBERT, José
1965   'Filiation des éditions françaises du Lazarille de Tormès
       (1560-1820)', Revue des sciences humaines, CXX:587-603
LAURENTI, Joseph L.
1968   Ensayo de una bibliografía de la novela picaresca
       española, años 1554-1964. Madrid, C.S.I.C.
MILLER, Stuart
1967   The Picaresque Novel. Cleveland, Case Western Reserve UP
MOLHO, Maurice
1968   'Introduction à la pensée picaresque', in his (ed.)
       Romans picaresques espagnols (Paris, Gallimard):11-142
REICHARDT, D.
1970   Von Quevedos 'Buscón' zum deutschen 'Avonturier'. Bonn,
       Bouvier
ROETZER, Hans Gerd
1972   Picaro, Landtstörtzer, Simplicius. Darmstadt, Wissen-
       schaftliche Buchgesellschaft
SIEBER, Harry
1977   The Picaresque. London, Methuen
TOURY, Gideon
1978   'The Nature and Role of Norms in Literary Translation', in
       J.S.Holmes et al. (eds.), Literature and Translation
       (Leuven, Acco):83-100
VLES, J.
1926   Le roman picaresque hollandais des XVIIe et XVIIIe
       siècles et ses modèles espagnols et français. (Thesis,
       University of Amsterdam)

TRANSLATED LITERATURE IN FRANCE, 1800-1850

José Lambert, Lieven D'hulst & Katrin van Bragt

1. Introduction

This essay attempts to assess the results of a collective research project carried out in the Department of General Literary Studies at the University of Louvain in the latter half of the 1970s.[1] The aim of the project was to study the literary function(s) of translations produced and distributed in France in the period from 1800 to 1850. We did not claim to be investigating the phenomenon of 'literary translation' or any particular number of translations in their own right. Rather, we were considering the entire system of relations (interferences and structural connections) between literature and translation within a given period of time. Indeed, we would prefer not to restrict the concepts of 'literature' and 'translation' to either the texts and their authors, or to the production and reception of individual texts. This implies that we regard 'literature' and 'translation' as complex communication systems, each aspect of which is worthy of careful consideration.

If it seems self-evident that no literature exists entirely in isolation from other literary systems (and from artistic, social and other non-literary systems; see Even-Zohar 1978:47-48), we may assume that no literature can deny the contacts it owes to translation. All literatures, at one stage or another, import texts that have been translated from other literatures. Of course, it may be that the translation of a given literary text is a non-literary or scarcely literary event; literal cribs or anthologies of translations, for example, often have an essentially pedagogical function. A useful distinction could be made between 'translations of literary texts', resulting in target texts of any non-literary type, and 'literary translations', which result in accepted literary texts in the target system (see Toury 1984:77 for this distinction). In certain circumstances, though, translations may become indistinguishable from 'original' literary texts. In other cases, translations, or at least certain translations, may constitute an entirely separate sub-group, remaining largely alien to the literary system of the target pole. It is our intention here to discuss to what extent translations fulfil a literary function, and, above all, what kind of literary function they have.

Although translation represents only one of the ways in which literatures enter into contact and interfere with each other, it is clearly a major one. As a methodological rule, the investigation of all such interferences, including translation, should start from the receptor (or target) pole (see Toury 1980:35-50). It is the individual in the target literature who selects the texts that are to be imported, as well as the systems and sub-systems from which the texts will be selected. It is the receiving literature that determines the translational method and its function. In the case of a 'literary translation' as described above, the translated text becomes an integral part of the target literature. If the translated text is not fully integrated into the receptor system, we shall have to determine its position with respect to both the target and the source system. Total integration is a rare occurrence anyway. Indeed, it can be claimed that any translation is, to some extent, a 'non-text', i.e. a text which finds itself, initially at least, in a non-systemic position (Toury 1980). However, in one way or another it will come to form part of the target system.

Various concrete parameters allow us to establish these interferences and degrees of integration, to describe them and subsequently to define their evolution or variation. The identity of the translators (and readers) and the nature of the distribution circuit (publishers, reviews, collections, theatres in the case of plays) are obviously crucial factors in the interaction between 'original' and translated literature. On each level, we try to determine whether the function of a particular translation is conservative or innovative, and whether translation is a marginal or a central phenomenon with regard to the target literary system as a whole. It is not unusual for a given translation to play totally different roles according to the period, the genre, or the literary, social, religious or any other context.

The above hypotheses and postulates concerning the position and function of translations in the literary system - including, for instance, French literature in the first half of the nineteenth century - can be represented schematically on the basis of the possible relations within translational communication, the actual relations between translational and literary systems, and the relations between translational and other systems (see Lambert & Van Gorp, above).

This approach clearly distinguishes itself from the majority of existing studies of and comments on translation, because from the outset we suppose that every translation and every feature of the translator's activity can be situated within some translational (sub-)system. In so doing, we take it for granted that no translation or translator can be treated in isolation, since translations and translators inevitably operate in the context of collective norms and models. As a result, no translated text is studied on its own. Nor do we wish to restrict the investigation to the relation between a single original and its translation, for this would lead to a one-way analysis which would probably end up by being prescriptive as well. Instead, we take into account the presence of various models other than the original. These models may be derived from the translational system or from the 'original' literary system itself.

Our approach thus aims at being as open and flexible as possible with regard to the issue of translation within a well-defined period. Of course, we do not wish to deny that within this period there may be highly individual translations and translators. However, in contrast with many traditional approaches, which in practice or even explicitly rule out the possibility of relating individual translations to general patterns and schemes, our investigation tries to discriminate between the general and the particular; indeed, what is particular can only be discovered in relation to a more general rule. This view also applies to the evaluation of translations, which only makes sense in a broader historical context, and which can only be dealt with on a functional historical basis.

With regard specifically to most earlier studies of translation in France in the first half of the nineteenth century, we think we should take a radically new stand, in accordance with our methodological framework. Numerous articles and books have been written on translation in the Romantic age. Many of these studies pay considerable attention to the his-

torical situation of individual translators, their
publishers and their audiences, and are therefore
closely connected with the prescriptive attitudes
prevailing within the period itself. Accounts of this
type, consequently, are characterized by much controversy, which, moreover, often has a literary origin
and corresponds with certain well-defined literary
trends. The problem of nineteenth-century translation
in France has rarely, if ever, been viewed in its entirety, not even by twentieth-century scholars. We
have deemed it necessary to question both older and
more recent studies of translation, because even our
modern specialists usually start from somewhat intuitive premises, and thus exclude many aspects of
the problem. Yet it would be unwise to overlook or
ignore these - often mutually irreconcilable - accounts and comments. In the same way as translators
comment on their own activities, we have interpreted
this large body of texts as investigations which are
prior to the scholarly approach itself, and which
allow us to formulate hypotheses that are useful to
our own research. For instance, the contradictions
which surface again and again in the traditional criticism and evaluation of translation point, among
other things, to conflicting trends within the nineteenth-century narrative system. Rather than putting
these existing studies aside as irrelevant, we should
make use of them in order to detect situations of
conflict that translational (and literary) problems
come to fore most clearly.

2. Translation and Literary Evolution

In the French literary system of the first half of
the nineteenth century, one can expect translation
to play a role in the so-called struggle for Romanticism.[2] Some obvious questions immediately arise. Are
the literary ruptures and conflicts influenced, perhaps even occasioned and oriented by translators and
translations? Do the conflicts within the translational system take on the same aspect as those within
the indigenous literary system? For about a decade,
between 1820 and 1830, the translations of plays and
the translations of poetry are central to the Romantic conflict (D'hulst 1982a; Lambert 1982), to such
an extent that sometimes the borderline between translation and original work (or adaptation) begin to
vanish. Here we may mention the *Théâtre de Clara Gazul*
(1825) and *La Guzla* (1827) by Prosper Mérimée, both
pseudo-translations with a parodic effect, as well
as *Le More de Venise* (1828) by Alfred de Vigny or *Macbeth*
(1826-   ) by Emile Deschamps and numerous other trans-

lations by such figures as Adolphe Loève-Veimars,
Amédée Pichot, Gérard de Nerval, Claude-Charles
Fauriel, Abel Hugo, the brothers Emile and Anthony
Deschamps, and others. *Wallenstein* by Benjamin Constant
and even Mme de Staël's *Geneviève* had been precursors
more than ten years before.

Most of the advocates of Romanticism tried to
influence drama, and most of them wrote theoretical
treatises alongside their dramatic output. In the
case of drama translations, the urge to theorize man-
ifested itself with the same vigour, and some essential questions were discussed with regard to translations rather than to indigenous French works (Vigny,
Lettre à Lord ***; Deschamps, preface to his *Macbeth*;
Constant, preface to *Wallenstein*). Reflections on foreign literature, as inaugurated by Mme de Staël, were
transformed into reflections on translation and on
drama in general. Moreover, observations on the art
of translation were functional rather than technical:
the translations appeared as 'dramatic works' and
not as 'translated works'.

The strategy used by the translators was very
much the result of the contemporary constraints of
the stage, i.e. of the strict rules which regulated
the French theatre of the time, and which the Romantic avant-garde attempted to abolish. Thus the unorthodox alexandrines used by Deschamps in his *Macbeth*
and by Vigny in his *More de Venise* constitute the 'new'
verse form cultivated by the Romantics, and more
specifically by Victor Hugo. The translation of foreign works (Schiller, Shakespeare, the Spanish playwrights) bears all the ambiguously innovatory features of original Romantic works. Nevertheless, even
Shakespeare in alexandrine guise became a revolutionary author - more revolutionary even than Casimir
Delavigne or Hugo. In fact, the translations of foreign drama became the most daring plays that the
French stage could offer to the public. As a result,
theatre directors often refused 'adapted' translations, or else would accept them only if they were
modified in accordance with traditional precepts.
This explains Deschamps' suggestions between 1826
and 1844, when he was dreaming of an *ad hoc* stage upon
which all forms of experimentation would be allowed.
Stendhal, in the years 1823-1826, alone promoted the
idea of a really 'natural' theatre, which would resolutely renounce verse. In deciding in favour of prose,
however, the dramatist of the Romantic age effectively
abandoned the French dramatic system altogether. The
translators who preferred prose thus openly acknowledged that their text was not meant to enter the

theatrical circuit. The works translated into prose
functioned in an intermediary zone set apart from
the stage and from drama itself. We have to wait until about 1829 (Dumas and then Victor Hugo) before
the formal constraints of verse are really dispensed
with. But notions like "le théâtre dans un fauteuil"
(Musset) and "drama at liberty" (Hugo) illustrate
that even after 1830 prose drama was still generally
regarded as 'non-drama'. We may therefore conclude
that the conflicts and dilemmas within French drama
were similar to those within the translations of foreign plays.

As a consequence of their a-systemic position,
then, translations often played a primary role in the
development of a new dramatic art. The change from
verse to prose was inevitably accompanied by a series
of innovations such as 'local colour', the use of
idiomatic speech and variations in linguistic register and the preservation of features belonging to foreign genres and traditions. All of this eventually
led to the abandonment of the prevailing dramatic
conventions. If drama played a crucial role in the
debate on Romanticism, the part played by foreign
works in translation should not be underestimated:
the triumph of Romanticism owed much to their influence. Still, it would be wrong to generalize too
quickly from this statement, for it is only in the
more élitist sectors of the new theatre that translation acts as a driving force. The innovatory impulse
remained more or less absent in popular drama (vaudeville and melodrama), except in the form of adaptations of texts which already existed in French and
which were indeed more often borrowed from the novel
than from drama. Within the world of classical drama
nothing new happened, either in terms of adaptation
or in terms of new productions. As a result, the new
translations of classical plays remained utterly re-
moved from the stage: they were part of literary education rather than of literature.

In short, the translations of plays reflect in
a symptomatic manner the structures of French drama
at the time. And, as the Deschamps file shows,(see
Lambert 1982), there is not even room to talk of a
true revolution around 1830; there is simply a slightly more liberal attitude.

*

With regard to other aspects of literary life, too,
we need to investigate ruptures and shifts in patterns
of translation. We have analyzed systematically the

various translations of great foreign 'classics' in the period 1800-1850, in order to determine whether or not they are revised around 1830. It seems likely that the events which marked the flourishing of literature around 1830 did not really influence the way translators and the reading public were assimilating foreign literature in general. The French continued to read Virgil, Homer, Dante and Boccaccio as if nothing had happened, and translations dating back to the eighteenth century were still frequently reprinted: the crisis of literary values did not have too great an impact on the world of translations, to the extent that the Shakespeare plays in the Ducis version of 1780 continued to be performed until the end of the nineteenth century. In other words, there is a large number of translations which played no more than a marginal role in the literary life of the Romantic era.

If there is a revolution, it reveals itself paradoxically where it is least expected. Between 1820 and 1850, a series of contentious writings drew the attention of contemporaries to the necessity of rejuvenating the art of translation, and to the need to restore it to its old splendour. There writings, which commented on texts from Antiquity and not on modern works, thus came right in the heart of the literary debate of the time. Paul-Louis Courier (about 1820) and Emile Littré (after 1845) denounced the artfulness of classical diction as it had been perpetuated in French versions of Homer, Herodotus, Sophocles and others since Mme Dacier and the seventeenth-century translators. Translation here became a weapon pointed at the linguistic, literary, cultural and even political traditions of France. In order to take a stand against the Boileau version of classical orthodoxy, Herodotus and Longus were presented in a pastiche rural language of the seventeenth century, or a gibberish which nc French writer would ever consider using. Homer (1847) and even Dante (as late as 1875) were rendered in a pastiche medieval language borrowed from the poets who filled the Romantics with enthusiasm.

Such experiments may be exceptional, but they are of great interest. It is no mere coincidence that in 1833 Désiré Nisard recommends translation as a means to rejuvenate classical antiquity and as a way to liberate literature from the scourge of 'easy writing'. The translation of the Bible and of authors from classical antiquity had a very rich tradition indeed, and, like the translations of works by Shakespeare or Schiller in the Romantic age, it functioned as a way of experimenting with literary and linguistic forms in the seventeenth and eighteenth centuries. According to Nisard, translation was no longer an art. It is true that in the period we are discussing, the awareness of the artistic aspects of translation is the exception rather than the rule. It manifests itself most strongly in the world of drama, where the existing codification and the discussions were more sophisticated, but also with respect to the writers from antiquity, where the heritage of many centuries of classical culture made itself felt. The translator of Virgil or Sophocles had at his disposal a set of models and rules which he found it hard to ignore. He remembered the verse forms and outlines of Delille or his predecessors which his respect for tradition forbade him to violate. In contrast, the translator of, say, E.Th.Hoffmann hardly imagined that reading a German writer in French could be a real problem, and was not worried by genre constraints or stylistic principles, even if he unwillingly fell victim to them. In the field of prose, the two foreign writers who were most successful at the time, Walter Scott and Hoffmann, were the object of competing and aggressive initiatives of translation. In the press campaigns, the issue of translation was dealt with casually and never in any fundamental way. The translators, for their part, were in a position to copy without being taken to task for doing so. On the whole, the coexistence of different translations of modern texts in prose was the result of commercial rather than literary pressures, in contrast with translations of texts from antiquity or of dramatic or poetic work. This means that, for a time at least, prose found itself outside the traditional codifications, in short: outside art.

*

In general, the principles that determine the translation of drama also apply to poetic texts. The analogy between the poetic and the translational systems allows us to generalize our observations concerning the function of the opposition between prose and verse, between elevated and non-elevated models, and between innovating and conservative strategies. Admittedly, there are some incongruities between the two systems, but the fundamental mechanisms appear all the more prominent on this account. The controversy over prose and verse clearly takes on a different aspect in the case of translated poetry. Around 1825 the status of prose as a non-elevated form encouraged those who had appropriated the poetic models inherited from the eighteenth century (from Voltaire, and especially Delille). By 1830, however, the situation was somewhat different. From this year onwards, and much more markedly than is the case in the dramatic system, we can see a widening gap between prose, which was set aside for translations, and verse, which became the exclusive domain of poetry. Prose translations by Claude-Charles Fauriel or Amédée Pichot, which in 1825 were more highly estimated than the verse translations of Greuzé de Lesser or Népomucène Lemercier, at the same time outstripped the poetry of Delavigne, Guiraud and Millevoye in importance. From 1828 onwards the poets of the 'premier Cénacle', headed by Victor Hugo, managed to establish new poetic models that were capable of pushing prose translation aside. The latter nevertheless retained its position as the translation model par excellence well beyond 1835.

Significantly, the translation of great works from classical antiquity was subject to very sophisticated rules, while the translation of recent prose works could yield a great variety of results, without giving offence to either critic or publisher. In this respect foreign modern drama was closer to classical literature than to modern prose: the translator worked with circumspection, and often felt obliged to clarify and justify his method, or indeed to apologize for it. In the translations of classical literature, the translational principles stemmed from a long-standing tradition of translation, which weighed on every new rendering; the translator knew that he formed part of a translational system.

But this tradition was closely linked with the indigenous literary tradition and canon, so that the translational system functioned within certain (traditional) limits of the literary system. Anyone who translated Shakespeare, Schiller or Lope de Vega, had to take into account first of all the *literary* constraint. Earlier translations might, either positively or negatively, influence the new translations, and the translator and his readers might be aware that they were part of a translational system, but they were even more conscious of their position in the literary system. On the other hand, people like A.J.B.Defauconpret and Albert de Montémont in translating Walter Scott, or Adolphe Loève-Veimars and others in translating Hoffmann, could afford many picturesque words and expressions, and were allowed to introduce new themes and narrative techniques. Although they too were clearly aware of their responsibility, which was sufficiently emphasized by the critics, they did not feel in any way vulnerable in their position as translators, and they hardly needed to worry about the possible existence of earlier translations, or about their own translations being plagiarized. Both within the literary and the translational system they enjoyed a freedom which can only be explained by the renewal of French literature through prose, whereby the new literary forms imported from abroad functioned as a kind of 'non-system' until they had built their own traditions. Nonetheless, a degree of interference stemming from the canonized literary system can still be detected, as the prose translations often show figures of style and other rhetorical devices clearly borrowed from the dominant traditions in classical theatre and poetry.

3. Translations and Genres

To the extent that it was submitted to the constraints of genres, the art of translation lays bare certain crucial dilemmas of literature in the Romantic age. The translation of a play or a poem was subject to rules which the translation of a novel or short story could ignore with impunity. As a result, the translation of narrative prose was characterized by an extreme diversity of strategies. Mme Montolieu reduces certain texts by a third, whereas elsewhere she offers more or less complete versions; Loève-Veimars, Defauconpret, Pichot and Montémont prove at times to be very inconsistent, but often also very scrupulous. The reason, as suggested above, is that narrative prose itself escaped a familiar and restrictive codification. The diversity in the methods applied by the translators corresponds with a diversity, one might even say a hierarchy, in the relations between the genres. Writers and critics voluntarily joined the debate on drama and poetry, but narrative prose hardly gained access to books and reviews, at least before 1830. It is striking that the theoretical and critical comments on translations in this period deal almost exclusively with drama, and, to a lesser extent, with poetry, but hardly ever with prose.

That the concept of the genres determined the theory and practice of translation also becomes clear at the level of the external presentation of texts. The title page of translated works does not always specify either the precise origin of the text or the translator of the book in question. Ducis and some other 'adaptors' of original drama announced *Hamlet* or other plays as the fruits of their own imagination. Their pseudo-translations likewise hid their real origins, but in the opposite sense: they presented as

foreign what was in fact French, whereas Ducis appropriated for himself the authorship of foreign works
which the reader was expected nevertheless to know
to be foreign. Although pseudo-translations did at
times appear in the field of drama and poetry, they
were much more common in prose writing (and this from
the eighteenth century onwards; see Yahalom 1981).
On the whole, the translators of plays and of poetic
texts revealed themselves in that capacity, from the
title page onwards. In many cases they even emphasized that their translation was 'new', that it was
in verse, that it was an 'attempt' at translation,
or even an imitation. Their clarity and honesty with
respect to the foreign text is often confirmed by
the presence of a preface and/or translator's notes.
These very explicit specifications concerning the
role played by the translator ("new translation, an-
notated and commented by..."; "literal version...")
rarely occur in prose texts.

There is, however, another principle which may
override the concept of genre. The translators often
inform us about the nature of their intervention as
soon as the prestige of the source text or of the
source literature demanded it. In effect, though,
this principle only confirms the importance of generic categories, because the prestigious authors from
antiquity or the modern age were first and foremost
poets and dramatists. Indeed, the classical Latin
and Greek writers were rarely translated or translated
anew without at least some comment on the exact nature of the translation and, where appropriate, on
previous translations.

The importance of genres in the history of
translation reveals itself in yet another way. At
certain moments and in certain sub-genres (drama,
tales of the supernatural, women's novels), we see a
sudden proliferation of translations, whereas in
other sub-genres they remain virtually non-existent.
It therefore becomes necessary to draw a distinction
between, on the one hand, the genres and sub-genres
that are essentially 'French' (such as tragedy, if we
consider the plays from antiquity - which are never
performed - as a separate category; vaudeville and
any popular form of theatre; an entire spectrum of
lyrical sub-genres), and, on the other, the more
open genres and sub-genres, where translation often
plays a crucial part, to the extent that we can speak
of 'imported genres' (tales of the supernatural,.
Gothic novels, women's novels, popular novels before
1820, in short: many subcategories of prose, apart
from the contemporary novels of 1830-1850). The

presence or absence of translations in specific sub-
genres clearly shows that they play a functional role
within French literature, and that the sudden proliferation of translations is a sign of an innovating
influence (drama roughly between 1820-1830), whereas
the stability in the number of translations, in the
selection of texts (both in the past and in the present; in England and Germany), and in the translation
method points to a more conservative function. The
absence of any form of translation in a particular
(sub-)genre generally confirms the traditional and
indigenous character of the (sub-)genre in question.
Thus French classical tragedy has such strong traditions that the tragedies from antiquity are not fit
for performance, and the tragedies imported from modern literatures have to undergo a change of genre in
order to be admitted to the dramatic system (Shakespeare, Schiller, the Spanish playwrights of the Gold-
en Age). One can make a distinction between stable or
closed genres, which refuse translations or allow
them only in the form of 'acceptable' versions, and
flexible or open genres, where the translation method
shows itself to be very free and often inconsistent,
ranging from the most 'adequate' to the most 'acceptable' type of version.

4. Translators and Authors

Between 1800 and 1830, the majority of dramatists
were also translators. What is more, their translations are an integral part of their oeuvre, in which
literature and translation (or 'adaptation') imper-
ceptibly merge. It is also among the writings of
these dramatists that we find most of the theoretical
statements on the problem of translation, precisely
because this is an eminently literary matter. From
about 1830 onwards, these translators tend to concen-
trate on 'original' writing rather than translating.
From their point of view, translating has been a
phase in their development, an exercise in literary
experimentation. As such, translation represented a
means to an end - the manipulation of imported literature in the service of the avant-garde - rather than
an end in itself. Their ultimate aim was the production of a new art.
    Between 1800 and 1830 translation was a natural
field of interest among poets as well. Chênedollé,
Chateaubriand, Nerval, the Deschamps brothers, Henri
de Latouche and many others integrated translation
into their poetic activity. After 1830, it was rather
the second-rate or marginal innovating poets, i.e.
the least mentioned but nevertheless original ones,

160

who produced translations. They herald the poetry of the future - of Verlaine and the Symbolists. Among these translator-poets, we may note in particular Xavier Marmier, Nicolas Martin, Blaze de Bury and Gérard de Nerval (who was the first to translate Heine's *Lyrisches Intermezzo*, 1848).

It appears that the translation of poetry does not owe much to the great names in the poetic genre after 1830 - Musset, Vigny, Hugo. One of the rare events in poetic translation of the 1830s was the publication of Milton's *Paradise Lost* by Chateaubriand in 1836. But the shift to prose in the writing of an epic, as well as the accompanying defence of a new art of translation, give the impression of a revolution *post factum*: both the prose epics and the poetry in prose of Chateaubriand had been known since the beginning of the century. The fact that in 1835 Chateaubriand is still convinced that he is making a fresh start on the question of translation and poetry, shows that he has been out of touch with his epoch for several years.

The various subcategories of prose, where the quantity of translations was often very high, were almost exclusively in the hands of 'specialists', i.e. professional translators. These translations often stood alongside the great names in French prose of the time, or rather, they often took their place and served them as models. This world of translators of novels, and often even of tales, shows us a flourishing culture of mainly foreign books, stimulated by powerful and daring publishers (Pigoreau, Renduel, soon also Hetzel and Calmann-Lévy or Charpentier), who relied on prolific writers to provide them with an uninterrupted flow of reading-matter. Their epoch called them "distinguished writers", but the label should be taken with a grain of salt, since contemporaries still placed them well below figures like Mme de Staël, Charles Nodier, Honoré de Balzac, Victor Hugo, Eugène Sue, Alexandre Dumas or Georges Sand. We are dealing with figures such as Isabelle de Montolieu, Amédée Pichot, Elise Voïart, Amable Tastu, Adolphe Loève-Veimars, Auguste Defauconpret, Albert de Montémont. It is symptomatic that only a few of them ventured into the translation of poetry or drama, i.e. anything beyond the limits of prose. The publication of scores of prose volumes in translation within a few years suggests that they belong to a separate world, where glory was attained by people like Loève-Veimars, Auguste Defauconpret and Isabelle de Montolieu. However, none of the great translators of prose works has been admitted to the pantheon of writers who are canonized in literary history. And yet the circumstances might have been propitious for them, because each year the proportion of translations in the total number of publications was considerably higher in the prose sector than in any other.

On many other levels, the hierarchical structure of the genre system seems to weigh on the function of translations. Thus dilemmas like the one between 'elevated' and 'low' style appear to be less sharp in prose than in drama, and less rigid in comedy than in tragedy. The return to a picturesque, exotic, conversational and even dialectal diction was common in prose but inconceivable on the stage, at least in the elevated genres (though not at all in vaudeville). We have the translators and authors of prose works to thank for the gradual penetration of ordinary speech into elevated literature. Nevertheless, this process was still slow in comparison with other countries. Indeed, even at a time when Victor Hugo spoke in defence of an art that would combine 'Beauty' and 'Ugliness', writers and critics saw it as their duty to exclude from the sphere of art anything considered vulgar or trivial.

Nineteenth-century French literature may have reached its peak with authors like Flaubert, Zola and other writers in the realistic mode. This climax owes a great deal more to translated prose than one might expect, even though in many cases prose translators exerted their influence in complete obscurity. In France, the revolution in language and the revolution of literary genres have often been interpreted as subversive, and there is no doubt that this was one of the main functions of the translations within the period we are considering. In contrast with such stately works as the Shakespeare of the Schlegel brothers and their friends, translation in France between 1800 and 1850 often produced cladestine texts and movements which have since sunk into oblivion. More than a century later, we hope to have fulfilled a useful task by revealing these functions which the past seems to have been less mistaken about than the present.[3]

NOTES

1. The research project 'Littérature et traduction en France, 1800-1850', sponsored by the University Louvain, was carried out by Lieven D'hulst, José Lambert and Katrin van Bragt. Several interim reports have been published, as well as reports on particular areas and on methodological questions.

In the present article we provide for the first time conclusions about the main findings of the project; more detailed conclusions and discussions will be published in book form.
2. The question of 'Romanticism' will be discussed in similar systemic terms in a special issue of the *Journal for European Studies* (ed. José Lambert and Franco Musarra, forthcoming).
3. One of the most important aspects of our research which could not be discussed here concerns the quantitative distribution of translations according to various parameters (chronology, translator, genre or sub-genre, source literature, title structure, publisher, etc.). We refer to our bibliography (approximately 8,000 titles), which will be computerized.

REFERENCES

D'HULST, Lieven
1982a   'The Conflict of Translational Models in France (end of 18th - beginning of 19th century)', *Dispositio*, vii, nos. 19-20-21:41-52
1982b   *L'évolution de la poésie en France (1780-1830). Introduction à une analyse des interférences systémiaues.* Unpublished PhD thesis, University of Louvain (KUL)
EVEN-ZOHAR, Itamar
1978   *Papers in Historical Poetics.* Tel Aviv, Porter Institute for Poetics and Semiotics
LAMBERT, José
1975   'La traduction en France à l'époque romantique. A propos d'un article récent', *Revue de littérature comparée*, xlix:396-412
1978   'Echanges littéraires et traduction: discussion d'un projet', in J.S.Holmes *et al.* (eds.), *Literature and Translation* (Louvain, Acco):142-160
1981   'Théorie de la littérature et théorie de la traduction en France (1800-1850), interprétées à partir de la théorie du polysystème', *Poetics Today*, ii,4:161-170
1982   'How Emile Deschamps Translated Shakespeare's Macbeth, or Theatre System and Translational System in French', *Dispositio*, vii, nos. 19-2C-21:53-62
TOURY, Gideon
1980   *In Search of a Theory of Translation.* Tel Aviv, Porter Institute for Poetics and Semiotics
1984   'Translation, Literary Translation and Pseudotranslation', *Comparative Criticism* 6:73-85
YAHALOM, Shelly
1981   'Le système littéraire en état de crise. Contacts inter-systémiques et comportement traductionnel', *Poetics Today*, ii,4:143-160

THE SURVIVAL OF MYTH

Mandel'shtam's "Word" and Translation

Leon Burnett

> ... What is all art, if not
> the finding of lost things,
> the immortalization of
> things lost ?
>
> M. Tsvetaeva

1. Recognition

The third stanza of 'Tristia', the title-poem
of Mandel'shtam's second volume of poetry,[1] concludes
with lines that point to the central importance of
recognition (uznavan'e) for the author:

Все было встарь, все повторится снова,
И сладок нам лишь узнаванья миг.
(All was of old, all will be repeated anew,/And sweet
for us is only the flash of recognition.)

As if to reinforce this declaration, Mandel'shtam's
poetry abounds in the "recognition" of earlier poets
and, more extensively, of earlier traditions. It is
not by chance that the single phrase that has come
most tenaciously to attach itself to commentaries on
his poetry is Mandel'shtam's remark *à propos* of Akmeism,
the poetic movement with which he allied himself,
that it was "a nostalgia for world culture".[2]
According to Taranovsky, "the fundamental problem which stands before investigators of (Mandel'-
shtam's) poetry" is to "reveal all his literary subtexts" (Taranovsky 1976:114), to recognize his recog-
nitions. Recognition, in this circumscribed sense,
is either *direct* or, as is more often the case, *mediated*
to such a degree that it requires the acumen of the
critical investigator to bring the lost allusion to
the surface. Translation (such as the poet's rendering of four poems from Petrarch's 'Canzoniere' into
Russian[3]) constitutes the most obvious, extended form

of direct recognition, to which the kind of fragmentary quotation that has been defined (with respect
to Eliot's comparable practice in *The Waste Land*) as
παραδιορθωσις, namely "the adaptation of one poet's
line by another poet for a different use" (Bowra 1967:
181), may serve as a supplementary, abbreviated form.[4]
Mediated recognition consists of the "echoes and correspondences, reflections and refractions" (Gifford
1979:12) that enable the poet to reconcile what Eliot
saw as the complementary conditions of 'tradition'
and 'individual talent'. The direct and the mediated
forms of recognition, taken together, make up the
subtext of "poetic reminiscences" and "other voices"
in Mandel'shtam's poetry (Taranovsky 1976:v-vi),
which I propose to explore in this essay.

Recognition, for Mandel'shtam, was at once a
token of "historical sensitivity" (*istoricheskoe chut'e*;
CCPL:134; S-F,II:272)[5] and a means of establishing a
personal identity. In an essay written in 1922 on the
occasion of the first anniversary of the death of the
Russian Symbolist Blok, Mandel'shtam introduced the
striking metaphor of the badger to comment on the
crisis in contemporary literature, a crisis so much
more pertinent to the living than to the dead poet.
He wrote:

> Blok was a man of the nineteenth century and he knew
> that the days of his century were numbered. Greedily
> he extended and deepened his inner world in Time like
> a badger digging in the earth, building his home with
> two exits. The age is a badger's hole and a man of his
> age lives and moves about in a narrowly restricted
> space, frantically trying to expand his domain, valuing
> above all the exits from his subterranean hole.
> (CCPL:134-35; S-F,II:272)

The defining features of Mandel'shtam's badger
are its awareness of the threat to its survival and
its instinct for burrowing into the earth. The badger, as an emblem of the poet's plight, suited Mandel'shtam better than Baudelaire's albatross (which
he associated with the nineteenth century (CCPL:138;
S-F,II:276)) in two main particulars: it is homely
rather than exotic, and subterranean rather than em-
pyrean. Domesticity and descent are Mandel'shtam's
'instincts' at this period of his life.

The poet's innate disposition to 'recognize' is
analogous to the badger's instinct for survival and,
like the animal, the poet assigns a great urgency to
the availability of access to the surface, to his
"exits", in the perpetual work of construction. The
poet digs down into an "inner world in Time" in order

to retrieve the fragments to shore against his ruins.
The essay on Blok draws to a conclusion with the observation that

> Poetic culture arises from the attempt to avert catas-
> trophe, to make it dependent on the central sun of the
> system as a whole, be it love, of which Dante spoke, or
> music, at which Blok ultimately arrived. (CCPL:137;
> S-F,II:275)

Even if the image of the badger does not appear elsewhere in the essays and the poetry that Mandel'shtam
wrote in the period subsequent to the historical
events of the Russian revolution in 1917, it is still
possible to find the broader propositions of 'Badger
Hole' (*Barsuch'ia nora*) recurring in other analogues.
What they amount to, as a whole, is a myth of survival, in which, as I shall attempt to show, the survival of myth is a paramount concern.

In this respect, Mandel'shtam's poetry offers a
model of a comprehensive tendency in European Symbolist and post-Symbolist literature, namely the culturally determined preoccupation with a traditional
(and, therefore, a conservative[6]) mythology whose
roots are planted firmly in the cultural soil of
Classical antiquity. The potential that mythology
has for transformation acts as a pledge against the
spiritual bankruptcy threatened in a materialistic
age. The stabilising power of myth, in reducing the
"anticipation of disaster" (in Kluckhohn's phrase),
accounts for the common attraction, at a time of
crisis for European poets as diverse as Eliot, Mandel'shtam, Rilke, and Valéry, to the rich pasture-
land of ancient Greece. Within a year of each other
(1922-23), *The Waste Land*, *Tristia*, *Sonette an Orpheus* and
Charmes were all in print. Myth (in its transformational function) provided these four poet-craftsmen
with a similar emotional stimulus to that of nature
(in its organic aspect) for the Romantic poet-creator
in the early nineteenth century. The dominant recognition for Mandel'shtam in *Tristia* is generated by
the transformative property of myth, which became
the "central sun" of his system as a whole. As the
analogy of the badger indicates, the central sun is
located underground.[7]

2. Transformation

Kerényi has defined the Greek word, μυθολογια, as
"an art alongside and included within poetry (the
two fields overlap), an art with a special assumption
as regards its subject-matter", its subject-matter
(or material) being "tales about gods and god-like

beings, heroic battles and journeys to the Underworld
...tales already well-known but not unamenable to
further reshaping" (Kerényi 1951:3). He continues:

> Mythology is the *movement* of this material: it is
> something solid and yet mobile, substantial and yet
> not static, capable of transformation. (*ibid.*)

Mythology "provides a foundation" for the teller by
means of which he "finds himself in the primordiali-
ty that is his concern, in the midst of the αρχαι of
which he is speaking", and, he adds, each man "has
his own αρχαι, the αρχαι of his organic being from
which he continually creates himself" (*ibid.*:10-11).
In an image that parallels the architectural metaphors of Mandel'shtam's Akmeist writings,[8] Kerényi
concludes that "the great and paramount theme of
mythology" is to "rebuild the world" at the crossroads of man and nature (*ibid.*:13).

Myth, regarded in this perspective, is neither
symbolical (or what the Akmeists had dismissed as
pseudo-symbolist (CCPL:129; S-F,II:255 and Tracy 1981:
16-25)[9]), that is, standing for something else, nor
is it either euhemerist or aetiological, that is,
explanatory in intention; it is, rather, as Malinows-
ki has claimed, "living reality" (quoted in Kerényi
1951:7). Myth possesses *operative* status: it does not
so much *have* as *give* meaning. Mythological ideas "always contain *more* than the non-mythological mind
could conceive" (Kerényi 1951:152).

The same applies to poetry. It has become axio-
matic in modern, so-called *organic*, views of poetry to
assert that meaning is distorted, if not destroyed,
by any alteration in the order of the text. The
aphorism of Coleridge that sought to distinguish between prose (words in the best order) and poetry
(the *best* words in the best order) is but an early
instance of the 'organicist' approach that has come
to treat the text as inviolable. What is true of
poetry is true also of the translation of poetry.
Another aphoristic statement (one that we might perhaps designate, after its instigator, Frost's Law)
observes that poetry is that which is lost in translation. If this is indeed so (and practising translators tend to recall it with all the gusto of *Schaden-
freude*), then the proper response would seem to fall
either to Shelley's romantic acceptance of the vanity of translation (that "it were as wise to cast a
violet into a crucible that you might discover the
formal principle of its colour and odour, as to seek
to transfuse from one language to another the crea-
tions of a poet" (cp. Webb 1976:24-29)) or to what

167

we may take as the modern rejoinder, Tsvetaeva's rhetorical question: "What is all art, if not the finding of lost things?" (Tsvetaeva 1980:231).

Literary translation, as a species of creative transformation, is at its most accomplished when it is also an act of recognition. The translator does well not to impose himself on the text either as rival or as slave (which seemed the only options open to the Russian romantic translator-poet, Zhukovsky[10]). Instead, he should possess within himself a certain degree of negative capability, a magnanimity of the imagination. Whereas the poet is creative, the translator should be receptive – but with a badger's vigilance.

3. Translation

Mandel'shtam wrote of his receptivity in a poem of 1923 whose theme is discovery, 'The Horseshoe Finder' ('Nashedshii podkovu'):

> То, что я сейчас говорю, говорю не я,
> А вырыто из земли, подобно зернам окаменелой
>   пшеницы.
> (That which I now speak, speak not I,/But it is dug out
> of the earth, like grains of fossilized wheat.)

Beside affording an example of the *exhumation* motif (to be considered later), these lines may be cited in support of the argument put forward by Mureddu that, Mandel'shtam's teleology, in his later poetry, is close to the concept of confession found in Petrarch (and his model, Augustine), that is, the emptying of one's self in order to be possessed by the 'Other'. There is, however, an important difference, as she notes. It is

> a difference qualifying Mandel'štam as a modern and,
> at the same time, making his message less a solution
> than a way of seeking: the "Other" for Mandel'štam is
> no longer Petrarch's God, but the very essence of nature,
> in which every creature can find his true self and the
> meaning of his individual experience. (Mureddu 1980:62)

Mandel'shtam returned again and again to the idea that the earth is a sacred repository, but not in the stereotypical sense that it is a source of (organic) fertility, nor yet in the anthropological equivalent to this view as expressed in *The Waste Land*. His land is neither fertile nor sterile: the grains (*zerna*) of wheat are "fossilized", *sealed up* in a stone.[11] As Mureddu has written, it is "less a solution than a way of seeking". Or, in the mythological

schema of Kerényi, he "finds himself in the primor-
diality that is his concern, in the midst of the
αρχαι of which he is speaking" (Kerényi 1951:10).
    Translation is a border activity. It involves
the translator in a raid on the articulate in the
'other' language and a return from that primordiali-
ty to the security of self. So long as the axis is
horizontal this crossing over the threshold is no
more than a voyage of discovery, but as soon as the
axis is turned through 90° to the vertical then a
powerfully mythic dimension is opened to view.
Mureddu has pointed to Mandel'shtam's "apparently
strange longing to hear the earth's axis" (Mureddu
1980:63) in the final line of a poem, 'Armed with
the seeing of narrow wasps' ('Vooruzhennyi zren'em
uzkikh os', 1937):

    Услышать ось земную, ось земную ...
    (To hear the earth's axis, the earth's axis ...)

It is a significant part of the poet's "associative
semantics" (Ginzburg 1975:291) that the Russian word
for "axis" (*os'*) not only closely resembles the geni-
tive plural of "wasp" (*os*), which occurs in the first
line of the poem (cp. Taranovsky 1976:167), but that
it also recognizes the kinship of the poet through
his first name: Osip.
    Beyond the recalling of Osip, lies the figura-
tive transformation of another poet, a paler ghost,
already metamorphosed in the opening line of Mallarmé's 'Le Tombeau d'Edgar Poe': "Tel qu'en Lui-même
enfin l'éternité le change". In life, Poe's pathological fear was premature burial.

4. Survival

    Poe's literary survival was assured by the dedi-
cated offices of his French translator, Baudelaire,
a reader in vertical and horizontal correspondences.
In Russia, the Symbolist poet-translator, Bal'mont,
extended the range of Poe's influence. Parallel to
the translation of his works by poets, there took
shape the transformation of Poe's life by legend.
Baudelaire had a hand in this as well.[12]
    Translation emerges as the "afterlife" (*Fortleben*)
of the original (Benjamin 1973:71). As Benjamin has
stated succinctly: "... in its afterlife - which
could not be called that if it were not a transformation (*Wandlung*) and a renewal of something living -
the original undergoes a change" (*ibid.*:73). In the
same essay, 'The Task of the Translator' ('Die Aufgabe des Uebersetzers')[13], he insists (quoting from

Pannwitz, *Die Krisis der europäischen Kultur*) that the
translator should go back "to the primal elements of
language itself" ("auf die letzten elemente der
sprache selbst") and penetrate to the point "where
work, image, and tone converge" ("wo wort, bild, ton
in eins geht")(*ibid.*:81). As we have seen, this "pri-
mordiality" is also the foundation for the teller of
myths according to Kerényi. Translation and mythopoeia
share a common interest in αρχαι (*ibid.* :78; Kerényi
1951:11). The difference is that the source for the
translator is textual ("the point where work, image,
and tone converge"), whereas the source for the myth-
maker is non-textual ("at the crossroads of man and
nature"). In myth, it is the nuclear idea that constitutes the inner structure (or αρχη), and that
remains inviolable as *psychic reality*, whereas the myth
itself *changes with time* as a result of *natural decay*
(Kerényi 1951:145; his italics). Kerényi observes
that

> The idea ... can be likened to a nucleus. We have to
> understand, as it were, the structure hidden in the
> 'abyss of the nucleus'. (*ibid.*:148)

This inner structure is reminiscent of Mandel'shtam's
zerna (grains, kernels) of fossilized wheat dug out of
the earth.
Terras diagnosed Mandel'shtam's condition of
"nostalgia for primordial unity with the cosmos"
(Terras 1969:351) in a poem entitled 'Silentium',[14]
written as early as 1910. His diagnosis, when joined
to the poet's own retrospective comment on Akmeism
as "nostalgia for world culture", which was made in
the 1930s, suggests an enduring concern for origins
in Mandel'shtam that approaches pathological propor-
tions. His wife's memoirs tell us that Mandel'shtam
as a five-year-old child burst into tears on hearing
the unfamiliar word 'progress', even though at the
time he did not know what it meant (N.M.:256).[15]

5. Origins

Myth has been defined as the 'symbolic residue'
of an archetype or, more technically, of the "inner
dynamic at work in the phylogenetic psyche" (Stevens
1982:89). According to Kerényi, there are three stages
in the grounding (*Begründung*) of an archetype: when
"compulsion" (stage one) meets "monadic structure"
(stage two), then "consumation" (stage three) results in the rounded whole. "Only here do things come
to a standstill, achieve stability as a work" (Kerényi
1951:29). Kerényi's account of grounding is matched

by the three stages in poetic composition, which one
can derive from the terms that Mandel'shtam employed
on this subject. One of these - the "kernel" (*zerno*),
which stands in metonymic relation to the earth -
has already been introduced. It is the equivalent of
Kerenyi's "monadic structure" or *monad* (Frobenius).[16]
The two other terms are the subject of Harris's essay
'Introduction: The Impulse and the Text' (CCPL:3-49).
Harris considers the various "impulses" that, as it
were, compelled Mandel'shtam to produce the text (and
they include "autobiographical", "creative", "psychological", "esthetic" and "intellectual"). It would
seem, however, that the most powerful was the *philological* impulse (see section 8 of this essay).[17] The text
originates in the instantaneous "flash of recognition"
when impulse and word-kernel (monad) fuse. To recognize is to integrate (Stevens 1982:214), to discover
the hidden meaning in the very act of transforming
(reproducing) it. This is true for the source material, whether it be nuclear idea (resulting in myth
variant or allomorph (Friedrich 1978:46)) or subtext
(resulting in translation/parodiorthosis).

The following table recapitulates parallel
schemata that supply the model for a consideration
of operations along transformational axes (including
that of translation):

	Kerényi	Mandel'shtam	Stevens
1.	compulsion	impulse	psyche
2.	monad	kernel	archetype
3.	consumation	text	myth

It is not to be expected, of course, that Mandel'-
shtam would limit himself to any one set of terms in
discussing the inner dynamic of poetic production.
His dedication to the idea of convertibility meant
that his vocabulary was continuously open to conversion. To take a single example, the above groundplan
operates in the "earth" metaphor (of a poem written
in 1920), which is expressed tersely in the three
Russian words: "Vremia vspakhano plugom" ("Time is
turned up by the plough"). In this metaphor, the
psychic activity of "turning up" (or ploughing) corresponds to the impulse (compulsion) and "time", as
so often with Mandel'shtam, represents the archetypal
material (kernel/monad) to be transformed into text.
As Brodsky has written: "Song is, after all, restruc-
tured Time, toward which mute Space is inherently
hostile" (*Osip Mandelstam: 50 poems*; translated by Bernard

Meares, introductory essay by Joseph Brodsky, New
York: Persea Books, 1977, p.16).

6. Homeostasis

What the proposed model for creative transformation has not yet acknowledged is that it is a homeostatic system ("...at any given time a cultural or
semiotic system is both breaking down and becoming
internally differentiated and, on the other hand, is
growing together and internally synthesizing itself"
(Friedrich 1978:54)). Two-way movement is implicated
in the process of "recognition", which causes a new
hierarchy of words (or units of poetic speech - Mandel'shtam[18]) to come into being within the semantic
system of the poet. At its widest reach, this requires a re-adjustment of the macro-system that we designate by the term 'literature' - a re-adjustment that
Malraux has dubbed "the Eliot effect", following the
observation in 'Tradition and the Individual Talent'
that every major work of art forces upon us a reas-
sessment of all previous works (cp. Kubler 1962:35).[19]
This re-adjustment, at whatever level it operates,
is fundamental to the full understanding of the status
of recognition in Mandel'shtam's poetics. Recognition
defines the artist's responsibility as one of creative
receptivity (cp. Stevens 1982:203-4). For Mandel'shtam,
'cognition' is always 'recognition' or *re-cognition*, a
return upon itself, a "coming round again" (Greene
1980:9,88).
In a vivid affirmation of Borges's remark in an
essay on Kafka, that every writer *creates* his own precursors, Mandel'shtam wrote that "not a single poet
has yet appeared. We are free from the burden of
memories (*ot gruza vospominanii*). On the other hand, we
have so many rare presentiments: Pushkin, Ovid, Homer"
(CCPL:114; S-F,II:224). This explains his scornful
rejection of the notion of "progress" and also underlines the importance of the poetic image quoted at
the end of the previous section: *vremia vspakhano plugom*.
In 'The Word and Culture' ('Slovo i kul'tura', 1921),
Mandel'shtam glosses this image:

> Poetry is the plough that turns up time in such a way
> that the abyssal strata of time (*glubinnye sloi vremeni*),
> its black earth, appear on the surface. There are epochs,
> however, when mankind, not satisfied with the present,
> yearning like the ploughman for the abyssal strata of
> time, thirsts for the virgin soil of time... I want Ovid,
> Pushkin, and Catullus to live once more, and I am not
> satisfied with the historical Ovid, Pushkin, and Catul-
> lus (...) Classical poetry is perceived as that which

must be, not as that which has already been. (CCPL:113-14; S-F,II:224)

Remembrance (*vospominanie*) and oblivion (*bespamiatstvo*) take on pronouncedly new shades of meaning in the poet's lexicon. So, too, does recognition (*uznavan'e*):

> A blind man (*slepoi*) recognizes a beloved face by barely touching it with seeing fingers, and tears of joy, the true joy of recognition (*nastoiashchei radosti uznavan'ia*), will fall from his eyes after a long separation. The poem lives through an inner image, that ringing mold of form (*tem zvuchashchim slepkom formy*) which anticipates the written poem (...) Today a kind of speaking in tongues is taking place. In sacred frenzy poets speak the language of all times, all cultures. Nothing is impossible. (CCPL:116; S-F,II:226-27)

The essay terminates with recourse to the "grain" image and an ultimate homeostatic claim:

> They say the cause of revolution is hunger in interplanetary space. Grain (*pshenitsa*) must be scattered through the ether.
> Classical poetry is the poetry of revolution. (CCPL:116; S-F,II:227)[20]

7. Exhumation

The badger's instinct for burrowing as a way to avert the threat of contingency served us as the initial analogy in a series of which the common theme was a descent and a subsequent return to the surface, augmented by significant retrieval. Thus, the timorous badger secured the comfort of his double exit; Poe, fearing premature burial, was rewarded with belated metamorphosis;[21] and the fossilized grains of wheat were, by judicious manipulation of textual reference, scattered through the ether.

Yet, while each member of the series has helped to emphasize the prevalence (in Mandel'shtam and elsewhere) of the dual process of katabasis and resurrection, no attention has been directed so far in this essay towards the primary vehicle for the myth of survival in *Tristia* (1922). This primary vehicle, and the structural principle organizing Mandel'shtam's lyric sequence, is the fitting mythological arbitress, Persephone. Brown has stated: "The goddess of *Tristia* is Persephone, queen of the afterlife and wife to Hades, and Mandelstam's city, where she now presides and which ... he calls Petropolis ... is a place of burial" (Brown 1973:255). If Persephone rules the Underworld in Classical mythology,

then equally she may be taken to reign over the subtext in *Tristia* (see section 14).

8. Logos

Repeatedly, in her essay on the impulse behind
the Mandel'shtamian text, Harris draws attention to
the radical significance of *philology* for the Russian
author. For example: "Mandelstam's literal definition
of "philology" (*philia + logos*) as the immediate, intense, direct "love of the word" is presented as the
only genuine and fully conscious response to poetry,
history and life" (CCPL:14). In support of this statement, she quotes from Mandel'shtam's most 'philological' essay, 'On the Nature of the Word'('O prirode
slova', 1922):

> Literature is a social phenomenon, while philology is
> domestic, intimate... Philology is the family because
> every family clings to its own intonations, its personal
> references (*na tsitate*), and to its own special meanings
> of words defined in parenthesis. The most casual utter-
> ance within a family takes on a nuance (*ottenok*) of its
> own. Moreover, such perpetual, distinctive, and purely
> philological nuancing defines the atmosphere of family
> life... I would derive Rozanov's attraction to the
> domestic quality of life, which so powerfully defined
> the entire structure of his literary activity, from the
> philological nature of his soul... (CCPL:14; S-F,II:249)[22]

Whereas Harris is concerned mainly with Mandel'-
shtam's prose (and autobiographical) writings, Mureddu is interested in the author's poetry and translations. As a result, she relates the Rozanov reference
directly to the poetry that starts from *Tristia*:

> Every human permanence is under threat of annihilation.
> There is a shift - marking the increasing importance of
> the everyday nature of the humanism to be saved - from
> the poetic 'word' towards the simple (but not conventio-
> nal, bureaucratic) 'word'. In this Rozanovian attitude,
> 'stone' has been definitively replaced by 'word', and
> if a thing symbolizes the dying humanism, then it is no
> longer a living material or organism, but a 'horse-shoe':
> witness to life but also a useless bygone. (Mureddu 1980:
> 59-60)

The *word* (*slovo, logos*), then, functions as the
basic, homeostatic unit - part of the system that is
"both breaking down ... and internally synthesizing
itself" (Friedrich 1978:54) - at once "empty shell"
and "kernel" (see note 22) to be scattered through
the ether. The 'philological' impulse extends to the
task of translation viewed as a stage in the homeo-

static enterprise of poetry (for poetry, like myth, possesses its inviolable "inner image" (cp. Mandel'-shtam:CCPL:407;S-F,II:374) and an outer form that "changes with time as a result of natural decay"(cp. Kerényi 1951:145)).

Mandel'shtam explicitly includes translation as one aspect of the poet's philological mission (in 'Torrents of Hackwork';'Potoki khaltury', 1929):

> Translation is one of the most difficult and responsible aspects of literary work. It is essentially the creation of an independent speech system on the basis of foreign material. Switching this system over to the Russian system requires tremendous effort, attention, will power, a wealth of inventiveness, intellectual freshness, philological sensibility, a huge lexical keyboard (*filologicheskogo chut'ia, bol'shoi slovarnoi klaviatury*) and the ability to listen carefully to rhythm, to grasp the picture of a phrase (*khvatit' risunok frazy*) and to convey it; and what is more this must all be accompanied by the strictest self-control. Otherwise the translation is merely interpolation. (CCPL:284-5; S-F,II:427)

9. Word

"Word" (*slovo*) occurs in six poems in *Tristia* (1922), which comprises 45 poems in all.[23] Three of the occurrences are tangential to the present examination. The poem 'I on a level with others...' ('Ia naravne s drugimi...',1920) belongs to those love poems addressed to Ol'ga Arbenina, which enjoy a large degree of thematic autonomy from the remainder of the lyric sequence(s) in the volume.[24] All the same, the image in the lines - "No word slakes/My parched mouth" ("Ne utoliaet slovo/Mne peresokhshikh ust") - is not without thematic relevance in the wider context of the *oeuvre* (Taranovsky 1976:108,128). In the poem 'Menagerie' ('Zverinets',1916) and in the title-poem, 'Tristia'(1918), "word" is used somewhat neutrally as designator, as in "The rejected word 'peace'..." ("Otverzhennoe slovo 'mir'...') and "Who can know at the word - parting,/What separation faces us" ("Kto mozhet znat' pri slove - rasstavan'e,/Kakaia nam razluka predstoit...") respectively. These usages need not detain us beyond the awareness of the materiality that words possess in Mandel'shtam's system. (In both 'philological' essays, 'The Word and Culture' and 'On the Nature of the Word', Mandel'shtam has discussed the relationship between *word* and *thing*, but the discussion is conducted in a language of metaphorical discourse that hardly clarifies the issue.)[25]

Two further poems, 'Solominka'(1916) and 'In

Petersburg we shall meet again...' ('V Peterburge my soidemsia snova...', 1920), are linked by the presence of the shared epithet "blessed" (*blazhennoe*) that is applied to "word" (*slovo*). This recurrence merits closer attention. In the first of these two poems, the pre-revolutionary 'Solominka', the line - "I have learned you, blessed words" - appears twice (as the final line in the fifth and last stanza of Part I and as the opening line of Part II). The "blessed words" in this difficult, Symbolist poem are female names. I quote Part II of the poem in full:

Я научился вам, блаженные слова,
Ленор, Соломинка, Лигейя, Серафита,
В огромной комнате тяжелая Нева,
И голубая кровь струится из гранита.

Декабрь торжественный сияет над Невой.
Двенадцать месяцев поют о смертном часе.
Нет, не соломинка в торжественном атласе
Вкушает медленный, томительный покой.

В моей крови живет декабрьская Лигейя
Чья в саркофаге спит блаженная любовь,
А та, соломинка, быть может Саломея,
Убита жалостью и не вернется вновь.

(I have learned you, blessed words,/Lenore, Solominka, Ligeia, Seraphita,/ In the huge room the heavy Neva,/ And blue blood is streaming from the granite.

Solemn December shines over the Neva./The twelve months sing death's hour./No, not a little straw in solemn satin/Tastes the slow, oppressive peace.

In my blood lives December's Ligeia,/Whose blessed love sleeps in the sarcophagus,/But the other, the little straw, perhaps Salomeia,/Killed by pity will not return again.)

It is as if a hybrid subtext has been superimposed upon a creatively transformed reminiscence.[26] The autobiographical reminiscence has been traced to the actual Salomeia Nikolaevna Andronikova (S-F,I: 431; Brown 1973:244; Taranovsky 1976:148), a "famous Georgian beauty and once the toast of St Petersburg" (Brown), upon whose first name the poet plays subtle variations in the course of the poem.[27] The variations supply the poem's title - 'Solominka' - which is both an intimate form of address and a diminutive of the word for 'straw' (*soloma*). As such, it is a good example of 'philology' in the sense defined by Mandel'-

shtam: "every family clings to its own intonations,
its personal references, and to its special meanings
of words defined in parenthesis"(CCPL:124; S-F,II:
249).

Extensive work has been done on the subtexts to
this poem. Brown has studied the resemblance between
this poem (including those in the unquoted first part
of the poem) and Poe's tale *Ligeia* (1838). His closing
remark is:

> The central moment of Poe's tale involves the changed
> identity of the two female figures, the metamorphosis
> of one into the other, and the gradual revelation of
> this to the 'I' of the narrator, and this (...) is also
> the fundamental concern of 'Solominka'. (Brown 1973:243)

Khardzhiev has uncovered the subtext of Gautier's
essay 'Charles Baudelaire', which would have been
available to Mandel'shtam in the recent Russian translation published in Petrograd in 1915, in which the
French writer had drawn together (as examples of a
type of *eternal woman*) the three names that accompany
Solominka in the second line of Part II of the poem
(Khardzhiev 1974:272).[28] Taranovsky has demonstrated
that 'Solominka' is connected with a poem in *Stone* –
'Insomnia. Homer. Taut sails.'('Bessonitsa. Gomer.
Tugie parusa',1915) – by the motif of insomnia and
the imagery of water filling up the room (Taranovsky
1976:147-48). In the same commentary he has also am-
plified the scope of the reference to *Salomeia*,which
the two earlier scholars had treated, by suggesting
that the literary source was Wilde's *Salomé*.

In all these references to separate subtexts
dealing with death and decadence, it seems to me that
one important linkage has so far been missed. "Séraphita", we may presume, does refer to Balzac's philo-
sophical novel of 1835, whose eponymous hero(ine) is
"finally transfigured and taken into heaven" (Brown
1973:243-44). Yet it surely has a stronger affinity
with a poem that was written in 1912 and published
in *Stone*, in which Mandel'shtam refers to Poe: 'We
cannot bear the tense silence'('My napriazhennogo
molchan'ia ne vynosim'). The relevant passage is
contained in the second stanza:

Я так и знал, кто здесь присутствовал незримо:
Кошмарный человек читает Улялюм.
Значенье – суэта, и слово – только шум,
Когда фонетика – служанка серафима.

(I knew who was invisibly present:/A nightmare man
is reading 'Ulalume'./Meaning is vanity, and the word only
noise,/When phonetics is the maidservant of the seraphim.)

Whether or not this be seen as an autobiographical reminiscence of a reading of Poe (by Piast) that Mandel'shtam attended (Brown 1973:200), or even as alluding to Mandel'shtam's inability to follow the English (Taranovsky 1976:10), it should not be allowed to obscure the association set up (by way of the "seraphim" reference) between Séraphita and Poe, which points to the occasions of inarticulacy (*shum*) in language. An additional linkage is afforded by the 'insomnia' motif, to which Taranovsky refers, that is present in the expression "nightmare man" (*koshmarnyi chelovek*). The "seraphim"/"blessed word" link is further reinforced by the line in one of the 'Arbenina' poems of *Tristia* (S-F,I:90-91, but not included in the original 1922 edition):

> Сначала думал я, что имя - серафим,
> И тела легкого дичился ...
> (At first I thought that the name was a seraphim,/And felt shy of its light body...)

Mandel'shtam's "Lenore", the last of the "seraphic" names to be considered, is perhaps closer thematically as well as acoustically to the 'lost Lenore' of Poe's hypnotic ballad, 'The Raven', than to his tale of the 'spiritualised' woman in 'Eleonora'. Both ballad and tale were translated by Bal'mont,[29] 'philological imports' of the Poe-kernel that "sprout(ed) up among us like a tree from a palm nut which had crossed the ocean on some steamship" (CCPL: 125; S-F,II:251). "Lenore", however, contains an allusiveness that goes beyond Poe to the ballad written by the German poet Bürger and twice rendered into Russian by Zhukovsky, first in the free version of 1808 (as 'Liudmila'[30]) and later in a more literal version of 1831 (as 'Lenora'). The dominant motif of the ballad 'Lenore', the heroine's terrifying night gallop with her bridegroom corpse, reverses the sexual polarity of Poe's couple, but preserves the underlying theme of love that overcomes death.

A reference in Mandel'shtam's essay 'Conversation about Dante' ('Razgovor o Dante'), confirms the fact that Bürger's ballad formed part of the poet's catalogue of translated literature ("migratory anecdotes") that amounted, in effect, to a homeopathic treatment for nightmare and insomnia:

> ... Ugolino's story is one of those migratory anecdotes, one of those horror stories (*koshmarik*) which mothers used to frighten their children, one of those entertaining horror tales which are mumbled with great satisfaction

as a remedy for insomnia (*kak sredstvo ot bessonnitsy*) while tossing and turning in bed. It is well known as a ballad, like Bürger's *Lenore*, the *Lorelei*, or the Erlkönig. (CCPL:428; S-F,II:398)

It is conceivable that in Mandel'shtam's mind the nineteenth-century variants of the migratory 'Lenore' did not only parallel the dominant mythologem of Persephone in *Tristia*, but that ultimately they converged with it, for Taranovsky has suggested that Professor F.F.Zelinsky (Tadeusz Zieliński) of Petrograd University was the main source for Mandel'shtam's 'Hellenism' (Taranovsky 1976:146). Taranovsky refers only to the two books, *Religion of Ancient Greece (Drevne-grecheskaia religiia*, 1918*)* and *Religion of Hellenism (Religiia ellenizma*, 1922), both published in Petrograd, as Mandel'shtam's source, but in an earlier collection of essays, *From the Life of Ideas* (*Iz zhizni idei*, 1905), which appeared in its third edition in Petrograd in 1916, Mandel'shtam could have found a piece entitled 'Antique Lenore' ('Antichnaia Lenora'). In it the author traces Bürger's Romantic ballad to its alleged Classical origins in the widespread story of Laodamia's love for the dead Protesilaus. One detail of Zieliński's erudite study of this "migratory anecdote" touches upon Persephone. Translating from the Byzantine grammarian Tzetzes, Zieliński quotes:

> ... the mythographers say that Persephone, having seen his (i.e. Protesilaus) beauty and his grief on separation (*o razluke*) from Laodania, requested Pluto to return (*vernut'*) life to him and she dispatched him from the abode of Hades to his wife. (Zieliński 1916:253)

These "blessed words", the "seraphic" female names, have been truly 'learned' by Mandel'shtam. However far we wish to pursue them, they may be taken as evidence of the "philological sensibility" and "huge lexical keyboard" (see section 8), which Mandel'shtam required for the switch from an alien system into Russian in the act of translation. In effect, what Mandel'shtam has accomplished in the transformation of the name-kernels in 'Solominka' is the translation of foreign material, not in the sense of a formal rendition, but rather as the grasping of the "picture of a phrase" and its communication ("making each phrase sound Russian and agree with the spirit of the original"; CCPL:327).

Mandel'shtam's is a keyboard exercise. He elaborates the idea in 'Conversation about Dante':

> Erudition is far from being equivalent to a keyboard of references for the latter comprises the very essence of

education.

By this I mean that a composition is formed not as a result of accumulated particulars, but due to the fact that one detail after another is torn away from the object, leaves it, darts out, or is chipped away from the system to go out into a new functional space or dimension, but each time at a strictly regulated moment and under circumstances which are sufficiently ripe and unique. (CCPL:401; S-F,II:368)

The poem which may be taken to complement 'Solominka' with respect to the motif of "blessed words" is 'In Petersburg we shall meet again'. Although much poetry had flowed under the bridge in the meantime, it is noticeable how the post-revolutionary poem picks up where the earlier lyric had left off - with the concept of *return*:

В Петербурге мы сойдемся снова,
Словно солнце мы похоронили в нем,
И блаженное, бессмысленное слово
В первый раз произнесем.

(In Petersburg we shall meet again,/As if we had buried the sun there,/And the blessed, meaningless word/We shall pronounce for the first time.)

The two poems share a common *chronotope*[31]: wintry Petropolis. Yet the second poem marks a decisive change for the poet. It is dated exactly - 25 November 1920 - and is the only poem in *Tristia* (1922) to be thus circumscribed. Indeed, only two others are even assigned to a particular month.[32] Furthermore, for the first and only time in the volume, the "northern capital" is designated by its old, tsarist name. Elsewhere it is called by the 'literary' name of *Petropolis*, which evokes the city of Derzhavin and Pushkin.[33]

This poem, then, of all the lyrics in *Tristia* (1922) acknowledges most explicitly the poet's "fall" into time, in "the black velvet of Soviet night/In the velvet of universal emptiness".[34] In the clearly historical context of the Petersburg poem, the "blessed words" of 'Solominka' have been transformed into the "blessed, meaningless word". At an autobiographical level, this development might be read as a foreshadowing of the barren 'silence' (spanning five years from 1925 to 1930), when Mandel'shtam composed no poetry at all, a period on which Taranovsky has remarked that "Mandel'stam's second 'silence' is not a myth, not a 'lyrical subject'; it is a staggering truth of art and life" (Taranovsky 1976:125-26).

Opinions differ as to what the *signatum* of the "blessed word(s)" may be. Words of love (Ginzburg 1975:294), free poetry (Brown 1973:235) and an infant's babble (Taranovsky 1976:140) are all interpretations that acknowledge the joy of recognition whereby the poet was able to bridge the gap between the spiritual and the secular, and thus effectively heal for himself the "rupture of continuity" that accompanies transition (cp. Stevens 1982:151).

10. Amnesia

The final poem that I intend to consider in this essay is the sixth in the series of lyrics in which the "word" motif is explicitly present. It is a poem whose first line extends the field of reference from the "meaningless" to the "forgotten" word: 'I have forgotten the word that I wanted to say' ('Ia slovo pozabyl, chto ia khotel skazat''). The poem poses contextual difficulties, for, although it is the last of the six "slovo" poems in *Tristia* (1922), it is placed fourth in the same series in the chronological arrangement of the definitive Struve-Filippov edition of the *Collected Works*. Moreover, it is given there the specific date of "November 1920" as opposed to the bare "1920" of *Tristia* (1922). A further complication is introduced by the publication (Berlin, 1923) of three thematically related poems as a unitary sequence under the general heading of 'Lethean Verses' ('Leteiskie stikhi'). These three poems are neither contiguous nor even arranged in the same order in *Tristia* (1922). For the present investigation, the chronological principle at work in the Struve-Filippov edition means that its sequence may be disregarded. On the other hand, the theme-specific Berlin sequence may be enlisted to establish pertinent connections between the *word* and *Persephone*.

In 'Lethean Verses', the poem that introduces the sequence and the poem which concludes it both make direct reference to Persephone, and thus may be said to constitute two of the four 'key' poems for the mythologem.[35] In this way, the dominant Persephone mythologem is indicated as being thematically relevant to the framed poem. Conversely, the direct reference that the middle poem makes to the "word" (and this appears as the title in an autograph copy (Khardzhiev 1972:278))may be shown to be extended *via* mediating prose links to the two framing poems. The link with the first poem, 'When Psyche-life descends to the shades...' ('Kogda Psikheia-shizn' spuskaetsia k teniam...'), is forged through the reference to Psyche in 'The Word and Culture': "Is the thing really master of the word? The word is a Psyche" (see note 25); and the link with the third poem, 'Take for joy from my palms...' ('Voz'mi na radost' iz moikh ladonei...'), through the affinity with Gumilev's poem 'The Word' ('Slovo',1921) from which Mandel'shtam quoted for the epigraph to 'On the Nature of the Word'. Gumilev's poem and the third 'Lethean' verse share the image of "dead bees".[36]

If the context of 'Lethean Verses' establishes the unnamed presence of Persephone in 'I have forgotten the word that I wanted to say', then the title which this poem was given in *Tristia* (1922), namely, 'The Swallow' ('Lastochka'), demonstrates that the link with the Underworld was combined with other associations.[37] I quote 'The Swallow' in full:

1

Я слово позабыл, что я хотел сказать:
Слепая ласточка в чертог теней вернется
На крыльях срезанных с прозрачными играть.
В беспамятстве ночная песнь поется.

2

Не слышно птиц. Бессмертник не цветет,
Прозрачны гривы табуна ночного,
В сухой реке пустой челнок плывет,
Среди кузнечиков беспамятствует слово.

3

И медленно растет как шатер иль храм,
То вдруг прикинется безумной Антигоной,
То мертвой ласточкой бросается к ногам
С стигийской нежностью и веткою зеленой.

4

О, если бы вернуть и зрячих пальцев стыд,
И выпуклую радость узнаванья,
Я так боюсь рыданья Аонид,
Тумана, звона и зиянья.

5

А смертным власть дана любить и узнавать,
Для них и звук в персты прольется,
Но я забыл, что я хочу сказать,
И мысль бесплотная в чертог теней вернется.

6

Все не о том прозрачная твердит,
Все ласточка, подружка, Антигона, ...
А на губах, как черный лед, горит
Стигийского воспоминанье звона.

(1. I have forgotten the word that I wanted to say:/The blind swallow will return to the hall of shades/On clipped wings to play with the transparent ones./In oblivion the night song is sung.

2. No birds sing. The immortelle does not flower,/Transparent the manes of the nocturnal herd of horses,/In the dry river an empty canoe is drifting,/Among grasshoppers oblivious becomes the word.

3. And slowly it grows as if tent or temple,/Suddenly it will feign mad Antigone,/Then, dead swallow, it plunges down to one's feet/With Stygian tenderness and a green branch.

4. O, if only the shame of seeing fingers would return,/ And the cupped joy of recognition,/I so much fear the sobbing of the Muses,/Mist, ringing and hiatus.

5. Mortals are given the power to love and recognize,/ For them even the sound spills through fingers,/But I have forgotten what I wanted to say,/And fleshless thought will return to the hall of shades.

6. Still the transparent one talks of other things,/ Still swallow, friend, Antigone.../And on the lips, like black ice, burns/Remembrance of Stygian ringing.)

Read as the middle stage in a tripartite sequence, the lyrical action in this poem is perceived as taking place between katabasis (when Psyche-life *descends* to the shades) and resurrection, in which the return is augmented by significant retrieval (in the injunction to *take for joy* from my palms). The 'moment' of the poem - the same "flash of recognition" as in 'Tristia', when compulsion meets monad - is alluded to in the prose account of 'The Word and Culture':

> The poem lives through an inner image, that ringing mold of form which anticipates the written poem. There is not yet a single word, but the poem can already be heard. (CCPL:116; S-F,II:227)

"Recognition" (*uznavan'e*) is a noun that occurs in only two poems in *Tristia* (1922) - the title poem and 'The Swallow'. In the title-poem, with its Ovidian intimations of exile, the setting is also Grecian, but one that is within the historical Hellenism of the nocturnal Akropolis rather than within the mythic Hellenism of the Underworld. Thus the "sobbing of the Muses" in the Underworld poem becomes the "women's weeping (*zhenskii plach*) mingled with the Muses' singing" in 'Tristia', and it is a "fire" (and

not supernatural "black ice") that burns in the Akropolis. Nevertheless, the echoes and reminiscences
are sufficiently strong to suggest a thematic linkage. If the lyrical 'persona in Hades turns his
thoughts to the "seeing fingers" of mortals, then
the speaker in 'Tristia', watching the activity of
busy fingers at the shuttle (*chelnok*)[38] of the loom,
refuses to turn his mind to the goings-on in the
abode of Persephone: "It is not for us to conjecture
about Greek Erebus" ("Ne nam gadat' o grecheskom
Erebe"). The thematic bond, however, is most firmly
marked by the celebration in each poem of the "Joy"
(*radost'*) and "recognition" (*uznavan'e*) that form part
of the gift of language.

11. Remembrance

The Orphic *synthema*, or 'passport' for the dead,
carried the instruction that the deceased should
choose the fountain of Mnemosyne, remembrance, and
not the fountain of Lethe, forgetfulness (Kerényi
1951:213). This instruction has reappeared in many
guises over the centuries since the time it flourish-
ed in the two ancient mysteries of initiation - of
Dionysus and the vine, of Demeter and the ear of
corn,[39] rites of passage that asserted the power of
human love and community over death itself. In modern
poetry, it finds a particular resonance in David
Jones's long work, *The Anathemata* (1952), in the celebration of *anamnesis*, which the poet derives directly
from the Christian testament[40]

Remembrance, as a form of *anamnesis*, is so prevalent an imperative of the human psyche that no individual provenance may be singled out as the subtext
for the motif that encompasses *recognition* in Mandel'-
shtam's writings. All the same, it is of interest to
note that 'The Swallow', in moving from the lexicon
of Lethe in the opening line to that of Mnemosyne in
the closing line - "Remembrance of Stygian ringing"
- hints at a formulaic subtext in the oldest recorded
source for the Persephone mythologem. The hymn 'To
Demeter', the second of the so-called Homeric Hymns,
was composed *circa* 645-25 B.C.[41] The closing formula
in twelve of the thirty-four hymns, including the
longer ones 'To Demeter' and 'To Hermes', is "But I
will remember you and also another song" (Sargent
1973:viii). This formula is repeated from hymn to
hymn so mechanically that, on occasion, it strikes
an incongruous note of humour to the modern ear, as
in the conclusion to the hymn 'To Demeter':

May you and your daughter, surpassingly lovely Persephone,

graciously grant for the sake of my song a suitable
stipend. But I will remember you, goddess, and a new
song as well. (*ibid.*:14)

The first hymn, 'To Dionysos', provides the justification for repeating the formula from hymn to hymn:
"... for in no way at all/ If we forget you can we
recall sacred song" (*ibid.*:1). Mandel'shtam echoes this
'Homeric' credo in his poem 'The Horseshoe Finder'
('Nashedshii podkovu'):

Трижды блажен, кто введет в песнь имя

(Thrice blessed, who introduces a name into his song)

Such a song, which lives longer than others, is
"cured" of oblivion (*istseliaiushchei ot bespamiatstva*) in
this way.

In the historically more proximate subtext of
'Ligeia', which Gautier examples as presenting the
type of the *eternal woman* who is "spiritualised"
(*besplotnaia*; cp. 'Lastochka' 1.20), a similar foregrounding of recognition (*uznavan'e*) as a function of
the semantic continuum 'remembrance/forgetfulness'
and the mythological pairing 'Mnemosyne/Lethe' occurs.
The narrator's opening words concern *forgetting* ("I
cannot, for my soul, remember..." Poe II,310),
against which is immediately set the *name* as that
which survives ("... it is by that sweet word alone
- by Ligeia - that I bring before mine eyes in fancy
the image of her who is no more" (Poe ed.1978:310)).
Later,this process of recollection is further expati-
ated upon in the narrator's observation of the fact
"that, in our endeavors to recall to memory something
long forgotten, we often find ourselves *upon the very
verge* of remembrance, without being able, in the end,
to remember" (*ibid.*:313-14; his italics. Cp. Saussure's
remark in note 6).

12.'Keys

Mandel'shtam operated a 'huge lexical keyboard"
(CCPL:284; S-F,II:427). Certain keys bearing upon
translation have been identified in this essay.
Translation, however, is a diffuse concept in Mandel'-
shtam - he refers at one point to Bal'mont, slight-
ingly, as the "rare case of a typical translation
without an original" (CCPL:125; S-F,II:251) - and
the issue is not simplified by his anti-evolutionary
insistence that "we are free from the burden of memories", since "not a single poet has yet appeared"
(CCPL:114; S-F,II:224). It is entirely consistent
with Mandel'shtam's view that "a verbal representa-

tion is a complex composite of phenomena, it is a
connection, a 'system'" (CCPL:129; S-F,II:256) to
find (*pace* Mureddu's conclusion that Mandel'shtam
"succeeded in preserving a remarkable fidelity to
the semantic content and to the sound-structure of
the Italian texts" (Mureddu 1980:78)) that the com-
piler of the Soviet edition of the poetry has repeated laconically, in the notes to each of the four renderings of Petrarch, "free translation" (*vol'nyi pere-
vod*; Khardzhiev 1974:315).

Nevertheless, what has emerged from this study
of subtexts is that recurrent keys are sounded, and
that some of these keys coincide with the cultural
keys that constitute the central focus for literary
translation in Russia in the first quarter of the
twentieth century. The metamorphosis of Poe, initiated
in Europe by Baudelaire and soon afterwards enshrined
in the Symbolist diction of Mallarmé, which reached
the Russian public largely through the translations
of Bal'mont, is one specific instance. More pervasive-
ly, the recrudescence of the Hellenic spirit was accomplished in the Russian Symbolist era (1895-1910)
through the translations and imitations of the original Classical dramatists and poets in the works of
two of the most powerful influences on the early life
of Mandel'shtam, namely Viacheslav Ivanov and
Annensky. [42]

The teleological function of the translation as
an "afterlife" (according to Benjamin) is subsidiary
to Mandel'shtam's more extensive quest: to seek an
anodyne for his cosmic "nostalgia". In this quest,
the "heuristic" (Brown 1973:240) value of names and
naming was fundamental. As early as 1924, Tynianov
had observed that Mandel'shtam "loves personal names,
because they are not words, but nuances of words"
(Tynianov 1929:572), and he was one of the first
critics to draw attention to the indirect meanings
(*kosvennye znacheniia*) in the poet's semantic system:

> The semantic system in Mandel'shtam is such that *one*
> image acquires a decisive role for the entire poem,
> one verbal series also imperceptibly colours all the
> others - this is the *key (kliuch)* to all the hier-
> archies of images (*ibid*.:570)

Yet such 'keys', Tynianov explained, are not necessary. The 'missing link' is always supplied: "It is
created from *verse to verse*; the nuance, the colour of
the word in each verse is not lost, it is condensed
(*sgushchaetsia*) in the following one" (*ibid*. :571-72).
The same point is made by Brown, in a tone of mock
exasperation, when he attempts to separate *Tristia*

from *Stone*. "His poems won't stay apart", he complains (Brown 1973:207).

For Mandel'shtam, the spoken name is an aspect of the poetic shaping of reality. A name, in itself, may be a *nuance* (*ottenok*) - a "blessed, meaningless word", but "blessed words" are the nucleus of a living reality. The transformation of the name in 'Solominka' is its most salient feature, as it changes from Salomeia to the heroines of Bürger, Poe and Balzac - Lenore, Ligeia and Séraphita - all subject to transformation in their original texts.

13. Shades

Tynianov's statement that Mandel'shtam "loves personal names, because they are not words, but nuances of words" involves a play upon "nuance" (*ottenok*), which in Russian is etymologically linked to the word 'shade' (*ten'*), a lexically prominent unit in *Tristia*, where it is associated with Persephone's Underworld. When Tynianov writes of Mandel'shtam that "U nego ne slova, a teni slov", the sentence may be rendered in English by means of an equivalent idiom: "In him there is no meaning, only shades of meanings". The nuance of the unnamed presence, especially the female presence, in *Tristia* (1922), would seem to be grounded either directly or through mediation (parallelism) in death's chamber, the misty, underworld abode of Persephone.[43]

Kerényi, with reference to the "shade" of Patroclus (*Iliad*, Book XXIII), has written:

> Instead of a single terrifying shape, the whole kingdom of the dead rises up to oppose the entry of the soul of one not yet buried (...) the shadowy, amorphous kingdom seen as the congregation of all the souls (...). Taken individually, the souls are not amorphous: they are the *images of the departed* (...) but not corpse-like images. (Kerényi 1951:172-73)

Each εἴδωλον in the realm of the dead represents "the *minimum conceivable amount of form* ... the image with which the deceased individual, through his uniqueness, has enriched the world" (*ibid.*:173). In Kerényi's reading of the myth, the Persephone aspect is understood as constituting the *uniqueness* of the individual and the *enthralment to not-being* (*ibid.*:172). The correspondences with Mandel'shtam's transformation of the mythologem are striking.[44] Above all, the peculiar centrality of Persephone as the deity ruling over Mandel'shtam's city of Petropolis is justified in Kerényi's remark:

> Over the countless "images" of all that has once been,

now heaped together and merged into an indeterminate
mass there reigns *Persephone* - the eternally unique.
(*ibid.*:173)

14. Silence

The past, while ceasing to be present, does not
cease to exist, or rather *subsist*; it is *present in its
absence* (Capek 1971:160). As the Underworld is the
insubstantial counterpart to the world of the living,
so, we might say, the *underword* (or subtext) is the
counterpart to, and precondition of, the incarnated
word. The 'word made flesh' is the word (trans)formed.
Such is the ontological basis of Mandel'shtam's
'philological' poetics (CCPL:120-21: S-F,II:244-45).
Brown has defined this *underword* as the *silence* that
precedes Mandel'shtam's creativity: "The poems came
from silence where they were perfect: such is his
Platonic notion" (Brown 1973:175). While I would
agree with the identification of a silent, pre-formal
matrix for the Mandel'shtamian *logos*, I believe that
Brown errs in attributing it to the *anamnesis* of Plato,
for this deprives it of the attachment to the *eidolon*
of the Underworld. The notion is far more Plutonic
than Platonic. The Greek concept of 'not being' is
intimately associated with Persephone in her aspect
of αρρητος κουρα ("the Maiden not to be named").
Kerényi stresses the central significance of the
αρρητον[45] ("something worthy of note but not to be
named") in Demeter's *gift*[46] to mortals in the Eleusinian mystery cult. The Homeric hymn 'To Demeter', he
remarks, "is completely unthinkable without this
allusion to the mysterious, supreme gift of the goddess" (Kerényi 1951:160). Wordless knowing is the
possession of the visionary knower.

The 'moment' that the lyric utterance celebrates
in its act of recognition cannot be recalled into existence, but it may be re-cognized through the creative imagination, when the poetic impulse overcomes
the Orpheus-like temptation to look back too fondly
at non-being, towards the "hall of shades", and "for-
gets" the word. In that Underworld, "Persephone
reigns, the eternally unique one who is no more"
(*ibid.*:172), or, to allow the final word to Mandel'-
shtam:

> Богиня моря, грозная Афина,
> Сними могучий каменный шелом.
> В Петрополе прозрачном мы умрем,
> Здесь царствуешь не ты, а Прозерпина.

(Sea goddess, terrible Athene,/Take off your mighty stone
helmet./In transparent Petropolis we shall die,/Where you
do not reign, but Proserpine.

NOTES

1. The text consulted for *Tristia* is the Ardis facsimile
(Ann Arbor, 1972) of the original edition (Petersburg/Berlin,
1922) brought out by the Petropolis publishing house in a tirage
of 3000 copies. Part of my argument is based on the original
lyric sequence, an arrangement that differs significantly in
places from both the Soviet selection (Khardzhiev) and the
emigré collection (S-F) of Mandel'shtam's poetry, each of which
attempts to follow a chronological order of composition. Although I have seen no reason to preserve the old orthography of
Tristia (1922), the punctuation of that edition is preferred to
the emendations in S-F and Khardzhiev. For a history of the
editions of *Tristia*, see Brown 1973:159-60,219-20; Khardzhiev
1974:251-52 and S-F,I:371-73. All translations of Mandel'shtam's
poetry are my own.

2. Mandel'shtam's phrase (*toska po mirovoi kul'ture*) is
given, *inter alia*, in Akhmatova 1968,II:185. An account of
Akmeism, and further reference, is given in H.B.Weber (ed.),
The Modern Encyclopedia of Russian and Soviet Literature (Gulf
Breeze, Fl., 1977-),I:25-30, under the entry *Acmeism* (by H.W.
Tjalsma). See also CCPL:582-83.

3. The most authoritative study of Mandel'shtam as literary
translator is Mureddu's analysis of the principles at work in
the Russian poet's versions of Petrarch. Mandel'shtam's literary translations were extensive, his 'Translations and Imitations' occupying nearly sixty pages in S-F I (with additional
material in S-F II and IV). Mandel'shtam also wrote two prose
articles on translation: 'Torrents of Hackwork' ('Potoki khaltury') and 'On Translations' ('O perevodakh'), both 1929. See
CCPL:283-96; S-F,II:425-41.

4. Taranovsky lists 24 separate sources for "obvious reminiscences" and "enciphered subtexts" in Mandel'shtam's poetry.
His comment that "such reminiscences, and even direct quotations,
acquire a new quality in his work" (Taranovsky 1976:3) corresponds with Bowra's definition of *parodiorthosis*. Taranovsky's
whole essay ('Concert at the Railroad Station: The Problem of
Context and Subtext'(Taranovsky 1976:1-20), is a meticulous
corroboration of the view that "recognition" operates as a
crucial organizing principle in Mandel'shtam's poetry.

5. Translations from Mandel'shtam's prose are taken from
CCPL, and are accompanied by a reference locating the Russian
source in S-F.

6. Saussure's manuscript remark, the whole of which is
significant for Mandel'shtam's poetics, may be quoted: "one
must not (...) distrust the intention of the author to follow,
insofar as is possible, what was said before him. It is this

impulse which is responsible for a profound conservative tendency which dominates the realm of legend. But Imagination, *across a memory gap*, is the principal factor of change, given the will to resist change which is otherwise in the tradition" (J.Starobinski, *Words upon Words:The Anagrams of Ferdinand de Saussure*; (transl. O.Emmet; New Haven, Yale University Press, 1979)).

7. For a discriminating analysis of the nuances of the "central sun", see Taranovsky 1976:54-55,150-52. One instance of the "buried sun" in *Tristia* is quoted in section 9 of the present essay.

8. See the introductory essay ('Mandelstam: The Poet as Builder') in Tracy's translation of the *Kamen'* poems for a comprehensive treatment of *stone* and *building* as themes (and metaphors) in the early Mandel'shtam. For the text of 'Morning of Acmeism' ('Utro akmeizma'), the poet's Akmeist 'manifesto' written in 1913, but not published until 1919, see CCPL:61-65; S-F,II:320-25.

9. E.Rusinko, 'Acmeism, Post-symbolism, and Henri Bergson', *Slavic Review*, vol.41,1982:494-510, is a recent discussion of *post*-symbolist aspects of Akmeism.

10. See V.A.Zhukovsky, 'O basne i basniakh Krylova', in *Sobranie sochinenii v chetyrekh tomakh* (Moscow, 1960),IV:410.

11. Mandel'shtam's definitive statement (in 'On the Nature of the Word'; 'O prirode slova', 1922) is: "An image is merely a word that has been sealed up, which cannot be touched" (CCPL: 128; S-F,II:254). The hermetic property of poetry is the subject of his essay 'On the Addressee' ('O sobesednike', 1913; CCPL:67-73; S-F,II:233-40), in which he states that "the poem is addressed to 'the reader in posterity'" (CCPL:69; S-F,II:235).

12. For the extent of Poe's reception in Russia, see J.D. Grossman, *Edgar Allan Poe in Russia: A Study in Legend and Literary Influence* (Würzburg, 1973). Chapters IV and VI treat the Poe-Bal'mont connection. Grossman refers to Baudelaire's handling of the Poe legend and gives a list of earlier critical studies (*ibid.*:8-13,217). An omission from her list is P.M. Wetherill, *Charles Baudelaire et la poésie d'Edgar Allan Poe* (Paris, 1962).

13. Quotations from this essay are taken from Zohn's translation with reference, where necessary, to Benjamin's original German phrasing.

14. For further commentary on this poem, see Schlott 1981: 48-54 and Tracy 1981:216-17.

15. Mandel'shtam's severest indictment of 'progress' (in adult life) is contained in his essay 'On the Nature of the Word'. See CCPL:118-19; S-F,II:243-44.

16. Kerényi glosses the *monad* of Frobenius as "an *inability to see otherwise*" when in the "possession" of the natural world and cultural history (Kerényi 1951:27). In this connection, it is worth comparing Mureddu's reference to *confession* as the emptying of one's self in order to be possessed by the "Other"

(Mureddu 1980:62).

17. Harris derives the terms "impulse" and "text" from Mandel'shtam's essay 'Conversation about Dante'. Her comment that "one of the major impulses informing Mandelstam's esthetic vision is the idea of recurrence and its expression through metamorphosis" (CCPL:45) is substantially at one with the main argument of the present essay.

18. "Any unit of poetic speech, be it a line, a stanza or an entire lyrical composition, must be regarded as a single word (*kak edinoe slovo*). For instance, when we enunciate the word 'sun', we do not toss out an already prepared meaning – this would be tantamount to semantic abortion – rather we are experiencing a peculiar cycle" (CCPL:407; S-F,II:374).

19. Eliot wrote that "whoever has approved this idea of order, of the form of European, of English literature, will not find it preposterous that the past should be altered by the present as much as the present is directed by the past."

20. In a note (CCPL:613), Harris relates the 'grain' reference to the poem 'I love the gray silence under the arches...' ('Liubliu pod svodami sedyia tishiny...', 1921). Significantly, this is the last poem in *Tristia* (both in S-F(I:91) and, with a different opening, in the 1922 edition). The poem, and therefore *Tristia*, ends with the line: "The grain of deep, full faith" (*Zerno glubokoi, polnoi very*). Harris does not mention, however, the closer congruence of the "grain" reference with a line from a later poem 'And the sky is pregnant with the future...' ('A nebo budushchim beremenno...', 1923): "And the sky is pregnant with the future,/ With the wheat of sated ether" ("A nebo budushchim beremenno,/ Pshenitsei sytogo efira") (S-F,I:146). The 'wheat-ether' image is discussed by Taranovsky, who points to a subtext in Gurdzhiev: "Mandel'štam transformed Gurdziev's fantastic cosmology into a new poetic myth" (Taranovsky 1976:6).

21. Poe's 'exhumation', of course, belongs to the cultural history of the epoch and is not a part of the poet's private symbolic system. Yet it is interesting to find the following parallel in Mandel'shtam's prose: "Would you like to know the key to the epoch, the book which had positively become white-hot from handling, *the book which would not under any circumstances agree to die, that lay like someone alive in the narrow coffin of the 1890s* ... whose first page bore the features of a youth with an inspired hairdo, features that became an icon?" (quoted in CCPL:587; italics mine, L.B.). It is the poet Nadson (1862–1887) to whom Mandel'shtam alludes.

22. The sentence continues (although Harris does not quote it in her essay): "... which, in its indefatigable search for the kernel, nibbled and cracked his every word, every utterance, leaving us only empty shells" (CCPL:124; S-F,II:249). The word for "kernel" here is *oreshok*, the diminutive of 'nut' (*orekh*).

23. Brown (1973:220) counts 46, but Khardzhiev (1974:251) and the table of contents to *Tristia* (1922) agree on 45 as the

total number of poems.

24. Brown (1973:245-52) devotes a section to 'The Poems to Olga Arbenina', and Taranovsky (1976:108,164) discusses the influence that the actress had on Mandel'shtam's lyric poetry written at the end of 1920. Both scholars stress the *transformation* in the poetry of actual encounters with women whom the poet loved (Brown 1973:245; Taranovsky 1976:61,152).

25. In 'The Word and Culture': "The word is flesh and bread. It shares the fate of flesh and bread: suffering ... Is the thing really master of the word? The word is a Psyche. The living word does not designate an object, but freely chooses for its dwelling place, as it were, some objective significance, material thing, like the soul around an abandoned, but not forgotten body." (CCPL:115; S-F,II:226); and in 'On the Nature of the Word': "What can be done when a word is fettered to its denotative meaning: doesn't this amount to serfdom? But a word is not a thing. Its significance is not a translation of itself." (CCPL:129; S-F,II:255).

26. Compare: "The Russian language, just like the Russian national spirit, is formed through ceaseless hybridization (*iz beskonechnykh primesei*), cross-breeding, grafting, and external influences" (CCPL:120; S-F,II:245).

27. Brown (1973:237-45) deals at length with this poem and the problems inherent in translating its 'acoustics'.

28. Gautier wrote of the "ideal ever sought, never attained; highest, divine beauty incarnated in the form of a woman, etherealised, spiritualised (*besplotnaia* in the Russian translation (Khardzhiev 1974:272))(...) like Edgar Allan Poe's Ligeias (...) and Eleonoras, and (...) Balzac's Séraphita-Séraphitus" (quoted from *The Works of Gautier*, XII (Boston,1903): 68; transl. F.C. de Sumichrast).

29. The history of the translation of 'Eleonora' and 'The Raven' into Russian is treated extensively in Grossman (see note 12). It is perhaps significant that 'The Raven' is the example that Poe cites in his 'acoustic' account of poetic creativity in 'The Philosophy of Composition'.

30. Zhukovsky returned to the theme of Bürger's 'Lenore' in 1812, when he gave the heroine the Russian name Svetlana and the ballad the happy ending that his first version lacked. In 'Svetlana' the heroine, recognizing the power of love to reach across the limits set by mortality, achieves a victory over the dream-death that is Liudmila's fate.

31. For *chronotope*, see M.M.Bakhtin's essay (1837-38), translated as 'Forms of Time and of the Chronotope in the Novel' in *The Dialogic Imagination* (ed. M.Holquist; Austin, 1981):84-258, and found in Russian in M.M.Bakhtin, *Voprosy literatury i estetiki* (Moscow, 1975):234-407. Both Bakhtin and Mandel'shtam (in 'Conversation about Dante') use Dante as a point of reference in their exposition of the aesthetic time-place co-ordinate.

32. Both the poems ascribed to a specific month (December

1920) belong to the 'Arbenina cycle'. Of the remaining 42 poems, 17 are not dated and 25 are dated according to the year only (1916:10; 1917:4; 1918:3; 1919:3; 1920:4; 1921:1).

33. A useful review of the literary myth and historical reality of St Petersburg as a topos as it pertains to Mandel'-shtam is to be found in Schlott 1981:134-43.

34. "V chernom barkhate sovetskoi nochi/ V barkhate vsemirnoi pustoty". *Black velvet*, a popular poetic commodity of the period (it appears, for example, in the poetry of Annensky, Bely and Blok), recalls the "solemn satin" of 'Solominka' and the "red velvet" (*barkhat alyi*) of Bal'mont's 'Raven' translation.

35. Strictly speaking, Persephone occurs lexically in only *three* poems, the fourth reference being to "Proserpine" (in the poem quoted at the conclusion of this essay). For an analysis of the two framing 'Persephone' poems, with regard to Classical myth, see Schlott 1981:181-208.

36. The image of "dead bees", common to Mandel'shtam and Gumilev, is one that has wider ramifications in the (post-) Symbolist debate in Russia early in this century; see Taranovsky 1976:165-67 and Schlott 1981:198-99. For further discussion of 'Take for joy from my palms...', see N.A.Nilsson, 'Mandel'stam's Poem 'Voz'mi na radost'', *Russian Literature* 7-8,1974:165-80 (reprinted in his book, *Osip Mandel'stam: Five Poems* (Uppsala, 1974)); Ginzburg 1975:295-96; and Burnett 1981:414-17.

37. Ginzburg comments that the *swallow* is one of Mandel'-shtam's favourite images, and that its significance varies from context to context (Ginzburg 1975:305). In the poem that I quote, she interprets it as standing for the "unspoken word" (*ibid.*:295;cp.306). Other significant associations include the 'soul' in Classical mythology (Brown 1973:252; Schlott 1981: 184); Derzhavin's poem 'The Swallow' ('Lastochka', 1792; Taranovsky 1976:158; Schlott 1981:185); and Ol'ga Arbenina.

38. *Chelnok* has two meanings in Russian: (1) *canoe*; (2) *shuttle*. It is employed in the first sense in 'The Swallow' and in the second sense in 'Tristia'. Thus, a further connection between the two poems is established at the homonymic level of recurrence. *Chelnok* is not a frequent lexical choice in Mandel'-shtam's poetry. It occurs in only one other poem in *Tristia* (1922), a poem discussed at length by Taranovsky in his essay 'The Clock-Grasshopper' (1976:68-82).

39. "As a sacrificial victim and one who is doomed, Diony-sus is the male counterpart of Persephone" (Kerényi 1951:193); "The ear of corn sprouting and ripening with supernatural sud-denness belongs to the mysteries of Demeter just as the grape that ripens in a few hours belongs to the drunken festivals of Dionysus" (Otto, quoted in Kerényi 1951:255). Friedrich points to the close connection between Orphism and the cult of Demeter (contemporaneously intensified in the seventh century B.C.): "... the myth of Orpheus descending into Hades to retrieve Eurydice has been perceived as a transformation of the myth of

Persephone's abduction" (Friedrich 1978:153). In similar fashion, the two myths are contemporaneously intensified in modern poetry, by Rilke and Mandel'shtam, in 1922-23.

40. See Part VII of *The Anathemata*, 'Mabinog's Liturgy'. Compare: "Poetry is to be diagnosed as 'dangerous' because it evokes and recalls, is a kind of *anamnesis* of, i.e. is an effective recalling of, something loved" (Jones 1972:21). Jones's allusion to the Christian sacramental use of corn and wine in Part VIII of *The Anathemata*, "Sherthursdaye and Venus Day", draws the Persephone mythologem into the poetic network of references: "Upon a time/ the Daughter's torch/ Demeter's arch/ extinguished/ down/ in our streets/ where is corn and wine?" (*ibid.*:231-32). The image of the "Daughter's torch ... extinguished" may be glossed by recourse to Kerényi, who notes that the "doused torches in the dark" precede the "finding" of the Kore (Kerényi 1951:197).

41. R.Janko, *Homer, Hesiod and the Hymns* (Cambridge University Press, 1982) establishes the hymn 'To Demeter' as falling within the range of absolute dates 678-625 B.C. (*ibid.*: 231) and prefers *circa* 645-25 B.C.

42. J.West, *Russian Symbolism: A Study of Vyacheslav Ivanov and the Russian Symbolist Aesthetic* (London, 1970), examines the "dynamic" (or transformational) function of Classical myth in Ivanov's aesthetic theories and demonstrates the centrality of Ivanov's theories for the Russian Symbolist movement as a whole (although he does not extend his study to cover Mandel'-shtam and Akmeism). Setchkarev (1963) considers the influential translations and imitations from Greek myth (and French Symbolism) that Annensky produced in his career as a "classical philologist". (His mythological tragedy, *Laodamiia* (1906), provided Mandel'shtam with an additional source to that of Zielinski for the "antique Lenore" reference. Annensky's formulation in the foreword to his tragedy was "Thessalian Lenore" (*Fessaliiskaia Lenora*); cp. Setchkarev 1963:184). Mandel'shtam offers a remarkable appraisal of Annensky as the representative of "heroic Hellenism, martial philology" (CCPL:126; S-F,II:252) in 'On the Nature of the Word'.

43. Kerényi, in a reference to "the strange equation of marriage and death, the bridal chamber and the grave" (Kerényi 1951:179), singles out Antigone as a mortal counterpart to "beautiful Persephone". The heroines of Bürger and Poe would qualify readily as modern equivalents.

44. Mandel'shtam was, of course, familiar with the Homeric account of the "hall of shades" in *The Iliad*, which constitutes a clear subtext for the poem 'When Psyche-life descends to the shades...' ('Kogda Psikheia-zhizn' spuskaetsia k teniam...').

45. Setchkarev (see note 42) mentions Annensky's reference to the *arriton* in discussing Briusov's symbolic eroticism; "His forbidden words (αρρητον) are words par excellence, sound combinations knowing their own value, just as are his unutterable (αφατον) words, words seeking for a - perhaps forgotten - symbol"

(setchkarev 1963:222). Annensky, who translated all 19 surviving
tragedies of Euripides (*ibid.*:150), would have known at first
hand the "unutterable thing hinted at in the very name" of the
Kore figure Persephone – αρρητος κουρα – (Kerényi 1951:163),
for the Greek expression is from Euripides' *Helen*, 1307 (fr.63).
For a discussion of the unnamed Penelope in *Tristia*, in connection with the significance for Mandel'shtam of *logos* and of
"finding what is lost", see Burnett 1981:409.
    46. The meaning of Demeter's gift is *immortality* (Kerényi
1951:161). As such, it is the equivalent of the 'finding' of
what has been lost. In the Eleusinian mystery, this was the
place of the ευρεσις, the finding of Persephone: "In this finding something was *seen* – no matter through what symbols – that
was objective and subjective at once. Objectively, the idea of
the goddess regaining her daughter, and therefore *herself*,
flashed on the experient's soul. Subjectively, the same flash
of revelation showed him his own continuity, the continued existence of all living things" (*ibid.*:196). The *gift* (or transference of a valued object) is the theme of several poems in
Tristia (1922). In 'Take for joy from my palms...' the transference motif merges with the transformation motif: "Take then
for joy my wild gift –/ A rough, dry necklace/ Of dead bees,
which have transformed honey into sun" ("Voz'mi zh na radost'
dikii moi podarok –/ Nevzrachnoe sukhoe ozherel'e/ Iz mertvykh
pchel, med prevrativshikh v solntse").

REFERENCES

AKHMATOVA, A.
1968   *Sochineniia*. Ed. G.P.Struve & B.A.Filippov. Vol.2.
            Washington, Inter-Language Literary Associates
BENJAMIN, W.
1961   'Die Aufgabe des Übersetzers', in his *Illuminationen:
            Ausgewählte Schriften* (Frankfurt A.M., Suhrkamp):59-69
1973   'The Task of the Translator', in his *Illuminations*
            (ed. H.Arendt, transl. H.Zohn; London, Fontana/Collins,
            :69-82
BOWRA, C.M.
1967   *The Creative Experiment* (1949; repr. 1967). London
            Macmillan
BROWN, C.
1973   *Mandelstam*. Cambridge, University Press
BURNETT, L.
1981   'Heirs of Eternity: An Essay on the Poetry of Keats
            and Mandel'shtam', *The Modern Language Review* lxxvi:
            396-419
ČAPEK, M.
1971   *Bergson and Modern Physics*. Dordrecht, Reidel
CCPL = MANDEL'SHTAM, O.
1979   *The Complete Critical Prose and Letters*. Ed. J.G.
            Harris; transl. J.G.Harris & C.Link. Ann Arbor, Ardis

FRIEDRICH, P.
1978   *The Meaning of Aphrodite*. Chicago University Press
GIFFORD, H.
1979   'Dante and the Modern Poet', *PN Review* vi,4:11-14
GINZBURG, L.
1975   'The Poetics of Osip Mandelstam', in V.Erlich (ed.),
            Twentieth-Century Russian Literary Criticism (New
            Haven, Yale University Press):284-312
GREENE, J.
1980   *Osip Mandelstam: Poems*, comp. and transl. J.Greene;
            revised ed. London, Elek
JONES, D.
1972   *The Anathemata: Fragments of an Attempted Writing*
            (1952). London, Faber and Faber
KERÉNYI, C. (with C.G.JUNG)
1951   *Introduction to a Science of Mythology: The Myth of
            the Divine Child and the Mysteries of Eleusis*. Transl.
            R.F.C.Hull, London, Routledge & Kegan Paul
KHARDZHIEV, N. = MANDEL'SHTAM, O.
1974   *Stikhotvoreniia*. Ed. N.I.Khardzhiev. Leningrad,
            Sovetskii pisatel'
KUBLER, G.
1962   *The Shape of Time: Remarks on the History of Things*.
            New Haven, Yale University Press
MUREDDU, D.
1980   'Mandel'stam and Petrarch', *Scando-Slavica* xxvi:53-84
N.M. = MANDEL'SHTAM, N.
1974   *Hope Abandoned: A Memoir*. Transl. M.Hayward. London,
            Collins & Harvill
POE, E.A.
1978   *The Collected Works of Edgar Allan Poe. Volume II:
            Tales and Sketches 1831-1842*. Ed. T.O.Mabbott.
            Cambridge (Mass.), Belknap Press
SARGENT, T.
1973   *The Homeric Hymns: A Verse Translation*. New York,
            Norton
SCHLOTT, W.
1981   *Zur Funktion antiker Göttermythen in der Lyrik Osip
            Mandel'stams*. Frankfurt a. M., Lang
SETCHKAREFF, V.
1963   *Studies in the Life and Work of Innokentij Annenskij*.
            The Hague, Mouton
S-F = MANDEL'SHTAM, O.
1967-81   *Sobranie sochinenii*. Ed. G.P.Struve & B.A.Filippov.
            4 vols. Washington, Inter-Language Literary Associates
STEVENS, A.
1982   *Archetype: A Natural History of the Self*. London,
            Routledge & Kegan Paul
TARANOVSKY, K.
1976   *Essays on Mandel'stam*. Cambridge (Mass.), Harvard
            University Press

TERRAS, V.
1969   'The Time Philosophy of Osip Mandel'shtam', *The Slavonic and East European Review*, xlvii:344-54
TRACY, R. = MANDEL'SHTAM, O.
1981   *Stone*. Transl. & introduced by Robert Tracy. Princeton, Princeton University Press
TSVETAEVA, M.
1980   *A Captive Spirit: Selected Prose*   d. and transl. J.Marin King. Ann Arbor, Ardis
TYNIANOV, IU.
1929   *Arkhaisty i novatory*. Leningrad
WEBB, T.
1976   *The Violet in the Crucible: Shelley and Translation*. Oxford, Clarendon Press
ZIELINSKI, T.
1916   *Iz zhizni idei: nauchno-populiarnyia stat'i*, 3rd ed. Petrograd

THE RESPONSE TO TRANSLATED LITERATURE

A Sad Example

Ria Vanderauwera

The road translated books have to travel is the same
as for any other book at the target pole: publication,
distribution, exposure in the media - the "gatekeep-
ers between books-in-themselves and books-for-others"
(Hall 1979:48). Compared with originals, however,
translations are already a step ahead as "books-for-
others". They are made and commissioned to fulfil a
particular purpose: that of making known a foreign
literature to an audience which has no access to it
otherwise. But mere publication does not suffice if
the books do not reach the readers. The problem facing literary translation does not end with a translator handing in his manuscript, with an editor carefully revising certain passages, or with actual publication. Getting translated and published is one
thing, achieving a response is another. Yet in the
final analysis both are facets of the same problem,
that of a literature trying to gain access to a literary environment which is different from its original one.

In the period between 1961 and 1980, fifty or
so novels originally written in Dutch (the language
spoken in the Netherlands and the 'Flemish' part of
Belgium, and one of the languages used in Surinam
and the Netherlands Antilles) were brought out in
English translation by British and American publishers.[1] It is not an idle question to ask what actually
happened to them. Were they advertised, distributed,
reviewed, sold, read? Did they receive any response?
Whether they were sold and read is, of course, difficult to answer (not all publishing houses release
sales figures), but some observations can be made
about whether, and how, these books were visible or
present at the target pole. Presumably, the observations can in principle be extended to other cases of
'small' literatures trying to make inroads into a

'big' literature which is notoriously wary of translation.[2] In what follows I should like to look more
closely at the fate of the novels alluded to.

As it is, the mechanisms of the literary market,
and literary taste at the target pole appear to function as commercial and aesthetic censors affecting
the distribution and reception of translated literature. Dutch fiction is not written by political dissidents and it is not from or about the Third World,
two factors which seem to have some market value at
the Anglophone target pole (the Caribbean production
is interesting but represents only a small fraction).
Hence the importance of an institution like the
'Foundation for the Promotion of the Translation of
Dutch Literary Works',[3] which functions as mediator
and, if necessary (and it often is necessary), as
financial sponsor. As a result, translated Dutch
fiction is introduced into the target pole mainly
via the cultured circuit: as part of academically-
oriented series such as the 'Bibliotheca Neerlandica'
or the 'Library of Netherlandic Literature' catering
primarily for universities, or as 'quality fiction'
brought out by publishing houses renowned for their
literary profile or list of translations aimed at a
literary-minded audience. In neither case is a large
press-run or large-scale distribution to be expected;
between 2,000 and 5,000 copies is pretty much the
norm. Sometimes, of course, a wider audience is aimed
at. A paperback edition may then follow the customary
hardcover edition, in which case translated Dutch
fiction may even become available in the paperback
outlets of airports and supermarkets. But this is
the exception rather than the rule. As a matter of
fact, only one Dutch novel in the period considered
achieved bestseller status — *I Jan Cremer* (Dutch 1964;
English 1965). At the very outset, the book's sexual
explicitness and its (intended) resemblance to the
work of Henry Miller (then widely circulating) promised
commercial success, and its publishers were quite
ready to spend considerable sums to promote the book.

In most instances, however, distribution is
limited and promotion modest or non-existent. Small
publishing houses cannot afford to spend large amounts
of money on a book which has little chance of making
it. Even advertisements in the cultured circuit, in
The New York Review of Books or *The Times Literary Supplement*,
for example, are rare. However, exposure in the printed press is not without importance for books which
cannot hope for promotion via other channels, such
as television or radio. The appearance of authors on
talk shows on local and national radio and TV is be-

lieved to be instrumental in increasing a book's sales figures, especially in the US (cf. Whiteside 1980:88). Among Dutch writers, only Jan Cremer came close to being a public figure associated with the Beat scene, but he was actually living in the US. It is not unimaginable that an appearance of, say, Jef Geeraerts on American or British television, carefully tied in with Henry Miller's endorsement of *Gangrene*,[4] a book about a civil servant's erotic adventures in the former Belgian Congo, would have boosted sales figures. But in the absence of large-scale advertising, Dutch fiction has to rely on the goodwill of newspapers, magazines and literary journals to give it some exposure in reviews. These are also the only written records of target readers' reactions to Dutch fiction and as such valuable indices of target taste and appreciation. The latter may or may not agree with the prevailing norms or beliefs at the source pole and thus inhibit or stimulate the contact and communication between source and target literatures. Reviews can then tell us a great deal about the difficulties Dutch fiction encounters on its way to response elsewhere.

As for the quantity of reviews, the situation is none too bright. Most works receive brief mention in the professional journals of the book trade such as *Publishers' Weekly*, *The Library Journal*, *Book List*, *Best Sellers*, *Kirkus Review*, *Choice*..., which cater for retailers, librarians, teachers and college professors. The most faithful reviewer of translated Dutch fiction, and one which reaches a somewhat wider audience is *The Times Literary Supplement*, which also occasionally devotes a complete issue or part of it to comments and information on Dutch literature and culture generally. Comparable publications in the US, such as *The New York Review of Books* or *The New York Times Book Review*, do not match this interest. Similarly, British newspapers like *The Observer*, *The Sunday Times*, *The Guardian* and *The Scotsman* devote some space to Dutch translated fiction now and again, albeit mostly in group reviews, but no comparable coverage in US newspapers can be noted. Apparently, the target production there is too massive, and Dutch fiction is simply not 'interesting' enough.

As regards contents, most reviews are disappointingly short and superficial. The scant information they contain on the original author and source literature is often safely copied from the publisher's blurb - general practice among fast-working and badly-paid reviewers anyway. More adventurous critics occasionally have recourse to easy clichés and recall

whatever they can associate with the Low Countries.
References to Anne Frank, whose diary has been reprinted many times in English since 1952, are commonplace in reviews of novels dealing with the Jewish
plight in the Second World War. The Dutch and Flemish painters — the great 'knowns' of the Low Countries — keep popping up, such as in "a self-portrait,
as realistic as one of Rembrandt's" (*Saturday Review*,
2 July 1966) or "a picture still easily recognizable,
I should have thought, to Breughel" (*The Spectator*,15
November 1968). It is most unlikely that these critics would have been reminded of Rembrandt or Breughel
if the books reviewed had not been translated from
the Dutch.

The fact that in-depth comments are rare does
not differ so much from many other reviews of fiction
at the target pole. There is simply too much to review and not enough money, time and space available,
while more of all this is given to non-fiction or
known authors expected to have a wider appeal. Moreover, Dutch translated fiction hardly ever gains access to the top circles of the reviewing establishment, a relatively small circle of critics, often
writers in their own right, whose reviewing activity
is really a matter of in-breeding. They hold the
literary power, and channel and direct the literary
opinions of their cultured audience. *The New York
Review of Books* is a notorious example of such policies
(Kostelanetz 1973-74:8; Ohmann 1983:205). There is
hardly any room for foreign fiction in such an environment, unless, of course, it is written by East
European dissidents, or is from or about areas and
political situations which are 'fashionable' in the
leading cultural and literary milieu — none of which
applies to the Low Countries and their literature.

The actual value judgements by target critics
resemble those of most other books: some reviews are
favourable, some bad, others merely polite. Excessive
praise, such as the claim that this book is "very
close to being a work of genius (...) I can only im-
plore you to read it" (*The New Observer* on Geeraerts'
Gangrene, 10 May 1975), is most unusual. The books are
rarely if ever applauded as new or refreshing contributions to the target literature — the British
press response to Heere Heeresma's modest novella
A Day at the Beach is a notable exception about which
more below. All this is no surprise, however. Dutch
fiction is chosen for translation either in function
of the status the work has acquired at the source
pole or, in the case of 'popular' fiction, in function of assumed target taste. Either way the books

acquire a slightly epigonal flavour. In the second
case, Dutch fiction 'resembles' or 'imitates' existing target works and is seldom considered new enough
to elicit the kind of comment quoted above. But it
is generally more 'successful' than work chosen exclusively for the first reason: that it is considered
one of the contemporary or less contemporary 'classics' of the source pole. Most classics are at best
interesting yet 'marginal' curiosities to a target
pole which is largely indifferent to foreign work.
One Dutch classic was considered worthwhile reading,
but nevertheless "a curiously late example of the
naturalistic novel at its most painstaking" (*New York
Review of Books*, 28 October 1965). No wonder the Library
of Netherlandic Literature received little attention
among American reviewers. In Britain the situation
seems to be somewhat different. The first volumes of
the 'Bibliotheca Neerlandica' (with Heinemann as the
main publisher) were considered worthy attempts to
rouse target readers from their insular slumber. One
critic, clearly bored with the current fiction scene
in Britain, pointed out that the volume on Gerard
Walschap "might well provide our own fiction with a
blood transfusion we could very well use" (*The Guardian*, 19 June 1964). But in the long run, interest in
the 'Bibliotheca' subsided all the same.

In general, the prevailing tone in most reviews
of Dutch fiction could be described as mildly sympathetic, ranging from the polite "well worth reading",
"well worth getting to know", "well worth having",
to slightly more critical variants such as "this
gloomy, yet impressive book" (*Sunday Times*, 5 February
1967), "a fine example of naturalistic fiction in a
minor key" (*The Booklist*, 1976:985), "an interesting
novel that suffers somewhat from the confines of its
author's attitude" (*Irish Times*, 19 October 1968).

Comments on the translation proper (if present)
usually refer to the text's readability, or lack of
it. Reviewers — and, by extrapolation, target readers — appear to be particularly sensitive to any
kind of deviation from modern, standard and idiomatic
English prose; Americans, moreover, often object to
emphatically 'British' translations. Sometimes, the
fact that the book is a translation is not even
mentioned, which is probably a tactical point: translations have a reputation of not selling well at the
target pole.

While the generally lukewarm reaction to translated Dutch fiction may be due in large measure to the
target pole's general reluctance to accept foreign
work, some of the critical comments may also origi-

nate in the simple discrepancy between source and target literatures, in different ideas about what literature is or should be, what a novel is or should be, and what kind of writing can be done in it. Moreover, commentators may be rather more fastidious and cautious towards a foreign book which imposes itself on a familiar literary scene and hence more conscious of the poetological concepts in vogue at the target pole. On the other hand, while translated Dutch fiction is unlikely to be reviewed by top critics carrying clout, it may well be covered by more marginal reviewers whose patience with types of prose fiction foreign to those they know may be somewhat limited. But even patient and perceptive critics (or potential publishers and editors) may 'dislike' the kind of Dutch prose fiction they are confronted with, because it does not live up to their expectations about the genre.

Relatively short, artistic and mannered novels appear to be the favourite type in contemporary Dutch fiction. This format, reminiscent of the novella, is rather alien to the contemporary target pole, especially in the US, where more voluminous and substantial novels occupy the scene. Not only is the sheer format of Dutch books (quality paperbacks) different from their present-day English counterparts (first hardcovers, followed by bulky paperbacks), but source and target novels also operate with different literary procedures — theme, style, setting, character, etc. Novels at the target pole are generally complex (some say: too complex), they often have a recognizable socio-political setting and broad intellectual scope; they abound with intricate and sometimes bizarre characters and events, and are often quite funny. Compared to these profuse and world-oriented novels, Dutch fiction tends to be solipsistic, intimistic and 'provincial'. It betrays an intense preoccupation with matters of style, with neat structures, precious formulation and imagery — a bias for which there is a perfect label in Dutch: "sierproza", ornamental prose. The actual plot of most contemporary Dutch novellas or short novels is thin (some say: too thin); they tend to be built around few events and contain little action; their meaning is sometimes vaguely metaphorical or allegorical; as they are given to self-centred musing, the outer world tends to be reduced to the immediate daily environment, which is often recorded with cinematic precision.

Needless to say, this is only a very general picture; in reality the production is undoubtedly

more varied, on both sides. Older work, too, can be
quite different. Fiction written in the first half
of the century by Flemish authors like Stijn Streuvels
or Gerard Walschap, for instance, betrays a belief in
the novel as a solid epic genre. The above picture is
nevertheless largely valid for a lot of fiction being
written in Flanders and Holland today and for the
literary criticism which canonizes it. Attention to
matters of form and style is generally appreciated
at the source pole and often considered the trade-
mark of true literature, whereas fullness of theme,
'round' characters, intellectual scope and, last but
not least, humour carry far more weight at the target
pole.[5] The comments that translator and critic James
Brockway made about introducing Dutch writing to a
British audience apply to the whole Anglophone world:
"...to explain and describe in terms of contemporary
British writing clearly will not do. Dutch writing
differs too widely in its origins and traditions,
and even in its nature and its aim, which does not
always appear to be primarily to entertain or even
to engage" (Brockway 1966:1).

    With this in mind, let us have a look at some
of the reviewers' reactions. Objections to the pessi-
mistic and oppressive mood of Dutch fiction keep recurring: "dour is the inevitable word" (*TLS*, 19 December 1963), "by insisting that there is no more than
despair, Wolkers weakens the effect his main character
can have. And despair itself, when examined from so
fixed a position, at such stiflingly close quarters,
becomes all too often merely oppressive and dreary"
(*Saturday Review*, 15 April 1967, on Jan Wolkers' *A Rose
of Flesh*), and "Mr.Ruyslinck succeeds, perhaps too
well, in presenting Stefan's colourless, featureless
world but unfortunately he fails, by a narrow but
essential margin, to make it convincing to those who
see life in a different and brighter light" (*Irish
Times*, 19 October 1975 on Ward Ruyslinck's *Golden
Ophelia*). It seems unlikely that this type of remark
would be heard from critics at the source pole.

    Meagre plots are given short shrift in "the
economy of style cannot disguise the dearth of material, a bland undirected monologue which has limited
yield" (*The Observer* , 13 September 1970), "this plot-
less, often pointless song of sorrows is tough to
read ... there is little to recommend this work"
(*Library Journal*, 1973:2144). Minute and slow observation is objected to in "'cinematic in style' says
the blurb ... Here is perhaps the source of its
finally being rather unsatisfying. It relies too
much on the pathos of visible 'things', not enough

on the pathos of character" (*New Society*, 1967:968),
and "the relentless and generally unselective piling
up of physical details palls over long stretches ...
an anticipation, perhaps of Robbe-Grillet's *chosiste*
approach, but the result is frequently tedious" (*New
York Review of Books*, 28 October 1965).

Precious imagery and formulation is handled with
circumspection. Reviewing Harry Mulisch's *Two Women*, a
critic remarked that "occasionally an image fails to
work: 'suddenly a tiredness covered me as a dropped
parachutist is covered by his parachute'" (*New States-
man*, 3 October 1980), perhaps implying that the translator might have modified the perfectly 'literal'
rendition of the image of the source text. A similar
objection is heard in the comment on Ward Ruyslinck's
The Reservation, which "is not made easier or cheerier
by a translation from the Dutch that faces one with
— for example — an 'acajou fringe of a beard like a
damp flat swingle'" (*The Observer*, 2 July 1978).
Wolkers' *The Horrible Tango*, on the other hand, is appreciated because "more sparingly than in his first
novel translated into English, *A Rose of Flesh*, Jan
Wolkers's predilection for surrealist imagery ('a
small piece of chewing gum lay like minute brains on
the iron table top') is kept in tune with the narrator's fevered awareness" (*TLS*, 1970:1155). In Heere
Heeresma's *A Day at the Beach* "there is the usual sense
of wastage in having poetic images in prose, but the
rate is economically controlled here" (*New Society*
1967:968), and one translator is complimented on his
restraint for not indulging too much in Ruyslinck's
verbal dexterity: "a master of nuance, (the author)
manipulates language with virtuosity and relishes
inventing new words. The translator R.B.Powell has
served the author well by not being colorful at the
expense of clarity" (*World Literature Today* 1979:304).

Excessive artistry is often considered superfluous: "an ingenious puzzle and scarcely anything
more" (*World Literature Today* 1978:483), "a confusing
and unnecessary rejuggling of time" (*The Times*, 27 November 1980), "exercises in modernist gimmickry without
bringing any part of (the author's) soul to the work"
(*Library Journal* 1980:1406), or "the only weakness is
the neatness of the dénouement which makes the whole
seem too perfectly integrated: the novella is liable
to appear even more arbitrary in its ending than the
novel and one is more tempted to think beyond it and
to question its validity" (*TLS* 1970:1155). The latter
is actually a carefully pondered remark about the
genre of the novella and its "afflatus".

Radically experimental fiction — if translated

and reviewed at all — provides a welcome opportunity
for critics to vent their feelings towards this type
of prose. Bert Schierbeek's *Shapes of the Voice*, a collection of experimental work (actually more poetry
than prose) and Ivo Michiels' *Book Alpha/Orchis Militaris*,
both published in the Library of Netherlandic Literature, received little attention. Mark Insingel's
Reflections, brought out by Calder and Boyars in London
and Red Dust in New York, elicited some interesting
controversial comments, however. The American *International Fiction Review* was obviously taken with it, "one
of the most challenging and interesting works of
modern fiction", but "the reader of traditional
novels" was warned that the "book would not appeal"
to her or him (1974:68-69). In Britain, the *TLS* review started by hinting darkly that "we are still
defensive about experimental art, giving it the benefit of every doubt which may arise," and ended with
a delightful pastiche of the book's central idea,
the multiplicity of fictional possibilities:

> Suppose, and it is a conservative estimate, that on
> average we are called on to weigh up twenty contra-
> dictions of the 'opposite (the same)' kind per page
> of *Reflections*. By the end of this slim novel we shall
> be entertaining 2^{1800} different plots, pictures, *Welt-
> anschauungen*, or whatever. For the sake of Marina/Janna,
> the prima/ultima donna of the Flemish/Walloon masterpiece/
> drivel as she sits astride the bidet and beckons you
> in — It is just not worth it. (*TLS* 1971:935)

Without Calder and Boyars, Red Dust brought out
another work by Insingel, *A Course of Time*. *Choice* could
still appreciate "its interesting architectonics,"
and the once enthusiastic *International Fiction Review*
sounded still favourable, yet more subdued: "after
a thorough examination of *A Course of Time* one has to
welcome it as a worthy addition to the fast growing
canon of experimental and heterodox narratives" (1978,
1:67-68). But as this comment shows, Dutch fiction
had acquired 'epigonal' status: *A Course of Time* was
just one among many narratives of its kind. A year
later, Egbert Krispyn, the editor of The Library of
Netherlandic Literature, observed in the introduction
to Michiels' *Book Alpha/Orchis Militaris* that "recent
trends in world literature indicate that, after the
frantic experimentation of the 1960s, there is a
general tendency to return to the more orthodox form
of the novel". The original Dutch versions of *Het Boek
Alfa* and *Orchis Militaris* were published in 1963 and 1968
respectively, their translations (two 'thin' Dutch
novels appropriately combined into one English hard-

cover) in 1979. By that time, of course, they had
lost their innovative value and had become 'modern
classics' of Dutch fiction. At the target pole,
Michiels was inevitably seen as an epigone of "the
practitioners of the *nouvelle roman*", as the dustjacket
erroneously had it. The *nouveau roman*, it should be
pointed out, never quite made it in the Anglophone
world.

Of course, it is not true that no experimental
fiction is written in English at all. Works by John
Barth, Thomas Pynchon, Donald Barthelme and William
Gass, for instance, do away with traditional narrative, revel in stylistic and structural artifice,
and are much appreciated by the critics. But there
is a difference. First, this is 'home' production
and the target pole is more tolerant of it. Secondly,
and this is more important, most of these books are
quite substantial, and exceedingly funny and satiri-
cal — "humor might make us persevere," wrote one
critic about a Dutch novel (*Library Journal* 1973:2144).
On the other hand, novellas are, of course, published
and appreciated at the target pole. For instance,
translated short fiction by the Italian Cesare Pavese
enjoys reasonable success. But again there is a catch:
Pavese played an important role as mediator between
American and Italian culture and literature (as a
translator, among other things) and as such he has
an exceptional cultural-historical appeal.

All this is not to say that the target response
to Dutch fiction is entirely negative. It is not,
but it is most certainly not positive either and
hardly ever quite forceful enough. Commercial success
is rare. Critical success both quantitatively (the
sheer number of reviews) and qualitatively is moderate, and any views as to the nature of modern Dutch
fiction are either non-existent or conveniently
stereotyped. A combination of three factors is basically responsible for this situation. As a matter of
fact, they are the same factors that made the English
publication of the novels so difficult in the first
place. First, patronage: the tough publishing and
distribution situation which has prevailed at the
target pole since the 1960s favours (potential)
bestsellers, preferably in the nonfiction area, at
the expense of more 'literary' work (cf. Sutherland
1973, Whiteside 1981). Second, status: literature
which comes from an area which is at present of
little socio-political or even cultural interest
does not elicit great excitement in a target pole
which has from the very outset been largely indifferent to foreign work; so it is relegated to a 'marginal'

position. Third, poetics: source and target literature hold slightly different opinions about literature, prose fiction, and the novel in particular.

Such a climate obviously does not favour the
publication of translations from the Dutch. Neither
does it prompt export-hungry authors or literary-
minded editors and translators to venture onto a
scene which is hard to gain access to anyway. A
government-subsidized institute — the above-mentioned
Foundation for Translations — is expected to do the
job instead, which seems a simple and convenient solution. This is not to say that there are no solitary
initiatives at all, only that the general climate is
hardly an ideal breeding ground. Jef Geeraerts'
Gangrene owes its publication to a considerable extent
to the zeal of its editor (Richard Seaver) and its
translator (Jon Swan), but the Foundation was still
called upon to take care of the financial side.

After publication, the same 'constraints' con-
tinue to thwart the distribution of Dutch work and
its access to the reviewing columns of newspapers
and journals. Factors number two (Dutch literature
is marginal, or curious at best) and three (Dutch
novels are not 'real' novels; the novella is an alien
format) function as aesthetic censors, so to speak,
preventing Dutch fiction from receiving serious attention, even from the literary-minded. As a consequence (factor number one), publishers assume little
interest, give the work a small press run and little
publicity. In its turn this yields only a limited
number of reviews, since "quality alone (...) has
never insured the media's notice or even the attention of regular book reviewers, for the enterprise of
reviewing extends not from literature out but book publicity" (Kostelanetz 1973-74:103). The few reviews
of translated Dutch fiction which do actually get
written further reflect factors number two and three.
They are by no means unanimously unfavourable, but
their basic stance is one of mild, sometimes even
warm, but seldom enthusiastic sympathy. Readers on
their part are not likely to pay much attention to
books which are merely 'interesting achievements'
when their own literature presents them with a massive stream of 'original' work.

As a result, we are faced with the proverbial
vicious circle. By providing financial assistance,
the Foundation for Translations tries to create ope-
nings on the level of publication. But while it is
still possible to get Dutch fiction published in
English translation, it is far more difficult to get
it distributed and to give it some exposure.[6] The

Foundation has no control over what happens to the
books after publication. Moreover, it may well be
that its financial support has a reverse effect on a
publisher's promotional efforts: there is no great
incentive to activate potential reviewers and buyers
if the money problem has been discreetly solved, for
the firm breaks even anyway. The purchase of a sizeable number of copies by the subsidizing institutions
at the source pole is another frequent practice; it
too defies its purpose. Only a few of the copies
thus sold reach an audience, via gifts to scholars
or diplomats, for instance; the rest is left to
gather dust in the storehouse. In England, Calder
and Boyars sold 500 copies of Mark Insingel's *Reflections*, including 200 to the Belgian Ministry of Dutch-
Language Culture; Red Dust sold fifty copies of the
book in the US, including twenty to the Foundation
for Translations.

*

In the preceding paragraphs I have emphatically *not*
tried to suggest that the reason for the 'poor' response to Dutch literature in English translation is
the 'poor quality' of that literature; neither have
I suggested the opposite, i.e. that the failure to
extend a warm welcome to translated Dutch work deprives Anglophone readers of the finest achievements
in world literature. It is not the researcher's or
the scholar's task to take a position here. As has
been shown in recent developments in the study of
literature, the reception and appreciation of literary works is not primarily a matter of their inherent qualitative inferiority or superiority, but
hinges on a series of interrelated factors ranging
from poetics to economics, from prestige to profit.
In what follows, I would like to suggest that while
such factors are indeed manipulating literary traf-
fic, they in turn may be manipulated.
    The sorry situation sketched above can be dealt
with in two ways. The easy one is to play to the
gallery by translating and promoting works that fit
assumed demand and taste at the target pole, thus
neutralizing aesthetic as well as commercial objections. The more difficult and hazardous one, and one
that will require some patience, is to try and project a certain image of Dutch fiction. This would
mean a concerted attempt to create attention for the
specific nature of Dutch prose, making editors, publishers and reviewers aware of the fact that there
is this particular format in contemporary Dutch fiction, halfway between the novel and the short story,

which derives its peculiar character from its suggest-
iveness, from its intimistic themes and precious
imagery, and which for that reason may have something
to contribute to the target literature. Fiction, it
has been observed, 'sells' better when it comes pack-
aged - as a recognizable genre, for example.

The first tactic could imply a deliberate policy
of tuning in, say, to the present interest in topical
work from and about the Third World. Jef Geeraerts'
Gangrene and *Black Ulysses*, set in the former Belgian
Congo, met such interests. The current 'Library of
the Indies' (University of Massachusetts Press),
which contains work dealing with the former Dutch
East Indies, responds to the challenge on a more
academic level, tying in with the popularity of Third
World Studies on university campuses. The Foundation
for Translations has, to a certain extent, also ad-
justed its earlier basically source-oriented policy.
It professes a readiness to take into account the
prevailing cultural taste at the target pole - without, of course, entirely relinquishing its source
criteria of 'excellence'. A target-oriented approach,
however, does not guarantee critical and commercial
success in the cultured or popular circuits. Literature does not function in quite such a mechanistic
way. It does mean, however, that in view of a number
of restraining factors of a commercial and aesthetic
nature, Dutch work from, say, Surinam or the Antilles,
if well promoted and publicized, may have a greater
chance of success at the target pole than the translation of the umpteenth clever experiment which was
nevertheless widely acclaimed at the source pole.

A suggestion: the work of Frank Martinus Arion,
an Antillean for whom the Third World is an important
topic. His novels are complex and run to considerable
length; they have an international setting, intellectual substance and a definite political flavour. I
fancy that the blurb could run like this:

> Like the Trinidadian author V.S. Naipaul, Frank Martinus
> Arion, an Antillean who writes in Dutch, is fascinated
> by the confrontation between the peoples, cultures and
> political beliefs of the Western and the Third World.
> Like Naipaul, Arion is capable of translating his striking
> perceptions into masterpieces of fiction which never fail
> to captivate the reader.

One may think this is somewhat preposterous. Perhaps
it is. But why not, if it helps Arion to reach a
wider audience? One may also deplore the philosophy
behind such policies, i.e. the wholehearted acceptance of target taste and standards, and the growing

internationalization of fiction, possibly at the expense of artistic value. Indeed, "there is some question whether quality fiction can adapt to the market-
ing techniques needed to sell it internationally
without damaging artistic concessions. Integration
which does not involve subjugation of the weaker
culture to the stronger, or subtle forms of prosti-
tution, is tricky" (Sutherland 1978:62). In the actual case of Geeraerts, however, or the suggested case
of Arion, there is, presumably, no danger of such
concessions, but then again, what is literary value,
and who determines it?

The second, perhaps more utopian tactic requires
that certain constraints be bypassed, rather than
challenged head-on. It is clearly absurd to believe
that literatures, literary systems, are such mechanistic wholes that, given a number of 'constraints',
one can predict the direction which fiction, translation, criticism, literary contacts, etc. will take.
Writers, critics, scholars, translators, editors and
publishers can take the relevant environmental factors into account, consciously or unconsciously, and
act accordingly; they may prefer to ignore them, or
actively try to challenge and change them. In the
latter case their 'unorthodox' writings and opinions
may simply disappear for ever, but they may also produce surprise successes, or even trigger new literary
developments in due course. It may well be that the
poetics underlying contemporary Dutch fiction are
presently coming under pressure, judging from a number of critical voices recently heard attacking them[7]
But that is not our problem here. The point is that,
in spite of unfavourable environmental conditions,
Dutch fiction, with its specific format and artistic
flavour, might still be able to attract serious attention at the Anglophone target pole and trigger
comments which go beyond mere sympathetic assessment.

Such a development is not entirely hypothetical.
An attempt along these lines was the English publication of a suggestive novella by Heere Heeresma, *Een
dagje naar het strand* (1962) as *A Day at the Beach* (1967).
James Brockway, who translated the work for sheer
pleasure, was well aware of the difficulty its particular length would pose to publication. It appeared nevertheless in a then relatively new paperback
series of poetry and short fiction as London Magazine
Edition number ten. The reviews were mostly favourable. There were the usual polite formulas (the book
"recommends itself as a work of genuine merit from a
writer never before published in Britain", *The Spectator*, 9 June 1967), but the small work also drew atten-

tion to its special format — "It is extremely short, a mere 117 small pages, but within its limits a *tour de force* of such intensity that its horror is almost unbearable" (*Sunday Telegraph*, 28 May 1967), and "short though *A Day at the Beach* is, it contains more wisdom, and art, than many novels self-consciously worked out at full length" (*Sunday Times*, 11 June 1967); finally, the reviewer in *The Spectator* (1967:686) noted that with the publication of *A Day at the Beach*, *London Magazine* had provided "a particularly congenial format for the novella — a form for which there are all too few available markets."

The fate of *A Day at the Beach* is exceptional.[8] It was introduced at the weaker of the two main target poles (with respect to fiction, that is) and may have profited from a temporary death-of-the-British-novel climate. Ward Ruyslinck's novella *The Deadbeats*, brought out a year later as a hardcover by Peter Owen (London) and favourably reviewed as well, did not elicit similarly outspoken comments on genre and format. Clearly, *A Day at the Beach* had taken advantage of a particular avant-garde publishing venture, the paperback series of *London Magazine*. Which only goes to show that initiative - at the target pole - by an inventive editor (Alan Ross) and an enterprising translator can, with luck, produce remarkable results and defy the mechanics of literary market and environment.

Whether Dutch fiction will eventually find a niche in the Anglophone cultural scene remains an open question. That translation is a first and necessary step in that direction, is illustrated by Heeresma's endeavours to have a film made out of his book:

> I am the kind of person who really believes that you should give your compatriots the first chance, but when all the attempts by everybody here to make a film out of it were not getting anywhere, I took a very big, very luxurious box of chocolates, threw out the chocolates, put in the English translation of the novel, and sent it off to Polanski. (Heeresma in *Skoop* VII,5:20; my translation, R.V.)

It is good to know that a film was eventually made. Roman Polanski wrote the script on the basis of the English translation.

NOTES

1. My doctoral dissertation *Fiction in Translation: Policies and Options. A Case Study of the Translation of Dutch Novels into English over the Last Two Decades* (University of Antwerp UIA, 1982) is an extensive study of the selection and

formulation of these translated novels, and of the response they received.

2. This has been amply illustrated with figures and statistics by Robert Escarpit 1969 (1965).

3. The Amsterdam-based 'Foundation' is an independent institution which works with funds made available jointly by the Dutch and Belgian Ministries of Culture.

4. On the publication of *Gangrene* (1975), Henry Miller sent a congratulatory telegram to its publisher (Viking). His enthusiastic review appeared in the *Los Angeles Times* (18 May 1975) and was subsequently reprinted nationwide in a number of local papers.

5. The Dutch literary periodical *De Gids* (1981 nos 2/3) devoted a whole issue to the discrepancy between Dutch and American fiction. Most contributors, no matter which side they took in the argument — pro-American or pro-Dutch fiction — implicitly recognized that there were indeed significant divergences, and generally agreed on their nature (solipsistic versus world-oriented, gloomy versus funny, preoccupation with style and the 'craft' of fiction versus broad thematic sweep).

6. This is a perfect illustration of the observation that "our literary system is very good at publishing books but much less efficient in distributing them" (Hall 1979:116), and "in totalitarian societies, a book is censored at the point of production; in literary-industrial societies, censorship occurs at later points along the communication line" (Kostelanetz 1973-74:196).

7. See the polemical exchanges in *De Gids* mentioned in note 5.

8. Another recent case of a Dutch 'novella' apparently making it is Cees Nooteboom's *Rituelen*, translated by Adrienne Dixon as *Rituals*, first published in the US by Louisiana State University Press (1983; 145 pp.) and scheduled to appear in Britain as a King Penguin at the end of 1984.

REFERENCES

BROCKWAY, James
1966   'Do the Dutch have writers, too, then?', *The Scotsman Weekend Magazine*, 12 November 1966:1
CREMER, Jan
1965   *I Jan Cremer*. Transl. R.E.Wyngaard & Alexander Trocchi. London/New York, Calder & Boyars/Shorecrest (Dutch: *Ik, Jan Cremer*, 1964)
ESCARPIT, Robert
1969 (1965) *La révolution du livre*. Paris, Presses universitaires de France/UNESCO
GEERAERTS, Jef
1975   *Gangrene*. Transl. Jon Swan. London/New York, Weidenfeld & Nicolson/Viking (Dutch: *Gangreen*, 1968)

HALL, John
1979   *The Sociology of Literature*. London/New York, Longman
HEERESMA, Heere
1967   *A Day at the Beach*. Transl. James Brockway. London,
            London Magazine Editions (Dutch: *Een dagje naar het
            strand*, 1962)
INSINGEL, Mark
1971,72   *Reflections*. Transl. Adrienne Dixon. London, Calder
            & Boyars (1971); New York, Red Dust (1972)(Dutch:
            Spiegelingen, 1968)
1977   *A Course of Time*. Transl. Adrienne Dixon. New York,
            Red Dust (Dutch: *Een tijdsverloop*, 1970)
KOSTELANETZ, R.
1973-74   *The End of Intelligent Writing*. New York, Sheed & Ward
MICHIELS, Ivo
1979   *Book Alpha and Orchis Militaris*. Transl. Adrienne
            Dixon. Boston, Twayne (Dutch: *Het boek Alpha,* 1963;
            Orchis militaris, 1968)
MULISCH, Harry
1980   *Two Women*. Transl. Els Early. London/New York, John
            Calder/Riverrun (Dutch: *Twee vrouwen*, 1975)
NOOTEBOOM, Cees
1983   *Rituals*. Transl. Adrienne Dixon. Baton Rouge, Louisi-
            ana State University Press (Dutch: *Rituelen*, 1980)
OHMANN, Richard
1983   'The Shaping of a Canon: US Fiction, 1960-1975',
            Critical Inquiry, vol.10, nr.1:199-223
RUYSLINCK, Ward
1968   *The Deadbeats*. Transl. R.B.Powell. London, Peter Owen
            (Dutch: *De ontaarde slapers,* 1957)
1975   *Golden Ophelia*. Transl. David Smith. London, Peter
            Owen (Dutch: *Golden Ophelia*, 1966)
1978   *The Reservation*. Transl. David Smith. London, Peter
            Owen (Dutch: *Het reservaat*, 1964)
SCHIERBEEK, Bert
1977   *Shapes of the Voice*. Transl. Charles McGeehan. Boston,
            Twayne (anthology)
SUTHERLAND, J.A.
1978   *Fiction and the Fiction Industry*. London, University
            of London/Athlone Press
WHITESIDE, Thomas
1980   'Onward and Upward with the Arts. The Blockbuster
            Complex' (Part 1), *The New Yorker*, 29 September 1980:
            48-101
1981   *The Blockbuster Complex*. Middletown (Conn.),
            Wesleyan University Press
WOLKERS, Jan
1966   *A Rose of Flesh*. Transl. John Scott. New York, George
            Braziller (Dutch: *Een roos van vlees*, 1963)
1970   *The Horrible Tango*. Transl. R.R.Symonds. London,
            Secker & Warburg (Dutch: *Horrible Tango*, 1967)

WHY WASTE OUR TIME ON REWRITES?

The Trouble with Interpretation and the Role of Rewriting in an Alternative Paradigm

André Lefevere

I

The academic, or not so academic activity known as 'literary interpretation' is in trouble, and for various reasons. It is in trouble because it has, of late, been pushed to what may well turn out to be its outer limits: "recent critical theory has placed undue emphasis on the limitlessness of interpretation. It is argued that, since all reading is misreading, no one reading is better than any other, and hence all readings, potentially infinite in number, are in the final analysis equally misinterpretations" (Said 1983:39). The question then becomes whether there are any rules left in this "gigantic game of one-upmanship" (McCanles 1981:271) which interpretation has become, or does an interpretation really "not always have to be true or justifiable to be interesting. Sometimes a reader is strong enough to make *anything* he or she writes about a text interesting" (Stout 1982:7).

If that is the case, the cat is truly out of the bag. There have always been writers who have been strong enough to make anything they write about - any aspect of the world - interesting. What would be the difference between them and strong readers or writers who can make anything they write about a work of literature interesting? If your interpretation, the horror-stricken argument goes, does not need to be true or justifiable but merely interesting, you may as well write anything you like about literature, just as you may write anything you like about life, and get away with it. In this case the interpreter himself or herself tends to become simply a writer in his or her own right, but one who chooses to write about books, rather than about reality – as if you could ever write about reality without referring to books. The horrible point of it all is, of course, that, if this is true, it would make the in-

terpreter a writer, and no longer a scholar; and interpreters, certainly those of the professional kind,
have always prided themselves on the fact that they
are scholars, not writers who can get away with saying anything they want, as long as what they want to
say sounds interesting enough.

We have had strong readers with us for centuries, whether they have been professionals, producing
the kind of interpretation that tends to get published in learned journals under the guise of criticism,
or amateurs, strong readers one hears on occasion
holding forth in bars, on buses, planes or other
means of public transportation, but who feel little
compunction to publish their readings. Interpreters,
whether strong or weak, have always been convinced
that their interpretation did, at the very least,
represent an attempt to get closer to either the
true or the justifiable, and preferably both. They
did, in other words, share the belief that there was
something 'out there' which would, in the final analysis, serve as a guarantee for their interpretation,
something which would underwrite what they had written. Take that something away and interpretation,
though undoubtedly still as interesting as ever,
loses its claim to be numbered among those writings
traditionally deemed to belong to the category of
scholarship.

Interpretation or, to stick to its published
variant, criticism has, at its best, always been interesting, illuminating and vastly erudite, and critics have genuinely believed that what they had written would be underwritten by truth, that it would
find its own justification. The fact that a sizeable
number of often mutually antagonistic, often uneasily
coexisting truths and justifications have appeared
and disappeared over the centuries, has not really
been able to deter interpreters. You could rational-
ize the fact that you were, really, choosing your
own truth, your own justification, rather than the
one-and-only truth, the one-and-only justification,
in at least one of two ways. Either you could regard
the proliferation of truths and justifications as a
healthy sign of pluralism and progress, which would
bring a tangible advantage into the bargain, since
"the equation of publishing with prestige institu-
tionalizes a need for the proliferation of criticism,
and gives every critic a stake in the idea of criticism's inexhaustibility, the potential infinity of
interpretation, the need for as great a plurality as
possible" (Pratt 1981:184). Or you could say that
interpretation simply has not reached the truth yet,

216

that it has fallen short of the ultimate justification because it simply isn't good enough yet, and
you call theory to the rescue, if by theory you mean
"the attempt to govern interpretations of particular
texts by appealing to an account of interpretation
in general" (Knapp & Michaels 1982:723).

In both cases you would never have to face the
fact that you were putting your talent, your time
and your erudition in the service of *a* truth, *a* justification that you yourself selected, not one that
is given to you, eternal, but one that was made for
you, transient. Interpretation, a way of reading a
work of literature which sometimes leads to writing
about that work of literature, rewriting it to some
extent, has never been an enterprise of cast-iron
scholarship and erudition only, but always of scholarship and erudition in the service of something else.
There has, in other words, never been a truly autonomous criticism, responsible only to the truth, the
eternal, the one-and-only. There have always been
different attempts at interpretation undertaken on
the basis of a certain concept of what the world
should be like (ideology) as well as a certain concept of what literature should be like (poetics),
and these attempts, neo-classical, romantic, existential, psychoanalytic, have always been temporary,
transient. They have accepted or rejected works of
literature on the basis of the ideology and the
poetics they happened to be serving but, much more
often, they have adapted works of literature, 'rewritten' them until they happened to fit their own
poetics, their own ideology.

There is nothing wrong with that. "Literary
theories are not to be upbraided for being political,
but for being on the whole covertly or unconsciously
so - for the blindness with which they offer as sup-
posedly 'technical', 'self-evident', 'scientific' or
'universal' truth doctrines which with a little reflection can be seen to relate to and reinforce the
particular interests of particular groups of people
at particular times" (Eagleton 1983:195). Works of
literature exist to be made use of in one way or another. There is nothing wrong, or right, about using
them in a certain manner, all readers do it all the
time. It is simply part of the process by which a
work of literature is absorbed into the reader's
mental and emotional framework.

What *is* wrong, though, or at the very least
dishonest, is for criticism, any kind of criticism,
to pretend to be objective and to try to take on the
trappings of the scientific while remaining partisan

and subjective. And yet this is precisely what criticism, any kind of criticism, *has* to do if it either
wants to achieve a dominant position inside a given
literary establishment or system, or if it wants to
maintain that position once it has succeeded in establishing it. To impress on people in the field,
and also on those outside the field who have a certain interest in it, that it is 'right', criticism,
any criticism, will have to act as if it, and it
alone, is in possession, maybe not of the ultimate
truth and/or justification, but at least of the key
to those, which makes the rest seem a mere matter of
time. There is, therefore, simply no point in dam-
ning one kind of criticism while praising another,
since the succession of critical schools which occupy a dominant position for a few years or a few centuries, can keep going on until human ingenuity itself is utterly exhausted, which appears rather unlikely, since that ingenuity has, to goad it on, that
most powerful of motivations, the glorious trinity
of jobs, remuneration and fame.

Rather, it looks as if a sharp dividing line
should be drawn, not between "scholarship (by which
is meant what I would call 'philology'), locating
and assembling the historical and philological facts
necessary to edit the works of, say, Bartholomew
Griffin, and 'criticism' as a reasonable division of
labor" (Herrnstein-Smith 1983:2), since criticism of
the professional kind has always been adamant about
its status as 'scholarship', but much more so between the endless succession of different schools of
scholarship-cum-criticism, and an analysis of the
factors which make it possible for those schools to
succeed each other. It must, in other words, be
accepted that "literary criticism represents an institution situated 'outside' a science of literature
...an institution which acts according to its own
rules and the goals it has set itself. These goals
guide literary criticism towards special ways of
participating in the literary system, not towards a
scientific analysis of that social action system"
(Schmidt 1982:51).

Criticism, which has often given the impression
that it is trying to describe and interpret works of
literature or whole historical epochs from the outside, should be seen for what it is: an attempt to
influence the development of a given literature in a
certain direction, the direction which happens to
coincide with the poetics and ideology of the dominant critical school of the moment. To do so, criticism, in its historical avatar, will not hestitate

to rewrite history until it fits the said ideology and poetics, nor will it give up trying to influence the way in which a reader reads a certain work of literature.

Deconstructionist criticism is, at last, beginning openly to acknowledge this state of affairs. Criticism is put squarely where it belongs: with literature, not with any kind of analysis of literature as a social phenomenon and not, as has been the case for too long, somewhere in between, occupying a fundamentally ambiguous position, and forced to occupy that position by the interplay of systemic constraints (how else could it ever hope to become and/or remain dominant?), yet obscuring the workings of those constraints by the very position it occupies. The realization that criticism is part of the rough and tumble of the development of a literary system, not a description of that system, may prove productive in opening the way for an analysis of literary systems as such. "Since", in Paul de Man's words, "they are not scientific, critical texts have to be read with the same awareness of ambivalence that is brought to the study of non-critical literary texts" (1979:110). They should no longer be taken for what they are not.

To recognize the fact that criticism, being part of a literary system, can never be autonomous, will not spell the end of literary studies, as those who produce interpretations and swear by them would have us believe, but it may spell the end of a study of literature in which interpretation functions as the central concept. It may also spell the breakthrough of another kind of study of literature which would not only take into account the literature that is written, but also the ways in which what is written gets rewritten, in the service of which ideology, which poetics, and with what results.

The study of literature would then no longer consist of the rewriting of literature in various ways, and the theory of literature would not be "the attempt to govern interpretations of particular texts by appealing to an account of interpretation in general". Rather, literary theory would try to explain how both the writing and the rewriting of literature are subject to certain constraints, and how the interaction of writing and rewriting is ultimately responsible, not just for the canonization of specific authors or specific works and the rejection of others, but also for the evolution of a given literature, since rewritings are often designed precisely to push a given literature in a certain direction.

219

Think, for example, of the often quoted rewritings of T'ang poetry in Pound's *Cathay*, which have helped to push the evolution of modern English-language poetry in a certain direction. And if we were able to find out about the evolution of a given literature, if we could discover certain regular, recurring patterns, we might even try to formulate a theory of what makes literature tick, a theory that would not focus primarily on "literary practice as an intimate mental process of writing" (Dubois:1978:34), since a few decades of focusing primarily on that aspect seem to have made us sadder rather than wiser, but on "the concept (and the reality) of a socialized apparatus that takes literature in charge and organizes it" (*ibid.*). This does most emphatically not mean that the writer is now relegated to the periphery, banished from the limelight for ever, but merely that he or she will have to share the limelight with rewriters, since they share the responsibility for the evolution of a literature, and to no small extent.

In what follows I would like to propose the outlines of such a theory, only it is not a theory as such, for the very sound reason that although I may be convinced of its explanatory power, others definitely are not. What follows is therefore a hypothesis, a tentative statement that says, in short: look at all the things we would be able to explain if only this hypothesis was - no, not true, but more generally accepted, since hypotheses are not primarily true or false. Rather, they tend to be accepted or rejected by a consensus, a majority or a minority of people working in the same field with the idea - at first it is little more than bare faith - that work done along the lines suggested by the hypothesis may turn out to be more productive, capable of explaining more features than work based on other hypotheses and, in doing so, actually take a few steps towards vindicating the hypothesis by testing its usefulness in the field.

If, at any moment, the minority described above turns out to be a majority, or rather, to have become a majority, we are faced with at least an attempt at a paradigm change. A paradigm is superseded by another when the newcomer "solves problems, eliminates others, and provides a guide for further research" (Mattesich 1978:154). Paradigms are constructed on the basis of observation (i.e. of things that are known to have happened), but also on the basis of previous paradigms. They do, moreover, contain some empirical corroboration in which the paradigm seems to be actually vindicated, which basically means that the way things happen tends to make more sense when they are seen to happen inside the framework of the paradigm and which implies, of course, that they might make even better sense when seen to happen within the framework of another paradigm.

Paradigms can be vindicated in certain instances, and other instances can no doubt be quoted to show that they are not all they are supposed to be. The problem then is to decide - the decision rests with those in the field - whether these instances invalidate claims made in the core of the paradigm or in its periphery. Paradigms are constructed around a core (the concept of system, to quote this particular instance), which is the part they simply cannot give up without ceasing to exist. All the rest, examples and counterexamples, is 'negotiable' so to speak, to be tested against the core, and the core itself can be tested not against some absolute yardstick 'out there', but in the field itself. There is, quite simply, no way of knowing whether it is more or less 'true' than its rivals are. There is, however, a way of finding out whether it is more or less 'useful': does it describe the same phenomena its rivals describe, does it describe more of them, does it describe them in a more consistent manner and are these descriptions conducive to further integrated research?

Yet, since paradigms are accepted or rejected by people, not yardsticks, acceptance or rejection does not take place on the basis of argument or rational exchange alone, since people, even when they are being scholars, are by definition not only rational. On the contrary, *an argument becomes effective only if supported by an appropriate attitude and has no effect when that attitude is missing* (and the attitude I am talking about must work *in addition* to the readiness to listen to arguments, and it is independent of an acceptance of the premises of arguments)" (Feyerabend 1978:8). One of the most blatant examples of this state of affairs in literary history is the availability, as early as the twelfth century, of a Latin translation of Aristotle's *Poetics* by William of Moerzeke. The book remained relatively unnoticed for another two centuries, mainly because the Middle Ages, which, as Cervantes reminds us, "Aristotle never dreamed of, Saint Basil never mentioned, and Cicero never dealt with", had developed their own attitude towards literature, their own 'poetics', after which it went on to become the central text of Renaissance poetics in the original Greek - attitudes had, quite obviously, changed.

It is because the acceptance or rejection of paradigms depends at least as much on attitude as it does on argument that exchanges between proponents of new paradigms and defenders of old paradigms tend to be rather acrimonious at times. Add to this that the only foolproof way to eternalize a certain orthodoxy, any kind of orthodoxy, is through the use of power, subtle or less so, and it becomes easy to understand why people in positions of power, who owe those positions to no small extent to their allegiance to a certain paradigm, will be rather reluctant to change their attitude and welcome a challenger to that paradigm. As a result, a struggle goes on for a number of years, not only in print, but also among those who decide what gets printed and what does not, or who gets appointed to which position and who does not.

A new paradigm tends to be 'in the air' for a number of years, in a number of similar or analogous versions, before it crystallizes in one or more versions which then become 'authorized'. We seem to have reached a moment in the evolution of literary studies when the attitude of a sizeable number of people working in the field has evolved towards one of dissatisfaction with the central position of interpretation, and one of relative willingness to try out alternatives. These alternatives would recognize the importance of rewriting in all its forms, among them translation, to a much greater extent than the interpretation-based paradigm could ever do.

II

Various proponents of alternative paradigms for the study of literature would agree that "the realities of power and authority - as well as the resistance offered by men, women and social movements to institutions, authorities and orthodoxies - are the realities that make texts possible, that deliver them to their readers, that solicit the attention of critics" (Said 1983:5). They would also agree that these realities need to be analysed, that meaningful work in the field of literary studies lies in that direction, rather than in the production of still more interpretations of individual works of literature, supplemented by still more theories of interpretation proposed in "publications on method that belong to the present theory wave" in which "no original suggestions, certainly not *a primis fundamentis*, are systematically worked out and defended...; rather one gets a presentation of a whole spectrum of outdated methods and concepts, in ever changing selections" (Koppe 1978:158).

The burning question is, of course, how? How does one reconcile, for example, the incontrovertible assertion that "criticism and interpretation, the arts of explanation and understanding, have a deep and complex relation with politics, the structures of power and social value that organize human life" (Mitchell 1982:iii) with the no less incontrovertible statement that "it is less certain that the emulation of Callimachus by Virgil and Horace can be fully explicated by social analysis" (Von Hallberg 1983:iv)? A systems approach to literature could, in my opinion, greatly clarify matters at this point and help establish a framework inside of which these realities can be analysed in a less fragmented way than they have been up to now. A systems approach to literature is consistent, relatively easy to explain (which has important pedagogical implications) and potentially productive: research that is based on it could be seen to move towards the solution of the problems it deals with. It is also plausible, i.e. "compatible with other theories currently deployed" (Kuhn 1971: 158) in other fields, which might help counteract the growing isolation of literary studies as a discipline. It does, moreover, provide a neutral framework for the description of literature as a social phenomenon, which means that it need not remain tied to Eurocentric concepts of literature, and that it can integrate literatures produced in other cultures than those of Europe and the Americas, without offending sensibilities.

In modern literary theory the concept of system goes back at least as far as the Russian Formalists. Marxist criticism, criticism based on communications theory, and reader-response criticism have each done much to pave the way for thinking about literature in terms of systems. Recent attempts at elaborating a systems approach have been made by Claudio Guillén, Itamar Even-Zohar, Felix Vodička, Ronald Tanaka and Siegfried J. Schmidt.

When I use the word 'system' in these pages, the term has nothing to do with System (usually spelled with a capital S) as it is increasingly used in everyday language to refer to the more sinister aspect of the powers that be, and against which there is no recourse. The way I want to use the term, .system has no such Kafkaesque overtones. It is merely intended to be a neutral term, used to designate a set of interrelated elements which happen to share certain characteristics which set them apart from other elements perceived as not belonging to the system. In other words, "a system is a portion of the world that is perceived as a unit and that is able to maintain its 'identity' in spite of changes going on in it" (Rapoport 1975:46).

What lies outside the system can be called that system's environment. A teaching situation, for example, can be described in terms of a system. Its elements would be the teacher and the students relating to each other. A janitor wandering in by mistake would not be perceived as belonging to the system, nor would he or she perceive himself or herself to do so. The system consisting of teacher and students tends to be rather short-lived. It breaks up after a few hours, at the most, to be reconstituted later, or not. The place where the teaching goes on is the environment of the system. It could be a classroom, or a shady spot under a tree as in most Taoist teaching, or the countryside Aristotle used to walk through with his disciples. The environment is obviously capable of influencing the system: if somebody were, say, to run into the classroom and shout 'Fire!', that action would lead to a speedy disintegration of the system. Or else the environment can withhold the necessary funding, which would also lead to the break-up of the system. Alternatively, the system is capable of affecting the environment: what is said in the teaching situation may lead to changes in the way students (or teachers) perceive, or act in their environment. The system we are talking about here is, therefore, an open system, i.e. one which interacts with its environment.

General Systems Theory, the body of thinking about systems which has constituted itself in the wake of the pioneering efforts of Ludwig von Bertalanffy, has, over the years, tended to grow progressively more vague and, at the same time, more dogmatic. It is therefore not my intention to subject the unsuspecting reader to the full rigours of GST, or to assail him or her with the full arsenal of terms developed by it, merely because these terms happen to exist. I shall only introduce the terms which appear, to me at least, directly relevant to the study of literature. The others will be neatly cut off with Ockham's razor, which teaches us not to multiply items beyond necessity.

These pages are not intended as a contribution to General Systems Theory. They would, however, like to try to show to what extent a much less ambitious handling of the concept of system, a part of the

"loosely organized and undogmatic endeavour called
the systems approach, or systems *research* in the
broadest sense" (Mattesich 1978:282), might be able
to provide some answers to problems in the study of
literature which other approaches have to gloss over
or even ignore.

A final word of warning before we plunge in:
systems, or a system, in the sense used here, simply
do(es) not exist. The word system is used here to
refer to a heuristic construct that does emphatically *not* possess any kind of ontological reality. At
most it is a concept in the mind of a student of
literature, or the collective construct a group of
students of literature has chosen to make use of.
The word system is merely used to designate a model
that promises to help make sense of a very complex
phenomenon, that of the writing, reading and rewriting of literature.

Literature - a literature - then, can be analysed in terms of a system. Systems research would
call it a contrived system, because it consists both
of objects (books, say) and human beings who read,
write, rewrite books. The fact that literature is a
contrived system should caution us against "making
an exact analogy between it and physical or biologi-
cal systems" (Kast & Rosenzweig 1972:20) which are,
on the whole, amenable to a somewhat more rigid description.

Literature is not a deterministic system, not
something that will somehow 'take over' and 'run
things', destroying the freedom of the individual
reader, writer or rewriter. That misconception can
be traced back to the everyday use of the term system mentioned above, and it must be dismissed, quite
firmly, as irrelevant. Rather, the system acts as a
series of 'constraints', in the fullest sense of the
word, on the reader, writer and rewriter. He or she
çan, therefore, choose to 'go with the system', so
to speak, to stay within the parameters delimited by
the constraints - and much great literature does precisely that - or, alternatively, he or she may choose
to go against the system, to try to operate outside
the constraints of his or her time, by reading works
of literature in other than the received ways, by
writing them in ways different from those considered
great at a particular time and in a particular place,
by rewriting them in such a manner that they tend
not to fit in with the dominant poetics or ideology
of his or her time and place, but with an alternative ideology, an alternative poetics. At most, then,
literature is a stochastic system, one whose "behav-

iour cannot be prognosticated unambiguously but only in statements for which no more than a certain likelihood is claimed" (Czayka 1974:45).

Literature is one of the systems which constitute the (super)system known as society, which also encompasses other systems, such as physics, law, and many more. A further word of warning may be in order here: I use the term system with a fair degree of flexibility, ranging far and wide in history (the Medieval System in Western Europe, say) and geography (the Euramerican system, or the Islamic system). I trust that the reader will read the term with a corresponding flexibility of mind, the result of a willing suspension of attitude, so to speak.

Alternatively, a society, a culture is the environment of a literary system. The literary system and the system of society are open to each other, they influence each other. There is, in fact, a control factor in the literary system which sees to it that that system does not fall too far out of step with other systems the society consists of. Or rather, it would be more accurate to say that this control function is shared by two elements, one of which belongs squarely in the literary system, whereas the other is to be found outside of that system. The first element tries to control the literary system from the inside, within the parameters set by the second element. The first element is represented by interpreters, critics, reviewers, teachers of literature, translators. They will occasionally repress certain works of literature because these works go all too blantantly against the dominant concept of what literature should (be allowed to) be - the poetics - and of what society should (be allowed to) be - the ideology, the world view - of a certain society at a certain moment. But these rewriters will much more frequently adapt works of literature until they can be claimed to correspond to the poetics and the ideology of their age. French neo-classical translations of Homer, for example, in which all that was felt to be 'uncouth', such as the entrails of both men and animals, was resolutely left out, are an obvious example of the process, as long as we realize that these features of the original were not left out because the translators knew no Greek, or because the Greek-French dictionaries of the period were strangely deficient in certain areas, but because the 'uncouth' simply ran counter to the dominant poetics/ideology of that period - to such an extent even that when Leconte de Lisle translated Homer about a hundred and fifty years later, and with all entrails in place, he was seriously accused, in certain quarters, of having mutilated the original, whereas he was, in fact, restoring it.

The second control factor, the one which operates mostly outside the literary system proper, will be called 'patronage' here, and it will be understood to mean something like 'the powers (persons, institutions) which help or hinder the writing, reading and rewriting of literature.' Patronage is usually more interested in the ideology of literature than in its poetics, or it could be said that the patron 'delegates' authority to the interpreter where poetics is concerned. A paradigmatic example of this, which will serve to make matters clearer, may be found in the relationship between the critic Sainte Beuve and his patron, the later Napoleon III. As Chris Baldick puts it, "the political 'strong man' for whom Sainte Beuve was to be the literary equivalent was Louis Bonaparte and it was in the (far from 'disinterested') Bonapartist journal *Le Constitutionnel* and the official government paper *Le Moniteur* that he published his *Causeries*" (Baldick 1983:13).

Patronage consists of three elements, which can be seen to interact in various combinations. There is an ideological component, which acts as a constraint on the choice and development of both form and subject-matter. There is also an economic component: the patron sees to it that writers and re-writers are able to make a living, by giving them a pension, appointing them to some office (Chaucer, as is not too widely known outside the circles frequented by medievalists, acted as "the King's envoy, the controller of customs on wool, hides and sheepskins or the subforester of North Petherton," cf. Bennett 1952:5), paying royalties on the sale of books, or employing writers and rewriters as teachers and reviewers. There is, finally, also an element of status involved: "acceptance of patronage signaled integration into an elite and acceptance of the style of life associated with that elite" (Clark & Clark 1977:201). Goethe's Tasso provides us with perhaps the most succinct description of this element when he exclaims: "here is my fatherland, here is the circle/ in which my soul is pleased to dwell/ I listen here, I pay attention to every hint/ here speak the voices of experience, science and taste" (lines 449-452). "Here" is, of course, the court of Ferrara, and Goethe himself had, as is well known, found a patron in another court. In more recent times, on the other hand, acceptance of patronage may simply mean integration into the lifestyle of a support group, or subculture, which certainly need not always be described in terms of an élite.

Patronage can be exerted by persons (not necessarily the Medici, Maecenas or Louis XIV), groups of persons (a religious body, say, or a political party), a social class, a royal court, publishers (whether they have a virtual monopoly of the booktrade or not) and, last but not least, the media: "the BBC is the richest and largest patron in history" (Hall 1979:62). Patrons rarely try to influence a literary system directly. They usually operate by means of institutions set up to regulate the writing or at least the distribution of literature: academies, bureaus for censorship, critical journals and the educational establishment. Critics who represent the 'reigning orthodoxy' at any given time in the development of a literary system are close to the ideology of the patrons dominating that phase in the history of the social system in which the literary system is embedded. Or, to put it somewhat bluntly: "the history of literature is to a great extent the history of the generosity of individual rulers and aristocrats" (Schücking 1961:92) - and of course also the history of their lack of generosity towards those they did not elect to support, often on the advice of the leading critics of their day: the names of Kleist and Hölderlin come to mind. It is also the history of those they elected to suppress, whether by outright physical extermination or by means of a more subtle nature. Nor should that history be limited to rulers and aristocrats, for that relegates the part played by patronage in literary systems to the more or less distant, more or less 'safe' past, and obscures the fact that the function of patronage, once performed mainly by rulers and aristocrats, is still a major factor to be reckoned with in any literary system: it simply has been taken over by patrons of a different kind.

Patronage can be differentiated or undifferentiated, or rather, literary systems can be controlled by a type of patronage which is either differentiated or undifferentiated in nature. Patronage is undifferentiated when its three components - the ideological, the economic and the status component - are all dispensed by one and the same patron, as was the case in most systems in the past, and as is the case in contemporary totalitarian states. Patronage is differentiated when economic success, for instance, is relatively independent of ideological factors, and does not necessarily bring status in its wake, at least not in the eyes of the self-styled literary

élite. Most authors of contemporary bestsellers tend
to illustrate that point rather well, none perhaps
more so than Harold Robbins whose economic success
is secure, whose books operate within the parameters
of the ideology generally accepted in his native
country, and who probably could not care less whether
the *New York Review of Books* crowd thinks he is a great
writer or not. In short, patronage is differentiated
in nature when the three components it consists of
are not necessarily dispensed by one and the same
person or institution.

A literary system also operates with a code,
which makes (at least potential) communication between author and reader possible. This code is called
a poetics, and it can be said to consist of two components: one is an inventory of literary devices,
genres, motifs, symbols, prototypical characters and
situations, the other a concept of what the role of
literature is, or should be, in society at large.
This concept plays an important part in the selection of themes, which must be relevant to society
for the work of literature to be noticed. In its
formative phase a poetics reflects both the devices
and the 'functional view' of the literary production
dominant in a system at the time when its poetics
was first codified. Once a poetics is codified it
exerts a tremendous system-conforming influence on
the further development of the system. A "systematic
poetics emerges in a culture after a literary system
proper has been generated and when important critical conceptions are based on a then flourishing or
normatively considered genre. The coinciding of major
critics with the considered genre generates the critical system. It is because Plato and Aristotle took
drama as the norm that they considered imitation the
essential character of literature" (Miner 1978:350).
And since they did so, they proceeded to invent an
appropriate critical vocabulary, many of whose terms
are still in current use in most European languages,
even though they were first thought up in Greek more
than two thousand years ago.

The functional component of a poetics is obviously closely tied to ideological influences from outside the sphere of the poetics proper, generated by
ideological forces in the environment of the literary system. In African culture, for instance, with
its emphasis on the community and its values, literature was not supposed to be conducive to personal
fame or personal immortality for its creator. In
fact, all traditional African literature is, by Western standards, 'anonymous' and classified under the

229

name of the tribe (the community), not that of the individual, the author, whose name remains unknown.

In the codification of the poetics of a literary system, then, practice precedes theory. Codification occurs at a certain point in time, which implies both the selection of certain types of current practice and the exclusion of others. Or, to put it in systems terminology, the principle of formative preference applies, which means that only certain possibilities which exist at a given time are, in fact, actualized. The codification of the poetics is the work of critics, though not necessarily of the kind we would now almost automatically associate with that term. Codification in African literature did occur in the 'classical' system, the literatures of Sub-Saharan Africa as they developed from about the beginning of our era to the advent of the white man, and beyond, but the absence of written records in the African system did prevent the rise of a group of professional critics. It did not, however - and this is a sobering thought - prevent the production of literature as such.

It would be a mistake to think that 'important critical conceptions' always find explicit expression in all literary systems. They do not in the African system, even though they are most certainly at work in it. They are also not explicitly formulated in the Chinese and Japanese literary systems, at least not in the way readers of Western literature would expect them to be. In the formative stages of both the Japanese and the Chinese systems, these critical conceptions were not written out in discursive prose or verse, but rather implicitly contained in anthologies, such as the *Shih Ching* and the *Chu Tzu* in the Chinese system, the *Manyoshu* and the *Kokinshu* in the Japanese system. The process of codification is probably more apparent in those systems, where teaching tended to rely more on written example than on precept, than in others where codification did take the form of discursive prose or verse, codifying varieties of existing practice mainly by abstracting their 'rules' and then 'prescribing' these rules for future writers to follow - the kind of textbook poetics familiar in the Indian, the Islamic and especially the Western literary systems. Yet in both cases codification of the poetics did take place, and in both cases it took place by means of the intermediary process of rewriting, not on the strength of the works of literature alone.

Codification of the poetics also leads to canonization of the output of certain writers whose work

is seen as conforming most closely to the codified
poetics. The work of those writers is then used as
an example for future writers to follow, and it occupies a central position in the teaching of literature.
Rewritings tend to play at least as important a part
in the establishment of canonized works of literature
as those works do themselves. Plato and Aristotle
have already been mentioned above, but probably the
most arresting example of canonization is that of
the *mu allaqat*, the original seven great qasidas of
the Islamic system, cast in gold and suspended from
the Kaaba in Mecca. They could hardly have achieved
the status they now occupy through the efforts of
the poets who composed them only. Canonization was
at least as much the result of the efforts of the
rawis, the apprentice-poets, who started out learning
their trade as professional reciters and spread the
fame of the masters to whom they were apprenticed.

In systems with a differentiated patronage, different 'critical schools' will try to elaborate different canons of their own, and each of the schools
will try to pass off its own canon as the only 'real'
one, i.e. the one that corresponds to its poetics,
its ideology. One of the most recent examples of the
process has been described by Terry Eagleton as follows:

> With breathtaking boldness *Scrutiny* redrew the map of
> English literature in ways from which criticism never
> quite recovered. The main thoroughfares on this map
> ran through Chaucer, Shakespeare, Jonson, the Jacobeans
> and Metaphysicals, Bunyan, Pope, Samuel Johnson, Blake,
> Wordsworth, Keats, Austen, George Eliot, Hopkins, Henry
> James, Joseph Conrad, T.S. Eliot and D.H. Lawrence.
> This *was* 'English literature': Spenser, Dryden, Resto-
> ration drama, Defoe, Fielding, Richardson, Sterne,
> Shelley, Byron, Tennyson, Browning, most of the Victo-
> rian novelists, Joyce, Woolf and most writers after
> D.H. Lawrence constituted a network of "B" roads inter-
> spersed with a good few cul-de-sacs. Dickens was first
> out and then in; 'English' included two and a half
> women, counting Emily Brontë as a marginal case; almost
> all of its authors were conservatives. (Eagleton 1983:
> 32-33)

Needless to say, such a canon becomes effective only
when actively propagated through teaching, a fact
Leavis was quick to realize, as T.S. Eliot, who was
elaborating his own canon of English and world literature at more or less the same time was not, failing to see "the importance of the educational system
as an agency of cultural continuity. As a result of

this failure, he proved incapable of carrying through any sustained cultural project of wider scope than the tiny readership of *The Criterion*" (Baldick 1983:131).

Codification takes place at a certain time, and once it has occurred the poetics takes on a life of its own, increasingly divorced from the environment of the literary system. A poetics is also subject to change, even though most poetics tend to present themselves as eternal and immovable, paradoxically by appealing to their own formative phase as the basis of their authority even when, at the time the appeal is made, their functional component has become quite different indeed from what it was in that formative phase. The change in the poetics of a literary system very rarely occurs at the same pace as that prevailing in the environment of that system. Sonnets began to be written when the horse was the fastest means of transportation, and they are still being written, albeit with slight modifications, in the age of jet travel.

Once a literary system is established it tends to try to reach a steady state, as all systems do, a state in which all elements are in equilibrium with each other and with the environment. Strictly regulated systems even appoint individuals to institutions especially created to bring that state of affairs into being, such as the Académie Française and other academies. Yet there are two factors, in the literary system as in all other systems, which tend to counteract this development. Systems evolve according to the principle of polarity, which holds that every system eventually evolves its own countersystem, the way Romantic poetics, for instance, eventually stood neo-classical poetics on its head, and the principle of periodicity, which holds that all systems are liable to change. The evolution of a literary system is the complex interplay of the tendency towards a steady state, the two opposing tendencies just mentioned, and the way in which the system's regulatory component (patronage) tries to handle these opposing tendencies. It is my contention that rewritten literature plays a vital part in this evolution.

III

All writing of literature takes place under the two constraints mentioned above, patronage and poetics, to which two more constraints must be added. One is what linguists often call 'universe of discourse' these days, i.e. the knowledge, the learning, but

232

also the objects and the customs of a certain time, to which writers are free to allude in their work. The other is the natural language in which the work is composed. For rewriters a fifth constraint must be added, namely that of the original work itself. The original is the locus where ideology, poetics, universe of discourse and language come together, mingle and clash.

All rewriting of literature, be it interpretation, criticism, historiography, the putting together of anthologies, or translation, takes place under at least one of the constraints mentioned, and implies the others. Philology of the traditional kind, for example, operated mainly under the third and fourth constraints, explaining linguistic difficulties and making clear again for the reader what was obvious in the writer's universe of discourse as he or she was writing. When Catullus notes at the end of his 64th poem, celebrating the wedding of Peleus and Thetis, that the bride's collar now no longer fits her neck, the readers needs to be told that the Romans believed that the successful consummation of marriage made the bride's neck swell slightly, or otherwise he or she will not be able to understand what is actually going on in the poem.

Since it operates mainly under the third and fourth constraints, philology seems at first sight to have little to do with either poetics or ideology, but both make themselves felt in the actual selection of texts for editing, and in the ways in which the editing itself is done. To take one example among many:

> The pioneering Hellingrath edition of Hölderlin, initiated before the First World War, embodies the the ideology of the Stefan George circle, to which Hölderlin owes his revival and to which Hellingrath belonged ... The Stuttgart Hölderlin edition, completed after the Second World War, shows a distinctly nationalist bias (the late hymns are grouped under the title 'The Patriotic Hymns'), and the strict division of final versions from earlier drafts and fragments reveals that conception of the individual poem as an autonomous entity which prevailed at the time. The Frankfurt Hölderlin edition reflects the leftist bias dominant among German scholars in the late 1960s and 1970s; not only does it highlight Hölderlin's sympathies with the French Revolution, but through its presentation of early and later drafts in the order of composition it suggests a notion of poetry as process, characteristic of our

own time. (Lindenberger 1981:222)

Interpretation, criticism, interpretation-cum-criticism, on the other hand, tend to be more concerned with the first and the second constraint. They tend to try either to salvage the text under discussion for productive integration into the system, or to dismiss it as a potentially pernicious influence, which is likely to upset the steady state and must therefore be left out. In actual practice, of course, most criticism cum interpretation is situated somewhere on the sliding scale that joins the two extremes described. Historiography tends to do for the whole oeuvre and the actual status of writers what criticism cum interpretation does for individual texts. Writers and their oeuvre are either subsumed in the ideological and/or poetological mainstream, or else they are reduced to 'minor' authors who have, at best, produced works that provide interesting footnotes to the period under discussion. The putting together of anthologies tends to reflect 'the judgements of literary history' where it really matters: in shaping the taste of a wider audience and, most importantly, in education. It is by means of anthologies that students are introduced to the 'masters' of their own and the 'giants' of world literature, and exclusion or inclusion often spells survival or oblivion. That anthologies are shaped by ideological and poetological constraints can be made clear by the following examples. Anthologies of German poetry during the Nazi era had to omit Heinrich Heine because he was a Jew. At best they could include his well-known Loreley ballad, but only if they managed to pass it off as 'anonymous'. It is also a well-known fact that most of the early battles of modernism in Anglo-American poetry were fought by means of anthologies, Imagist, Georgian and other. Rewriting, then, in all its forms, can be seen as a weapon in the struggle for supremacy between various ideologies, various poetics. It should be analysed and studied that way.

Translation is probably the most obvious instance of rewriting, since it operates under all four constraints. Yet all different forms of rewriting tend to work together in a literary system. No translation, published as a book, is likely to give you just the translation. It is nearly always accompanied by an introduction, which is a form of criticism cum interpretation. If the translation is successful, acclaimed, taken up into the mainstream, it is sure to be anthologized sooner or later, and historians of literature writing on literatures other than those of which they know the languages, will rely on translations to get their impressions of what a work is like. No one form of rewriting alone can establish or disestablish, make or break the reputation of a writer and/or a work inside the receiving culture, just as functional and inventory innovations in the poetics of the receiving literature may be initiated by translation, but they are then reinforced by other forms of rewriting.

Translation operates first of all under the constraint of the original, itself the product of constraints belonging to a certain time. Second, the language changes, quite dramatically. Third, the universe of discourse very often poses insuperable problems for any kind of so-called 'faithful' translation. Universe of discourse features are those features particular to a given culture, and they are, almost by definition, untranslatable or at least very hard to translate. They can be things, like 'bistro' in French, or concepts, like 'völkisch' in German. They belong to a certain time, like 'völkisch' in German or 'tunica' in Latin, and they go under with their time as far as their language of origin is concerned. In translation, however, they need to be resuscitated, though nobody is quite sure in what form: loan translation, calque, footnote, a combination of the three?

Voltaire's translations of Shakespeare provide us with a good example of the poetological adaptation works of literature are forced to undergo: the alexandrine takes the place of the iambic pentameter and the alexandrine does, of course, rhyme. Shakespeare, in other words, has to sound a lot more like Racine in order to be acceptable as Shakespeare for the French audience of Voltaire's time. In Victor Hugo's time, on the other hand, Shakespeare does not have to sound like Racine any more - proof of the fact that no poetics remains dominant in a given system for ever. The same fact also highlights the relationship between patronage and poetics: the poetics of Victor Hugo's time is so different from that of Voltaire's time because the patronage has shifted dramatically: the people who extended patronage to Hugo were the people who, among other things, survived the French Revolution and even profited from it. Many of the people who were Voltaire's patrons, and went to applaud his tragedies which are now almost completely forgotten, did not.

Writers are rewritten when their work passes from one literature into another, just as they are rewritten inside a given literature. But why, it may be asked, do writers have to submit to these indignities? First of all, they don't really submit. In many cases they have long been dead, in most they have precious little say in the matter. Writers are powerless to control the rewriting of their work, which may be a bad thing; but so, in the long run, is anybody else, which may not be such a bad thing after all. Second, if the writer does not 'submit', he or she will simply not exist in the receiving literature at all. Third, these indignities usually stop after a while. True, the foreign writer may have to adopt the native guise, but once he or she is established in the receiving literature, new translations tend to be made with the aim of revealing him or her on his or her own terms to the receiving literature, and no longer on terms dictated by the receiving literature itself. The example of Brecht's *Mother Courage* in English/American, which I have analysed in more detail elsewhere (Lefevere 1982), is instructive in this context.

It is and remains a fact of literary life that patrons and critics are, in the final analysis, influential in deciding what will 'make it' in a given literature and what will not. They do the screening and they pronounce the verdict. The fight to influence that verdict one way or the other is fought with weapons taken not primarily from the writings of the author in question, but by means of rewritings of all kinds, which are used against each other until a certain consensus is reached in systems with differentiated patronage. In systems with undifferentiated patronage the matter is usually settled with more efficiency and dispatch: what does not fit in with the dominant poetics or ideology is simply labelled 'denatured', or 'vile', or 'trivial', or even 'popular and entertaining'.

Whether or not a literature dictates its terms to potential imports will often depend on the self-image that literature has developed. If, like French literature in the eighteenth century, it was convinced that it represented the very epitome of wit and elegance, it would have every reason to screen out whatever did not fulfil its requirements, or else change it in such a way as to make it acceptable. It did that to foreign works by means of translations, it also did that to French works written in a French that was not quite the French of Paris (and therefore dismissed as 'popular', even though, on occasion, 'charmingly naive'), and it also did that to French works not written to its specifications, ideological or otherwise, such as those of the Marquis de Sade.

If, on the other hand, the potential receiving literature does not have all that much of a self-image, like German literature in that same eighteenth century, it will not (and did not) dictate any terms at all. On the contrary, it will accept at least the poetics of the source literature as a potentially liberating influence and one that will, through patient imitation, allow it finally to emerge from the depths of obscurity and to play an important part on the stage of world literature as a whole.

Translation, then, is the visible sign of the openness of the literary system, of a specific literary system. It opens the way to what can be called both subversion and transformation, depending on where the guardians of the dominant poetics, the dominant ideology stand. No wonder, therefore, that there have been all kinds of attempts to regulate translation, to make sure that it does not exert any subversive influence on the native system, to use it to integrate what is foreign by naturalizing it first. Various historical periods, dominated by completely different poetics, have formulated rules for the translator to follow, different rules, of course, contradictory rules even, but rules nonetheless. In fact it could be said that long after the normative (handbooks of) poetics disappeared from Western literature – and those always contained at least one chapter on translation – translation remained the only literary activity still supposed to be bound by rules also, and with a vengeance, in the Romantic period which claimed to have abolished all rules of any kind in poetic composition.

It should be clear, by now, that translation does not manage to subvert or transform a literature all on its own. Translation does so in conjunction with other forms of rewriting, which explains why translation should also be studied in conjunction with other forms of rewriting, and not on its own. If the study of translation is to be made productive for the study of literary theory and, especially, literary history, it is quite clear that translation can no longer be analysed in isolation, but that it should be studied as part of a whole system of texts and the people who produce, support, propagate, oppose, censor them. Or, to put it differently, translation can be studied in isolation only if it is reduced to one half of one of the constraints under which it is produced: that of the locutionary level of language.

The translation of literature, then, must be heavily regulated because it is potentially - and often actually - subversive, precisely because it offers a cover for the translator to go against the dominant constraints of his or her time, not in his or her own name which, in most cases, would not happen to be all that well known anyway, but rather in the name of, and relying on the authority of a writer who is considered great enough in another literature so as not to be ignored in one's own, at least not if one wants to safeguard that literature against provincialism and other forms of atrophy. It goes without saying that all this holds equally true for other forms of rewriting; translation only makes it all so much more obvious, though still not as obvious as the production of drama. But then translations are more difficult to ferret out and destroy than drama. It is not too difficult to close down theatres, or to censor plays, or to forbid specific performances of specific plays. It is much more difficult to destroy all potentially subversive translations.

Not all translations produced do, of course, fit the mould described here. A fair number of them tend to be produced by 'technicians' rather than 'prophets' By technicians I mean scholars of literature who are able to make works of literature belonging to other systems available in their own systems through translations. This is a sorely needed contribution to literary studies, since in the present state of literary affairs the natural language in which a work of literature is written does not infrequently militate against that work being given wider exposure. As a result, certain systems of literature (particularly the Islamic one, in my opinion) are rather less well known than others, and generalizations in surveys and histories of literature are made on the basis of what is best known. Most generalizations about literature have, in fact, been made on the basis of a more or less unashamedly Eurocentric poetics, and, more precisely, of a certain historical phase in the evolution of that poetics.

It is clear, however, that 'literature' cannot be adequately studied if it is, in practice, restricted to the literature of Europe and the Americas, and that non-Western literary systems, so often relegated to the mysterious and therefore largely ignorable status of the 'exotic', are as vital for any understanding of literature as is the Western system on its own. Generalizations are, therefore, very often made in good faith, though just as often on the basis of the kind of ignorance that could be relatively easily remedied by translation.

It should also be clear that the translations I

have in mind at this point should be seen as a heuristic tool to profit the study of literature - which does, of course, not mean that they should be forbidden to delight and please the reader as well - and not as an 'interpretive' weapon in the struggle between rival poetics inside the receiving system. The aim of this kind of translation would be to make literature produced in other systems available for description and analysis, which is why it should, ideally, be a 'descriptive' rather than an interpretive translation. In practice, of course, translations will tend to be more or less descriptive or more or less interpretive, simply because nobody is ever able to escape from the ideology and/or the poetics prevalent in the literary system of his or her own time, to which his or her translation will be seen to belong.

IV

Regulation comes relatively easily to the translation of literature because, on one level at least, translation is regulated. I mean the level of language, to be sure. But here, too, things are not that simple and I need to explain the distinction currently made in linguistics between the locutionary and the illocutionary levels of language. The locutionary level is that of grammatical rules and semantic accuracy: you don't translate elephants by crocodiles and you don't ask questions featuring the "do you" pattern in German. This is, in other words, the level of the howler and the lack of competence. The illocutionary level, on the other hand, is that of the way in which language is used to achieve certain effects, to express what the writer has to say in such a way that it achieves maximum impact. Here regulation tends to become a lot more difficult, and rules more difficult to enforce, for the simple reason that different languages tend to achieve similar illocutionary effects in dissimilar ways, a well-known example being the effective use of word juxtaposition in highly inflected languages, which has to be feebly reconstructed by means of prepositions in languages less inflected. This state of affairs also helps to explain why translation is mainly taught on the locutionary level and this fact explains, in its turn, why so many textbooks purporting to teach translation turn out, after some scratching of the surface, to be little more than a rehash of currently dominant linguistic theories, combined with a dosage of stylistics and remedial language teaching. Another reason

why this is so should, in my opinion, be looked for
in the very classroom situation in which translation
is taught. The teacher is supposed to make competent
translators out of his or her students, and the only
level on which the teacher can judge that competence,
inside the classroom, is that of language, certainly
in its locutionary, to some extent also in its illocutionary use. The other levels far transcend the
classroom, as the student who produces the umpteenth
translation of Heine - which may actually be better
than most existing translations but fails to find a
publisher because of the copyright situation - will
soon find out. As a result, the teacher tends to limit competence to the only kind he or she can more or
less safely circumscribe in his or her capacity of
first person of an (un)holy trinity consisting of
teacher, grammar and dictionary. Since he or she is
powerless in the face of other constraints, he or she
might as well try to ignore them as much as possible,
although he or she can never do that completely and
is bound to run into contradictions sooner or later.

Teaching translation on the linguistic level is
not doing actual (or rather, potential) translators
a service. It consists mainly of teaching people a
number of skills which do not appear to be adequate
for dealing with complex situations outside the classroom, which leaves the recipients of this knowledge
rather disturbed and also rightly irritated at their
teachers, which, in turn, leads to a growing disenchantment with 'theory' among practising translators.
Teaching translation this way is to try to train
people so that they will fit in with the teacher's
abstraction of the many and variegated demands the
culture he or she teaches in is likely to make on
translators, without trying to make them understand
why those demands are made, why they must be so complex and why they are likely to change.

And yet the choice is not between a collection
of skills on the one hand and a theoretical edifice
without any practical relevance to the actual translator on the other. A valid way of teaching translation would show how the four constraints enumerated
above influence the writing and rewriting of texts.
It would open the practising translator's eyes to
the way in which texts are actually generated in the
culture he or she is part of, and which expects him
or her to regenerate a foreign text. The translator
will then be able to devise his or her own strategy
with respect to the constraints listed, in such a
way as to make the text take its place in the receiving culture, rather than to apply, in a more or less

mechanical fashion, a number of skills which are
necessarily limited and are not even designed to
match the multitude of actually occurring situations
calling for a multitude of different strategies. Once
he or she has been shown that translation is so much
more than the mechanical application of acquired
skills, the translator will be able to identify the
goal he or she sets out to reach, not as the result
of some hunch, some intuition, but rather as the result of an analysis of the source text and the culture it was generated in, with a view to regenerating
it in a different culture.

It is therefore perfectly acceptable to fill in
the general heuristic model of constraints with specific constraints actually operative at a given moment, and to act accordingly, depending on what you
set out to achieve. If you want to translate a text,
or texts, it will no doubt be of importance to you
to know what constraints are operative in your here
and now, and you may use the knowledge you have gath-
ered to write a textbook summarizing the present
state of affairs, as long as you emphasize that that
is, precisely, what it represents, and nothing more,
certainly nothing of the timeless and unchangeable
variety.

If, on the other hand, you see translation as
one, probably the most radical form of rewriting in
a literature, or a culture, and if you believe that
rewriting shapes the evolution of a literature or a
culture at least as much as actual writing, you will
analyze different instances of that process in different cultures at different times, to test your heuristic model and, no doubt, to adapt it. You can do
this within the cultural subsystem called literature,
and investigate to what extent rewriting is responsible for the establishement of a canon of core works
and for the victories and defeats of successive con-
stellations of poetics and ideologies, or you can decide that you don't have to stop there and that translation, like other forms of rewriting, plays an ana-
lysable part in the manipulation of words and concepts
which, among other things, constitute power in a
culture.

It is a sobering thought, in this respect, that
a somewhat pigheaded translator of the Bible into
German, a defrocked Augustine monk was, also because
of his translation, largely responsible for the
Reformation which changed the face of Europe for ever,
or that the Aramaic which Jesus Christ spoke has no
copula, no actual verb 'to be', even though theolo-
gians have haggled for centuries over the true mean-

ing of the 'is' which appears, in Greek translation, in phrases like 'this is my body' and that they have burned those who failed to agree with their rewriting whenever they had the power to do so.

REFERENCES

BALDICK, Chris
1983   *The Social Mission of English Criticism, 1848-1932.*
        Oxford, Clarendon
BENNETT, H.S.
1952   *English Books and Readers.* Cambridge, Cambridge UP
CLARK, P.P. & CLARK, T.N.
1977   'Patrons, Publishers and Prizes: the Writer's Estate
        in France', in J.Ben-David & T.N.Clark (eds.), *Culture
        and its Creators* (Chicago, Chicago UP):197-225
CZAYKA, L.
1974   *Systemwissenschaft.* Pullach, Verlag Dokumentation
DUBOIS, Jean
1978   *L'institution de la littérature.* Brussels, Editions
        Labor
EAGLETON, Terry
1983   *Literary Theory.* Oxford, Basil Blackwell
FEYERABEND, Paul
1978   *Science in a Free Society.* London, New Left Books
HALL, J.
1979   *The Sociology of Literature.* London, Longman
HALLBERG, R. von
1983   'Editor's Introduction', *Critical Inquiry*, x,1:iii-vi
HERRNSTEIN-SMITH, Barbara
1983   'Contingencies of Value', *Critical Inquiry*, x,1:1-31
KAST, F.E. & ROSENZWEIG, J.E.
1972   'The Modern View: a Systems Approach', in J.Beishon &
        G.Peters (eds.), *Systems Behavior* (New York, Harper &
        Row):14-28
KNAPP, S. & MICHAELS, W.B.
1982   'Against Theory', *Critical Inquiry*, viii,4:723-742
KOPPE, F.
1978   'Die literaturwissenschaftlichen Hauptrichtungen und
        ihr Ertrag für eine Gegenstandsbestimmung der Litera-
        turwissenschaft', *Zeitschrift für allgemeine Wissen-
        schaftstheorie*, ix,1:157-184
KUHN, T.S.
1971   *The Structure of Scientific Revolutions.* Chicago,
        Chicago UP
LEFEVERE, André
1982   'Mother Courage's Cucumbers: Text, System and Refrac-
        tion in a Theory of Literature, *Modern Language
        Studies*, xii,4:3-20
LINDENBERGER, Herbert
1981   'Criticism and its Institutional Situations', in

P.Hernadi (ed.), *What Is Criticism?* (Bloomington, Indiana UP):215-229

McCANLES, Michael
1981   'Criticism is the (Dis)closure of Meaning', in P.Hernadi (ed.) *What Is Criticism?* (Bloomington, Indiana UP):268-279

MAN, Paul de
1979   *Allegories of Reading.* New Haven, Yale UP

MATTESICH, R.
1978   *Instrumental Reasoning and Systems Methodology.* Dordrecht/Boston, D.Reidel

MINER, Earl
1978   'On the Genesis and Development of Literary Systems, I', *Critical Inquiry*, v,2:339-353

PRATT, Mary
1981   'Art without Critics and Critics without Readers', in P.Hernadi (ed.), *What Is Criticism?* (Bloomington, Indiana UP):177-188

RAPOPORT, Anatol
1975   'Modern Systems Theory - An Outlook for Coping with Change', in B.D.Ruben & J.Y.Kim (eds.), *General Systems Theory and Human Communication* (Rochelle Park, New York, Hayden Books):33-51

SAID, Edward
1983   *The World, the Text, and the Critic.* Cambridge (Mass.) Harvard UP

SCHMIDT, Siegfried
1982   *Grundriss einer empirischen Literaturwissenschaft.* Braunschweig, Vieweg

SCHUECKING, L.L.
1961   *Soziologie der literarischen Geschmacksbildung (1923),* Berlin/Munich, Francke

STOUT, J.
1982   'What is the Meaning of a Text?', *New Literary History,* xiv,1:1-12

GENERAL BIBLIOGRAPHY

The bibliography given below is highly selective. In principle, only publications by contributors to the present collection and by participants to the three colloquia mentioned in the Introduction are listed, with an emphasis on books, articles and preprints in English and French. Since, in practical terms, the descriptive and functional research carried out by members of this group is not necessarily incompatible with work done by other scholars in the field who do not share the theoretical presuppositions of the systems concept of literature, there are no hard and fast rules for selection on grounds of content alone.

For more general bibliographical data on translation studies, see, among others: Louis Kelly, 'Bibliography of the Translation of Literature', *Comparative Criticism* (ed. E.Shaffer), 6, 1984:347-359, which also mentions the most important existing bibliographies; James Holmes, 'A Basic Bibliography of Books on Translation Studies 1956-1976', in J.S.Holmes *et al.* (eds.) *Literature and Translation* (Louvain, Acco, 1978):236-260; and, above all, the very full bibliography compiled by Jeffrey F.Huntsman, *Translation Theory: A Comprehensive Bibliography* (Amsterdam, John Benjamins, 1985;600pp.).

BACCHILEGA, Cristina
1982   'Cesare Pavese and America: The Myth of Translation and the Translation of Myth', *Dispositio*, vii,19-20-21,1982: 77-84
BARRASS, Tine
1978   'The Function of Translated Literature within a National Literature: The Example of Sixteenth-Century Spain', in J.S.Holmes *et al.* (eds.), *Literature and Translation* (Louvain, Acco):181-203
BASSNETT-McGUIRE, Susan
1978   'Translating Spatial Poetry: An Examination of Theatre Texts in Performance', in J.S.Holmes *et al.* (eds.) *Literature and Translation* (Louvain, Acco):161-176
1980   *Translation Studies*. London/New York, Methuen

BRAGT, Katrin van
1982 'The Tradition of a Translation and its Implications:
      The Vicar of Wakefield in French Translation', *Dispositio,*
      vii,19-20-21,1982:63-76
BROECK, Raymond van den
1978 'The Concept of Equivalence in Translation Theory: Some
      Critical Reflections', in J.S.Holmes *et al.* (eds.) *Liter-*
      ature and Translation (Louvain, Acco):29-47
1981 'The Limits of Translatability Exemplified by Metaphor
      Translation', *Poetics Today*, ii,4, Summer-Autumn 1981:
      73-87
BROECK, Raymond van den & LEFEVERE, André
1979 *Uitnodiging tot de vertaalwetenschap.* Muiderberg, Coutinho
BURNETT, Leon
1976 *Dimensions of Truth: A Comparative Study of the Relation-*
      ship between 'Language' and 'Reality' in the Works of
      Wordsworth, Coleridge, Zhukovsky, Pushkin and Keats.
      Unpublished PhD thesis, University of Essex
1981a ''Obval': Pushkin's 'Kubla Khan'', *Essays in Poetics,* vi,
      1, April 1981:22-38
1981b 'Heirs of Eternity. An Essay on the Poetry of Keats and
      Mandel'shtam', *Modern Language Review,* lxxvi,2, April
      1981:396-419
D'HULST, Lieven
1980 *La ballade en France (1810-1830). Formation et évolution*
      d'un genre instable. Preprint. Dept. of General Literary
      Studies, University of Louvain (KUL)
1981 'Les variantes textuelles des traductions littéraires',
      Poetics Today, ii,4, Summer-Autumn 1981:133-141
1982a *L'évolution de la poésie en France (1780-1830). Intro-*
      duction à une analyse des interférences systémiques.
      Unpublished PhD thesis, University of Louvain (KUL)
1982b 'The Conflict of Translational Models in France (end of
      18th - beginning of 19th century)', *Dispositio,* vii,19-
      20-21,1982:41-52
ETKIND, Efim
1978 'La traduction et les courants littéraires', in J.S.
      Holmes *et al.* (eds.), *Literature and Translation* (Louvain,
      Acco):128-141
EVEN-ZOHAR, Itamar
1978 *Papers in Historical Poetics.* Tel Aviv, Porter Institute
      for Poetics and Semiotics
1979 'Polysystem Theory', *Poetics Today,* i,1-2,Autumn 1979:
      287-310
1981 'Translation Theory Today. A Call for Transfer Theory',
      Poetics Today, ii,4,Summer-Autumn 1981:1-7
GORP, Hendrik van
1978 'La traduction littéraire parmi les autres métatextes',
      in J.S.Holmes *et al.* (eds.) *Literature and Translation*
      (Louvain, Acco):101-116
1981 'Traductions et évolution d'un genre littéraire. Le roman

picaresque en Europe au 17e et 18e siècle', *Poetics Today,* ii,4,Summer-Autumn 1981:209-219

HERMANS, Theo
1979   'Translation, Comparison, Diachrony', *Comparison 9,* Spring 1979:58-91
1980   'P.C. Hooft: The Sonnets and the Tragedy', *Dutch Crossing* 12, December 1980:10-26. Also in *Dispositio,* vii, 19-20-21, 1982:95-110
1982   *The Structure of Modernist Poetry.* London/Canberra, Croom Helm

HOLMES, James S.
1969   'Forms of Verse Translation and the Translation of Verse Form', *Babel* xv, 1969:195-201. Also in J.S.Holmes *et al.* (eds.) *The Nature of Translation* (The Hague/Bratislava, Mouton/Slovak Academy, 1970):9i-105
1971   'The Cross-Temporal Factor in Verse Translation', *Slavica Slovaca,* vi,1971:326-334
1975   *The Name and Nature of Translation Studies.* Preprint. Amsterdam, Dept. of General Literary Studies, University of Amsterdam
1978   'Describing Literary Translations: Models and Methods', in J.S.Holmes *et al.* (eds.),*Literature and Translation* (Louvain, Acco):69-82

HOLMES, James S., HAAN, Frans de & POPOVIČ, Anton
1970   (eds.) *The Nature of Translation: Essays on the Theory and Practice of Literary Translation.* The Hague/Paris & Bratislava, Mouton & Slovak Academy of Sciences

HOLMES, James S., LAMBERT, José & BROECK, Raymond van den
1978   (eds.) *Literature and Translation. New Perspectives in Literary Studies.* Louvain, Acco

LAMBERT, José
1977   'Traduction et technique romanesque', in A.Varvaro (ed.) *XIV congresso internazionale de linguistica e filologia romanza (Napoli, 1974)* (Napoli/Amsterdam, Macchiaroli/ Benjamins), vol.ii:653-668
1978a 'Echanges littéraires et traduction: discussion d'un projet', in J.S.Holmes *et al.* (eds.) *Literature and Translation* (Louvain, Acco):142-160
1978b 'Echanges littéraires et traduction. Etudes descriptives vs études théoriques', in L.Grähs *et al.* (eds.) *Theory and Practice of Translation* (Bern, Lang):237-250
1980   'Production, tradition et importation une clef pour la description de la littérature et de la littérature en traduction', *Revue canadienne de littérature comparée,* vii,2, 1980:246-252
1981   'Théorie de la littérature et théorie de la traduction en France (1800-1850), interpretées à partir de la théorie du polysystème, *Poetics Today,* ii,4, Summer-Autumn 1981:161-170
1982   'How Emile Deschamps Translated Shakespeare's *Macbeth,* or Theatre System and Translational System in French',

Dispositio, vii,19-20-21,1982:53-62
1983   *Un modèle descriptif pour l'étude de la littérature. La*
       littérature comme polysystème. Preprint. Dept. of General
       Literary Studies, University of Louvain (KUL)
LAMBERT, José & BRAGT, Katrin van
1980   *'The Vicar of Wakefield' en langue française. Traditions*
       et ruptures dans la littérature traduite. Preprint. Dept.
       of General Literary Studies, University of Louvain (KUL)
LAMBERT, José & LEFEVERE, André
1978   'Traduction, traduction littéraire et littérature compa-
       rée', in P.A.Horguelin (ed.), *La traduction, une profes-*
       sion (Ottawa, Conseil des traducteurs et interprètes du
       Canada):329-342
LEFEVERE, André
1975   *Translating Poetry. Seven Strategies and a Blueprint.*
       Assen/Amsterdam, Van Gorcum
1977a *Literary Knowledge. A Polemical and Programmatic Essay*
       on its Nature, Growth, Relevance and Transmission.
       Assen/New York, Van Gorcum/Humanities Press
1977b *Translating Literature. The German Tradition.* Assen/
       Amsterdam, Van Gorcum
1978   'Translation: The Focus of the Growth of Literary Know-
       ledge', in J.S.Holmes *et al.* (eds.), *Literature and*
       Translation (Louvain, Acco):7-28
1981a 'Theory and Practice - Process and Product', *Modern*
       Poetry in Translation 41-42,March 1981:19-27
1981b 'Programmatic Second Thoughts on "Literary" and "Trans-
       lation", or: Where Do We Go From Here?', *Poetics Today*,
       ii,4,Summer-Autumn 1981:39-50
1982a 'Literary Theory and Translated Literature', *Dispositio*,
       vii,19-20-21,1982:3-22
1982b 'Mother Courage's Cucumbers: Text, System and Refraction
       in a Theory of Literature', *Modern Language Studies*, xii,
       4,Fall 1982:3-20
1983   'Poetics (Today) and Translation (Studies)', *Modern*
       Poetry in Translation, 1983:190-195
1984   'That Structure in the Dialect of Men Interpreted',
       Comparative Criticism 6, 1984:87-100
LEUVEN, Kitty van
1984   'The Methodology of Translation Description and its
       Relevance for the Practice of Translation', *Dutch*
       Crossing 23, August 1984:54-65
LLOYD, David
1982   'Translator as Refractor: Towards a Re-reading of James
       Clarence Mangan as Translator', *Dispositio*, vii, 19-20-
       21,1982:141-162
MOOIJ, J.J.A.
1979   'The Nature and Function of Literary Theories', *Poetics*
       Today, i,1-2,Autumn 1979:111-136
POPOVIČ, Anton
1970   'The Concept "Shift of Expression" in Translation

Analysis', in J.S.Holmes *et al.* (eds.), *Literature and Translation* (Louvain, Acco):78-87
1972   'Die Stellung der Uebersetzungstheorie im System der Literaturwissenschaft', *Slavica Slovaca*, vii,1972:378-395
1976a 'Aspects of Metatext', *Canadian Review of Comparative Literature*, 3,Autumn 1976:225-235
1976b *Dictionary for the Analysis of Literary Translation.* Pamphlet. Edmonton/Nitra, University of Alberta/University of Nitra
POPOVIČ, Anton & DENÉS, Imrich
1977   *Translation as Comparison.* Pamphlet. Nitra, Pedagogical Factulty, University of Nitra
ROSE, Marilyn Gaddis
1977   (ed.) *Translation in the Humanities.* Binghamton, State University of New York at Binghamton
1981   (ed.) *Translation Spectrum. Essays in Theory and Practice.* Albany, State University of New York Press
1982   'Walter Benjamin as Translation Theorist. A Reconsideration', *Dispositio*, vii,19-20-21,1982:163-176
SCHREURS, Bernadette
1978   'Roman - Parodie - Traduction: les *Tristram Shandy* français', in J.S.Holmes *et al.* (eds.), *Literature and Translation* (Louvain, Acco):214-233
SHAVIT, Zohar
1981   'Translation of Children's Literature as a Function of its Position in the Literary Polysystem', *Poetics Today*, ii,4,Summer-Autumn 1981:171-179
TOURY, Gideon
1980   *In Search of a Theory of Translation.* Tel Aviv, Porter Institute for Poetics and Semiotics
1982   'A Rationale for Descriptive Translation Studies', *Dispositio*, vii,19-20-21,1982:23-40
1984   'Translation, Literary Translation and Pseudotranslation', *Comparative Criticism* 6,1984:73-85
TYMOCZKO, Maria
1982   'Strategies for Integrating Irish Epics into European Literature', *Dispositio*, vii,19-20-21,1982:123-140
1983   'Translating the Old Irish Epic Táin Bó Cúailnge: Political Aspects', *Pacific Quarterly Moana* 8,1983:6-21
VANDERAUWERA, Ria
1980   'Texts and Contexts of Translation: *Max Havelaar* in English', *Dutch Crossing* 12,December 1980:34-54. Also in *Dispositio*, vii,19-20-21,1982:111-122
1982   *Fiction in Translation: Policies and Options. A Case Study of the Translation of Dutch Novels into English over the Last Two Decades.* Unpublished PhD thesis, University of Antwerp (UIA)
YAHALOM, Shelly
1981   'Le système littéraire en état de crise. Contacts inter-systémiques et comportement traductionnel', *Poetics Today*, ii,4,Summer-Autumn 1981:143-160

CONTRIBUTORS

Susan Bassnett-McGuire is a Lecturer in the Graduate School of Comparative Literature at the University of Warwick

Katrin van Bragt is a Research Assistant in the Department of General Literary Studies at the University of Louvain (KUL)

Raymond van den Broeck is a Professor in the Institute for Translation Studies at the University of Amsterdam

Leon Burnett is a Lecturer in the Department of Literature at the University of Essex

Lieven D'hulst is a Lecturer at the Institute for Translators and Interpreters of the University of Antwerp (RUCA)

Hendrik van Gorp is a Professor in the Department of General Literary Studies at the University of Louvain (KUL)

Theo Hermans is a Lecturer in the Department of Dutch at University College London

José Lambert is a Professor in the Department of General Literary Studies at the University of Louvain (KUL)

André Lefevere is a Professor in the Department of Germanic Languages at the University of Texas at Austin

Gideon Toury is Senior Lecturer in the Department of Poetics and Comparative Literature at the University of Tel Aviv

Maria Tymoczko is a Professor of Comparative Literature at the University of Massachusetts at Amherst

Ria Vanderauwera is a Lecturer in the Translation Section of the Institute for Higher Education in Maastricht

Printed in Great Britain
by Amazon

35525136R00145